CHRISTIANITY
AND
HISTORY

CHRISTIANITY
AND
HISTORY

Essays by

E. Harris Harbison

PRINCETON, NEW JERSEY

PRINCETON UNIVERSITY PRESS

1964

Publication of this book has been aided by the Whitney Darrow
Publication Reserve Fund of Princeton University Press.
Printed in the United States of America
by Princeton University Press,
Princeton, New Jersey

For John, Helen, and Meg

PREFACE

IT IS EASIER to say what is not here than to describe what is. This is not a collection of "research" papers. With the possible exception of the last two essays, few of these present "new facts" to the reader. Rather they are concerned with the understanding of what we already know.

Some years ago, I thought I would write a book on "the Christian understanding of history," emphasizing the Augustinian period, the Lutheran, and the present. Committed Christians are quick to exploit anyone within the walls of Academe who manifests any interest whatever in Christianity. Any unity or consistency which the following lectures and papers show thus is the result of a combination of personal concern and of public image which apparently brought me to mind as a suitable speaker when the subject was either the Christian understanding of history, or Christianity in history. Three lectures at Grinnell were a good excuse to sketch "the Christian understanding of history," and they were so titled. But the book never got written, and these are the fragments.

"Referred to the departmental Christian," my then chairman wrote jocularly on a letter. Today I am not so conspicuous as a departmental Christian, and the chairman in question has become a Roman Catholic. It is again respectable to raise the question of the scholar who is also a Christian. The question, "What has Athens to do with Jerusalem?" is still with us, and always will be. The best hope of the author is that the reader may find some good starting point for his own meditations on the subject in the lectures, essays, and papers that follow. My particular thanks are due to the Director of the Princeton University Press, Mr. Herbert S. Bailey, Jr., who was the first to pass on to me the suggestion of nameless friends that such a collection be made. To my old friend and colleague, Joseph R. Strayer, I owe special thanks.

E. HARRIS HARBISON

Princeton, N.J.
January 1964

CONTENTS

I

THE CHRISTIAN
UNDERSTANDING
OF HISTORY

1 · RELIGIOUS PERSPECTIVES OF COLLEGE TEACHING: HISTORY*

I

A THEOLOGIAN who had written an eloquent history of the Reformation is said to have met the historian Ranke in Berlin and embraced him effusively as one would a confrere. "Ah please," said the father of scientific history, drawing himself away, "there is a great difference between us: you are first of all a Christian, and I am first of all a historian."

It was with this anecdote that Lord Acton introduced the central argument of his inaugural lecture on "The Study of History."[1] The story dramatizes vividly the nineteenth century belief that history is a "science," and that science is knowledge of an utterly different order from religion. The "great difference" which Ranke saw between Christian and historian has undoubtedly narrowed in our own

* The titles of most of the essays that follow were chosen by organizations outside the university for special reasons, and this was no exception. In 1950 the Hazen Foundation was planning a survey of religious values in teaching the various academic subjects and asked me to do the chapter on history. The resulting essay was carefully done, therefore, and may serve as a starting-point for thought about the question. Its content owes something to my presence during the summer of 1949 at a conference at what became the Ecumenical Institute at Bossey, near Geneva, Switzerland. Certainly the professors and students present from all over free Europe to discuss the Christian understanding of history had an unseen hand in shaping the essay that follows. It appeared first as a Hazen pamphlet (1950), later as a chapter in *Religious Perspectives in College Teaching* (Ronald Press, New York City, 1952.) It is republished here by permission of the Hazen Foundation and the Ronald Press.

[1] Lord Acton, *A Lecture on the Study of History* (London and New York, 1895), p. 50 and note p. 115. Acton quotes an article of Victor Cherbuliez in *Revue des deux mondes*, XCVII (1872), 537, in which the historian is not identified.

[3]

day as historians have grown more conscious of the subjectivity of their interpretation and more uneasy about calling history a "science." But a difference still exists in the academic mind between one who would call himself "first of all a Christian" and one who would call himself "first of all a historian."

Many years ago men would have looked at the same difference from the other side of the gulf. Imagine Acton's anecdote in reverse: Ranke (in a previous incarnation) enthusiastically embraces a great medieval saint, let us say Bernard, as a comrade; but the saint draws himself away saying, "You are a chronicler of the City of Man, I am a citizen of the City of God; between us there is a great gulf fixed." The point is simply that in the Middle Ages the tables would have been turned. Sainthood once had the prestige which science (and "scientific" history) was to attain in the nineteenth century. St. Bernard, in the position in which we have imagined him, would have sensed the danger in Ranke's desire to clothe his secular scholarship with the aura of Christian sanctity. "You are first of all a historian," he might conclude, "I am first of all a Christian."

In letting the imagination play upon the apparent difference between professing Christian and professional historian, however, it is easy to oversimplify. We know, for instance, that Ranke himself was a deeply religious person. "In all history," he wrote at one time, "God dwells, lives, is to be seen. Every deed demonstrates Him, every moment preaches His name."[2] I can find little information about the effusive theologian in the story, but I am sure that if Ranke thought his history of the Reformation a bad job, it *was* a bad job. Assuming that what Ranke objected to was the distortion of events "as they actually happened" to

[2] James Westfall Thompson, *A History of Historical Writing*, II, 171.

[4]

fit the demands of sectarian prejudice, the cause of Christian truth certainly did not suffer through his rebuke. The eager quest from Bayle to Voltaire to cleanse the historical record of superstition and priestly distortion, the passion for accuracy, objectivity, and exhaustiveness in the nineteenth century German school of "scientific" historiography—these things were certainly not anti-Christian in and of themselves. It is far too simple to say that in our anecdote Ranke represents something called "history" and the theologian something called "Christianity." Each in a different sense was a *Christian historian*. The question as Ranke stated it was which comes "first of all," a man's vocation as Christian or his profession as historian.

II

There is a false sharpness in this apparent contradiction between "Christian" and "historian" which results from the survival of a naïve nineteenth century conception of "objectivity." Deep at the heart of the American academic world is the belief that the word "scholar" cannot tolerate any qualifying adjective like "Christian." Has not the scholar had to battle the priest at every step of the way in his fight for freedom of inquiry? Did not the Church burn Bruno and humiliate Galileo? And in the search for historical truth, were not the real heroes those who (like Valla) exposed the arrogant forgeries of Popes or (like Bayle) laid bare the superstitions on which Christians had been nourished for centuries? Once a man allows himself to be *anything* before he is "scholar" or "scientist," so the argument runs, truth flies out the window and prejudice fills the classroom. The adjectives most feared today are of course not religious, but pseudo-religious—not "Christian" and "Jewish" but "Communist" and "Fascist." Fascist, Nazi, and Bolshevist regimes have attacked the disinterested pursuit of truth for its own sake as not only

[5]

dangerous but fundamentally immoral, and it is no wonder that older convictions about the incompatibility of science and religion should be reinforced by the present-day evidence that disinterested scholarship cannot survive under the shadow of our great pseudo-religions. Such convictions are particularly strong among historians because they know what happens to the historical profession and the historical record in the hands of totalitarian governments. In any discussion of the hackneyed problem of "academic objectivity" it is important to remember that American academic communities are keenly aware of the overwhelming threat to the disinterested pursuit of truth which has driven a throng of scholarly exiles to our shores and onto our campuses. The jealous fear of coupling any adjective implying zealous faith with "scholar" is not altogether unjustified.

This was borne in upon me vividly at Bossey near Geneva during the summer of 1949, at a conference of professional historians and graduate students on "The Meaning of History." Years of totalitarian tyranny or war regimentation on the Continent have sapped any vitality which might have been left in the nineteenth century belief in "objectivity." Historians who lived under "thought control" learned to use "objectivity" as an escape from publicly committing themselves to the dominant political philosophy. Today their students have only contempt for the tendency they notice in the older academic generation to avoid commitment of any kind, on or off the lecture platform. On the other hand, they warm to teachers who believe something, even though it be a communism which most of them would reject. To most of them "objectivity" is either a hypocritical dodge designed to cover up unspoken assumptions or an immoral escape from the necessity of taking a stand on the vital issues of the day. Many European historians are so saturated in existential thinking as to deny the possibility of objectivity in any sense of the word. The only attainable objectivity, one member of the conference argued, is a frank and detailed confession of all subjective prejudices in the preface of a historical work. In other words, the dominant opinion in many European academic communities appears to be the opposite of the dominant American opinion. You must proclaim openly what sort of a historian you are—Communist, Bourgeois, or Christian. Words like "scholar" and "historian" must always and inevitably have qualifying adjectives attached to them or they have no meaning.

Contact with such thinking has a dual effect upon an American. On the one hand, it gives him a sense of pride and gratitude that belief in the possibility of disinterested inquiry is still alive and vigorous in American universities. On the other hand, it makes him sensitive to the naïveté and hypocrisy in much American talk about impartial objectivity. There is a sense in which "impartiality" has become a luxury which only those nations can afford which remained neutral or happened to avoid the worst physical and moral destruction during the late war. Swedish students at the conference mentioned were insistent that they and their friends were not a bit interested in the personal beliefs of their professors but solely in what they *knew*. Any teacher of history this side of the water will remember the same disposition in many students he has known. Faith in the possibility of "objective" knowledge is evidently still strong in these two parts of the world at least. But to most Europeans, and even to many Americans, teachers and students alike, impartiality is simply a pose adopted by fearful academicians with de-sensitized social consciences and dried-up emotions. Even in the United States all of us who face students in the college classrooms have at one time or another sensed the utter seriousness with which undergraduates ask, "But what is *your* relation to what you know? What is *your* concern with it? What do *you* think it's all about?" This is not the place to spell out what has happened to the concept of "objectivity" in recent epistemology—and only a philosopher would do the job well. It is enough to point out that the contemporary teacher and writer of history is confronted in fact by an audience which includes an increasing number who think that Ranke was not necessarily any more "objective" than his theological friend. Europeans are simply a few steps ahead of Americans in popular awareness of the truth that the knower is intimately involved in the process of knowing.

III

The question which haunts any historian today who is at all sensitive to the deeper currents of the age in which he lives, the question his students constantly ask of him by implication even when they do not put it into words, is the question of the meaning of history. A great many of the veterans who flocked into courses in history and the social studies in such swollen numbers after the war made it clear to advisers and teachers that they were looking for answers they thought neither the arts and letters nor the natural sciences could give. Somewhere in history, many of them thought, the answer to how it all came about was to be found. This search is still on on many campuses, at least so far as history courses are concerned. Students who would hardly think of asking "What is the meaning of nuclear energy?" or "What is the meaning of the artistic impulse?" will ask in one way or another "What is the meaning of human history?" What they really mean to ask, of course, is "Where are we all headed?"

Questions like this are not fashionable among professional historians, but when a man reaches the top of the profession and no longer has reason to fear the sneers of his colleagues, it is a well-established custom to reflect upon such matters. Kenneth Scott Latourette, delivering the presidential address before the American Historical Association in 1948 on "The Christian Understanding of History," pointed out that "a survey of the presidential addresses made before this Association reveals the fact that no one single topic has so attracted those who have been chosen to head this honorable body as have the possible patterns and meanings of history."[3] In a recent discussion with a fellow historian Arnold J. Toynbee remarked, "This job of making sense of history is one of the crying needs of our day—I beg of you believe me."[4] The philosophers and above all the theologians have been even more eager than the historians in recent years to make sense of history. Books on "The Meaning of History," "Meaning in History," "Faith and History," "Christianity and the Nature of History" have poured from the presses in fairly steady succession, particularly since the close of the war. The historian may perhaps be pardoned for thinking that this question of the whole meaning of his subject is pressed upon *him* more insistently these days by students and fellow scholars than it is upon any of his colleagues in other departments of higher learning.

There are two easy answers to this question of the meaning of history. One is to say that meaning is so woven into the texture of history that the pattern is self-evident to any interested and careful observer. All that is necessary is to study the historical record "objectively" and impartially, and a design of meaningful progress will become evident. The other is to say that there is no meaning in history and that the search for design is futile and stupid. The first is an attitude of assurance which is closely affiliated

[3] *American Historical Review*, LIV (Jan. 1949) 261.
[4] *Can We Know the Pattern of the Past?* Discussion between P. Geyl . . . and A. J. Toynbee . . . (Bussum, Holland, 1948), p. 30.

to the nineteenth century faith that if the facts are only heaped high enough they will amount to something. The second is an attitude of doubt which is generally born of disillusionment about the failure of exactly this kind of assurance.

It is not the purpose of this essay to present and preach a Christian "interpretation" of history. Rather it is to suggest that the question of meaning must be faced by every professional historian whether he likes it or not, both in his teaching and writing; that current secular answers generally end up either in a too-easy assurance or a too-abject doubt; and that there is a Christian way of looking at history which is something less than a philosophy of history but something more than a mere frame of mind, which constitutes the only really adequate alternative to either dogmatism or skepticism.

The men of assurance in the historical profession are perhaps not so numerous as they once were, but they are still an impressive group. They are generally the "social scientists" among historians, the heirs of a great hope, that science will save society. The study of history has always had its statistical side and the areas of it which are capable of semi-scientific treatment have received increasing attention during the past two centuries: geography, climate, demography, production and exchange, class struggle and social displacement. Historical study has profited immensely from this statistical emphasis, and the hard-boiled statisticians who keep reminding their colleagues of prices and wages, food production and population fluctuation, "forces" and "trends," are stimulating and indispensable members of any department of history. But the perception of trends and the drawing of graphs appear to exercise a fatal fascination on the academic mind. The trends become animated, and before we know it we are confronted with mechanisms and determinisms which "explain" history.

Any practicing historian knows how deliciously seductive these magnificent simplicities can be to students who for the first time encounter the historical interpretation of Marx, for instance, or Spengler, or Sorokin.

If the men of assurance seize upon one of the emotional attitudes of modern science—its self-confidence and optimism—the men of doubt seize upon another—its tentative, skeptical, inquiring attitude, Descartes' *de omnibus dubitandum.* History to them is an unintelligible and meaningless process. Any meaning ascribed to the course of history is totally subjective; any determination of cause and effect is difficult and dubious; even the concept of cause itself, many of them maintain, is best dispensed with. There is an intellectual honesty about these people, a refusal to be taken in, an ascetic renunciation of wishful thinking which are altogether admirable. But in the classroom this second attitude too often ends in a philosophy which proclaims that life is a mess, history a farce, and historical study a kind of intellectual game, interesting in a gruesome sort of way, but not enlightening and certainly not ennobling. All this is particularly appealing to a bewildered, disillusioned, and fearful post-war generation of students. In times of trouble pessimism is a surer balm than optimism. Men can enjoy misery if they know they have company in it. I have often seen students gain real emotional release through the discovery that a professor of history was more cynical and despairing about the state of the universe than they were themselves. But the anodyne is not permanent. And although doubt may be the beginning of wisdom, I know of no guarantee that it must end in wisdom. It is hard to nourish vigorous and creative historical thinking on the thin gruel of thoroughgoing skepticism.

IV

It should be the mark of a Christian attitude toward history that it resolves the antinomy of assurance and doubt about the meaning of the historical process on a higher plane. St. Augustine was the first Christian thinker to wrestle long and hard with the problem of how the Christian must look upon history, and it was Augustine who first saw clearly that to the Christian history is *neither* a deterministic system *nor* a meaningless chaos. The determinists of his day believed that history moved in cycles and that if only historians studied the process of recurrence carefully enough they could describe and predict the movements of history almost as they could predict the motions of the planets. Origen had seen that if this were true, then "Adam and Eve will do once more exactly what they have already done; the same deluge will be repeated; the same Moses will bring the same six hundred thousand people out of Egypt; Judas will again betray his Lord; and Paul a second time will hold the coats of those who stone Stephen."

"God forbid that we should believe this," Augustine wrote, "for Christ died once for our sins, and rising again, dies no more."[5] In other words, there is a decisiveness and unpredictability about history which is falsely annihilated in any view of history as mechanical recurrence, scientifically intelligible and predictable.

Augustine saw with equal clarity that history is not chaos. The rise and fall of states and civilizations is not meaningless process: "We do not attribute the power of giving kingdoms and empires to any save to the true God. . . . He who is the true God . . . gave a kingdom to the Romans when He would, and as great as He would, as He did also to the Assyrians and even the Persians. . . . And the same is true in respect of men as well as nations. . . . He who

[5] Augustine, *De Civ. Dei*, Book xii, chap. 13. The passage from Origen (*Peri Archon*, ii, chap. 3) is quoted by Lynn White, Jr., "Christian Myth and Christian History," *Journal of the History of Ideas*, iii (1942), 147.

gave power to Augustus gave it also to Nero. . . . He who gave it to the Christian Constantine gave it also to the apostate Julian. . . . Manifestly these things are ruled and governed by the one God according as He pleases; *and if His motives are hid, are they therefore unjust?*"[6]

The very essence of a Christian understanding of history, despite the many sectarian forms it may take, is in this last sentence. The Hebrew prophets and the Christian fathers agreed in believing the strange paradox that God both *reveals* and *conceals* Himself in history. There is too much revelation for a Christian to think that there is no judgment or mercy in history, no moral meaning, no spiritual significance. On the other hand, the divine concealment is of such a character that no Christian may think that the judgment or meaning or significance is unambiguously clear to him as a human being. To Luther, who wrote eloquently about this "hiddenness of God" in history, there is mystery as well as majestic purpose in the historical pageant; and the one is meaningless without the other. God is Lord of history to Luther, but He does not work openly and visibly in the historical process. In typically extravagant imagery, he speaks of history as God's "play," God's "mummery," God's "joust and tourney." The actual course of secular history cannot be identified with God's will—nor can it be wholly divorced from His will. God wills to conceal as well as to reveal Himself in the fate of empires, and above all in the unplumbed depths of two central events, the Birth and Passion of Christ. In a famous comparison of God's grace to a passing shower of rain, Luther suggested in a single brief passage the simultaneous revelation and concealment of the divine will, the unity-within-diversity of human history, the uniqueness of events, and the decisiveness of the present moment in history for the individual: "For this shall you know, that God's word

[6] *De Civ. Dei*, v, chap. 21.

[13]

and grace are a passing shower of rain, which never comes again where it has once been. It was with the Jews, but what is gone is gone, they have nothing now. Paul brought it into Grecian land. What is gone is gone again, now they have the Turks. Rome and Latin land had it also. What is gone is gone, they now have the Pope. And you Germans must not think that you will always have it. So grasp on and hold to, whoever can grasp and hold."[7]

V

In developing the implications of these basic Christian insights into history, Christian thinkers and Christian sects have not escaped the danger of falling into one or the other of precisely the same attitudes which we have described in the case of secular historians. We might say that in the Christian case these are the "heresies" of over-assurance and over-diffidence about the meaning of history, the one closely parallel to the sin of pride, the other to that of sloth.

To Christian historians the Biblical record has always appeared to reveal a broad pattern of the divine activity in history. A Swiss scholar, Oscar Cullmann, has sketched this pattern with brilliant strokes as he believes it to appear in the New Testament.[8] As he sees it, the God who created the universe is the Lord of redemption and so of history. By the dual process of "calling" and "substitution," he directs the drama of salvation through its various stages to triumphant conclusion beyond the historical vision of mankind. He first calls or chooses mankind to stand for creation; then calls a nation, the Hebrews, to substitute for man in general; then summons a remnant to represent that nation when it falls away; and finally fixes upon one man, the Christ, to stand for all humanity and creation. The

[7] Luther, *Werke* (Weimar ed.), xv, 32.

[8] See Oscar Cullmann, *Christus und die Zeit* (Zürich, 1946) (English trans., *Christ and Time*, Philadelphia, 1950), particularly Part 1, chap. VIII.

progressive reduction then gives way to progressive expansion and the process reverses itself. Through Christ the apostles are won, through the apostles the Church is founded, through the Church all mankind will be reconciled to God, and the new heaven and earth will complete the first creation. The fact that the Western world divides time into "A.D." and "B.C." is the most obvious evidence of the incalculable influence which this broad pattern of meaning envisioned by the early Christians has had upon historical understanding.

The point at which this pattern becomes controversial for Christian groups is naturally the concrete meaning given to the age in which we live, the age of the Church from the Resurrection to the present. Is the gradual unfolding of this age a significant part of the drama or not? Is God's hand still evident in every turn of events? If so, how and where and in what?

The answer has been clearest through the ages for the Roman Christian. For him, God's hand has been clearly evident in history since Pentecost in the Roman Catholic Church. There is a real progress in history: progressive unfolding of doctrines which were only implicit in New Testament times, progressive winning of the pagan, the infidel, and the schismatic in spite of all appearances of defeat. History has a central thread in Church history, in the growth of a visible divine institution—what Sir Thomas More called "the common, known church"—changeless in goal but constantly changing in its temporal position in relation to this goal. In different times and in different ways, such a conviction that God's hand in history is unmistakably revealed in a visible historical institution has been shared by Eastern Orthodox Christians as well as by Lutherans, Anglicans, and early Calvinists. Its remote source is undoubtedly the Old Testament Covenant of Jehovah with his chosen people.

Another form taken by Christian assurance about the meaning of history is the belief that God's hand is evident not so much in *institutions* as in *events*. In the Middle Ages, the most significant events were visions and miracles. To readers of the lives of the saints, God's love and power were constantly breaking in upon the ordinary course of human affairs in a direct and self-evident way. The successor to this belief in more sophisticated early modern times was the conviction, particularly evident in Oliver Cromwell and his Puritan contemporaries, that God's hand appears not so much in miracle as in the outcome of historical events like battles. This conviction that God guides men not by mystical vision or miraculous breaking of natural law but by his shaping of secular history, by what Cromwell called "dispensations," was rooted in the Hebrew prophets and widely prevalent among our seventeenth century American ancestors.

Among Protestants today assurance about the meaning of history is certainly not a besetting sin. Christians have never entirely recovered from the eighteenth century attack on the "theological interpretation" of history which had been dominant from Augustine to Bossuet. Nor should they, perhaps. Many of the things which Voltaire assailed in Christian historiography needed to be assailed: the narrow parochialism which funneled all ancient history into the story of "that miserable little people," the Jews; the neglect of non-Christian civilizations; the partisanship and axe-grinding so characteristic of monkish and priestly chronicle; the easy recourse to miracle as a short-circuit of causal explanation. Voltaire and his fellow-philosophers destroyed the older Christian pattern of meaning in history only to substitute another, that of secular progress. But the shattering experience of two world wars and the cold shadow of a third have effectually destroyed the naïve belief in inevitable progress, and most Protestant leaders today are concerned to extirpate the last traces of nineteenth century optimism about the course of secular history.

The result is a strong tendency on the part of Christian intellectuals today to adopt a kind of Christian skepticism about the meaning of history. Among Protestant theologians this group is clearly in the ascendancy today, in terms of prestige if not also of numbers. There is sound historical reason for this. Primitive Protestantism had at its center a passionate protest against identifying the will of God with any visible institution such as the Roman Church. Too often the result was simply to substitute the church of Wittenberg, Geneva, or England for that of Rome. But it is impossible in the long run for a Protestant to rest content with any theory of history in which a visible institution is the sole channel of God's grace. This is why Protestants turned so easily to something like Cromwell's doctrine of "dispensations." They soon abused this doctrine, to be sure, by seeing God's will in secular events or movements which pleased them, all the way from parliamentary government and democracy to liberalism and socialism. Led by Karl Barth, Protestant theologians today are moving in strong reaction to such tendencies. In spite of the widespread current interest in history among theologians, the deepest currents in Protestant theology, particularly in Europe, can only be described as *anti-historical*. These currents find their source in Kierkegaard, in Barth, in Berdyaev, and in secular philosophers of the existentialist school. Diverse as they are in their sources and present courses, they have some things in common: a deep distrust of everything associated with "progress"; a sense that God is the "wholly Other" and hence not to be identified with any historical institution or movement, whether it stem from Rome or Geneva or Moscow; a radical Christian relativism in viewing all historical achievements.

[17]

This Christian skepticism about the possibility of discerning any pattern of meaning in secular history bulks large in recent theological works. "There never has been and never will be," a recent writer concludes, "an immanent solution of the problem of history, for man's historical experience is one of steady failure. . . . History is, through all the ages, a story of action and suffering, of power and pride, of sin and death. . . . The importance of secular history decreases *in direct proportion to* the intensity of man's concern with God and himself. . . . A 'Christian history' is non-sense."[9] I have heard a similar view eloquently expressed by a deeply spiritual Danish professor of church history who was arguing "the impossibility of a Christian conception of history." Since real knowledge presupposes simultaneity, he maintained, we can never actually know the past and the past can never have real significance for us. The mere unrolling of history has no visible meaning for a converted Christian. "Christian belief," he concluded, "is to trust God in the uncertainty of life. It is the most abominable arrogance to make false certainties by interpreting history in a Christian way."[10] The trend toward a Christian agnosticism with respect to any self-evident meaning in the course of history is very strong indeed, particularly in Europe. Evidently the Christian historian does not avoid the twin dangers of dogmatism and doubt simply by being a Christian.

VI

The historian who happens also to be a Christian is thus besieged, as it were, by four attacking armies of colleagues, students, and friends who come at him from the four points

[9] Karl Löwith, *Meaning in History* (Univ. of Chicago Press, 1949), pp. 190-197. Italics mine.
[10] P. G. Lindhardt, of the University of Aarhus, Denmark, at the conference at Bossey mentioned above.

of the compass. His secular colleagues who have all the answers tell him to put aside childish things like religion now that he has become a man and to open his eyes to the great material mechanisms which determine history. A few of his Christian friends are perhaps equally dogmatic on the other side of the matter, exposing the naïve assumptions of the materialists and pointing out with equal assurance just where the hand of God is to be discerned in history. The agnostics among his colleagues both in history and in theology come at him from two different and opposite quarters—each with *Nescio* inscribed on their banners, but for quite different reasons. Each group maintains that history has nothing much to do with Christianity, the first because Christianity is nothing, the second because history is nothing. In this plight I think the Christian historian may well stand up and make a brief speech which might run something like this:

"I am neither a philosopher nor a theologian. I am interested as any educated man is in philosophy and theology, but as a professional historian you must not expect of me a fully-rounded philosophy or theology of history. Thanks to my training, I am suspicious of big words and big ideas. I believe that Marx was wrong in his interpretation of history for the same reason that the authors of saints' legends were wrong—that human history cannot be reduced to magnificent simplicities, either material or spiritual. I have a feeling that agnosticism, not assurance, is the first step toward wisdom, provided that it does not sink away into cynicism and despair. But I cannot agree that history has nothing to do with the religious insights of Christianity, or that Christianity has nothing to do with secular history. I could not long remain either a believing Christian or a practicing historian with my convictions about Christianity and history in water-tight compartments. I believe, in spite of secular skeptics, that Christianity offers a profound insight into the general nature of the historical process, even though both as historian and Christian I am too diffident to think that I can discern a clear-cut pattern. I believe, in spite of the theological skeptics, that secular history is important to the Christian and that Christianity always suffers when its historical character is minimized, because the immediate result is always a loss of ethical vigor among Christians. I think I see a fine traditional ambiguity in the word 'vocation' as the call of God both to religious commitment and to service in a job. I see no reason why I cannot find a reconciliation between my two 'vocations' on the practical working level of teaching and writing history, if not on the loftier levels of philosophy and theology."

VII

To the professional historian, much of what has been discussed thus far may seem highly theoretical and only very tenuously related to the practical work-a-day problems of the classroom. It is my conviction, however, that in any discussion of religious perspectives in teaching history—whatever may be true of other subjects—it is impossible to separate the theoretical and the practical, just as it is impossible to split apart the historian's dual function as teacher and writer. The real problem is to find a practical working form of Augustine's or Luther's understanding of history which takes account of the immense recent progress of historical knowledge and technique, which conforms to the idiom of twentieth century thought in general, but which remains true to the basic insights of Christianity into the nature of man, of God, and of time.

On this level the first illusion to be got rid of is the idea which I have heard expressed by enthusiastic theologians that being a Christian will make a man a better professional historian—nay, that it is the very condition of being a true historian at all, since it was Christianity which nurtured the modern historical sense of unique events happening in irreversible sequence in straight-line time. Christian belief is obviously no substitute for competent scholarship at the technical level, and it would be intolerable pride in a Christian to suggest that on this level his religion gives him an advantage over the non-religious historians. I cannot see how Christian belief contributes anything significant to the careful study of matters like the laws of Solon, medieval land-tenure, or the impact of gunpowder on the history of military tactics. Furthermore, sectarian prejudice has long been a notorious obstacle in the path of historical understanding.

There is an important truth, however, at the basis of this illusion, a truth most eloquently developed in Herbert Butterfield's penetrating and exciting lectures on *Christianity and History*. It is that the Christian understanding of the nature and destiny of man—created yet free, fallen yet redeemable, bounded by history yet able to transcend it by his imagination and creativity—cannot fail to deepen and enrich any historian's understanding of his subject. It cannot be said too often that historical understanding is never merely a matter of reading documents. A child cannot comprehend Luther's experience in the monastery until his own human experience and powers of imagination are mature enough to provide at least some common ground of understanding. A student cannot understand the complexities of the movement Luther started, its contradictions and confusions, the mixture in it of lofty ideals and base motives, until he has absorbed something at least of how the politics and mass movements of his own day operate. In the same way, the truly great historian cannot afford to ignore the thinking about human nature and the problem of evil which has been done by the most sensitive and intelligent observers. To the Christian, the profoundest view is the Hebraic-Christian as it has been developed from the prophets and Christ through the apostles and later teachers of the Church.

There is an opposite illusion which may also be dismissed briefly. This is that a man will be a better Christian for being a historian. Stated in this form, the proposition is of course absurd. Learning of any sort has never been a condition of Christian perfection. But again there is a truth at the basis of the illusion. The Christian faith was born among a people which had developed a relatively strong historical sense, and the New Testament is saturated with temporal terminology used naïvely: "then," "straightway," "when the time was fulfilled," "in the fullness of time." At the Last Judgment men are judged by what they have done in history, even though their righteousness or unrighteousness is not evident to them during their historical existence. The Apostles' Creed is a statement of belief about events which happened in time, not a statement of truths which are eternally true apart from time. To Augustine, as to the Hebrew prophets before him, there was significant development in time of God's purpose; and to Dante, the destiny of Rome was linked firmly and surely to the destiny of the Church.[11] In other words, the Hebraic-Christian tradition, unlike others which arose in India and China, is a history-valuing tradition; and it is no accident that when it became partially secularized, the result was the modern idea of progress. Except when Greek or Oriental influences have become dominant, Christians have never looked upon time as something to be fled or annihilated. There is a sense in which a man must be

[11] The most significant passages for study of the general problem seem to me the following: Acts II, III, X, XI; Romans VI; Galatians IV; I Corinthians XV. Augustine, *De Civ. Dei*, Book V, chap. 21; Book XII, chap. 13; Book XVIII, chap. 46. Dante, *De Monarchia*, and *Purgatorio*, cantos 16, 20.

historically minded in an elementary way in order to be a Christian.

Let us grant that Christian belief will not improve a historian's standing with his fellow scholars, nor professional historical knowledge a Christian's standing among the saints. On the practical level the gulf between Christian and historian is nevertheless by no means so wide as Ranke implied it was. There are some qualities and attitudes which are equally admired by Christians and by professional historians, and which may serve as guide-posts for the man who wishes he were both a better Christian and a better historian.

One of these is *universality* or catholicity of outlook. The best historians are not satisfied until by a rigorous intellectual asceticism they have risen as far as humanly possible above all parochialism of both time and place which narrows or distorts their historical vision. It was part of Ranke's greatness that he strove so hard and so self-consciously to rise above sectarian and national prejudice and to judge past ages by their own standards rather than by those of a later day. The most obvious source of this rationalistic universalism was the Stoic conception of the natural equality of all men and the eighteenth century cosmopolitanism so akin to it. This outlook blended easily with the catholicity preached by a religion which insisted from the beginning upon the fatherhood of God and the brotherhood of all men. The monotheism of the Hebrew prophets and the belief in the universal fatherhood of the Christian God formed the basis upon which the first clear conception of the *unity of history* was built in the West. Christian historiography, with all its failings, constituted a notable step beyond the parochialism and nationalism of Greek and Roman historical writing; and even if it developed a new parochialism of its own, it never entirely lost the belief that all local histories are really one history.

The Christian believed that though one nation may be "chosen," the mission of a chosen people is world-wide, more is demanded of it than of others, and if it falters, its mission may pass to the Gentiles. Amid all the welter of histories written in the interests of class, nation, race, or sect, this ideal of universality of perspective still stands as that of professional historian and Christian alike.

Closely related to universality is the difficult matter of *judgment*. The secular historian would dislike any theological terminology here, but a reading of the ablest contemporary historians I think would suggest that they believe in something very close to the Christian belief in a justice completed, though never annihilated, by mercy. Most historians are aware that they cannot avoid judgment of men and movements, either in their writing or their teaching. Monographs and textbooks which simply "give the facts" betray underlying judgments in the very choice and arrangement of such facts—especially when they are read after the lapse of a generation or so. Students are quick to sense the judgment implicit not only in the conscious choice of material for presentation but even more in the unplanned and half-conscious tone of voice or facial expression which betrays the teacher. Granted the necessity of making judgments, the real question is on what basis they are to be made, and here the historian and the Christian are in general agreement. Justice requires that all the relevant data be used and fairly weighed before judgment is given. The usual result of a long and honest attempt to get at all the historical evidence about any disputed event or personality is an overwhelming sense of the complexity and relativity of the issues, a sense of *tout comprendre, c'est tout pardonner*. The desire to be fair ends often enough in the desire to extend mercy, even on the level of purely secular historical labor. In the Gospels "Woe unto you, Scribes and Pharisees . . ." is balanced by "Judge not that ye be not judged." The historian knows—or should know—that the limits of judgment lie for him too between these same two extremes, between a sense of righteousness which refuses to blink the fact of evil, and a sense of mercy which follows from the complexity of human affairs and the frailty of human judgment.

To take a concrete case, any historian who writes, lectures, or talks with students about Luther is sooner or later forced to take up an attitude toward him. A Roman Catholic teacher may vent his righteous indignation upon the reformer; a pious Lutheran may make a spotless prophet of him; a Marxian may point out that Luther was a mere puppet in the grip of irresistible economic forces. It may be suggested, without any intent to blaspheme, that the best professional historian's ideal here is theoretically the same as the Christian's: to see Luther as nearly as possible as his own Lord saw him, in all his weakness and strength, his compromises and triumphs, his freedom and his compulsion, so that in the resulting judgment justice is perfectly tempered with mercy. As a matter of fact, close and persistent study of Luther and his whole age by professional historians has brought us closer at least to the possibility of such a judgment than was conceivable a century ago, simply because we knew too little then. Mere knowledge is no guarantee of sound judgment of men and movements, either in historical study or in ordinary Christian living, but it is often the beginning of true understanding. The kind of judgment the best historians strive for is not so far as some may think from the kind of judgment the truest followers of Christ have striven for.

A third quality or attitude which is characteristic of both historians and Christians on different levels is best described as *realism*. Generally it is the "humanists" among historians, not the traditional Christians, who are shocked by the realities of human nature as they are encountered in history. The historian and the social scientist habitually deal with human nature at its lowest level, the level at which "moral man" is absorbed in "immoral society." Much of the time they are concerned with the competition of groups for wealth and power, the game of power politics, the awful destruction of revolution and war. My guess is that the ratio of cynicism among historians is higher than that among, say, professors of literature or of physics. At any rate the historian is not apt to be a Pollyanna at the present moment of world history. Nor is the Christian. Both succumbed for a time to the eighteenth century belief in the goodness of human nature and the inevitability of progress, but a good many non-Christian historians today would be impelled to agree with Herbert Butterfield when he writes, "We have gambled very highly on what was an over-optimistic view of the character of man. . . . It is essential not to have faith in human nature. Such faith is a comparatively recent heresy and a very disastrous one."[12] The tough-mindedness about which many professional historians pride themselves is not so far from a Christian attitude toward human nature as a soft and idealistic optimism.

Tough-mindedness must be balanced, however, both with the historian and the Christian, by *open-mindedness*. By this I mean openness to unforeseen possibilities in human nature and history. The historian who is merely cynical is obviously going to be blind to the unexpected and unexplainable good in human nature, the movements which turn out better than their sordid origins would lead one to expect. "Good" events in history have a disconcerting way of producing unlovely results. But many of the results which we later call "good" have been the by-product

[12] Herbert Butterfield, *Christianity and History* (London, 1949), pp. 34, 47.

of selfish conflicts—civil liberties in English history, for
instance, were partly the product of self-interested squab-
bles over privilege by social or religious groups. The great
historians have invariably had a certain open-mindedness
to the infinite possibilities in human nature which is certainly akin to, though it is not identical with, the Christian's sensitivity to the redemptive possibilities in any
human situation. In the mental make-up of a historian,
realism must be balanced by a certain naïveté and wonder,
a sense of the kindliness in human beings that is the ultimate foundation of societies and of the resilience which
human beings keep demonstrating in the face of disaster
and evil. On a different level the Christian would call this
kindliness and resilience evidence of the workings of grace.
Luther's warning that to talk of the Law and forget the
Gospel is "to wound and not to bind up, to smite and not
to heal, to lead down into Hell and not to bring back
again," has its clear implications for the historian as well
as for the Christian.

Finally there is a sense in which both historians and
Christians are *relativists*. One of the major counts brought
against teachers of history by moralists in our day is that
they instill into the minds of our youth a corrosive
relativism, a feeling that there are no universal and unchanging standards and that moral codes are always relative
to time and place. In this view, for instance, there is no
justification for saying that Democracy is any better than
Naziism, or "civilization" any better than "barbarism."
Undoubtedly there are radical skeptics among historians (as
we have already pointed out) who appear to enjoy fostering the amoral relativism they find ready-made among
their students. But the Protestant Christian at least will
find some common ground more readily with one of these
relativists than he will with an absolutist who defies some
historical institution or movement or individual. The

Christian is too deeply rooted in history to be unconcerned about the strivings and achievements of his own class, nation, or civilization in history. But his nature and destiny can never be understood from the historical perspective alone since man transcends history in addition to being immersed in it. In other words, the prospect of the collapse of our civilization is important (as it is not to a Buddhist), but not all-important (as it is to a humanistic believer in progress). If God is really Lord of history, then no man or group or idea is lord of it. The Christian can never compromise with men who see the meaning of history exhausted, for instance, in the rise of the Aryan race to world empire under the leadership of a Fuehrer; but he can find a beginning of mutual understanding with men who refuse to deify any hero or cause in history.

In all this there is meant to be no implication that the attitudes of professional historians and of Christians are *necessarily* the same, or even that when parallel attitudes emerge they spring from the same underlying motives. It is simply to say that from the perspective of the mid-twentieth century, Ranke was wrong. There is no inherent and necessary contradiction between being a Christian believer and being a professional historian.

VIII

We are left with a final question. Is there anything *distinctive* about a historian who is also a Christian? What are his marks and how will he be known? How will he understand history as how will he attempt to teach others to understand it?

To many—students, colleagues, and friends—the chief test will be quantitative: the amount of time and attention a historian devotes in his writing and teaching to the place of religion in history. Important as this test undoubtedly is, I believe it is generally over-emphasized. A good historian, whether he is a person of religious belief or not, should give religion its due just as he gives every other factor—economic, political, intellectual—its due in his study of the historical process. The current tendency is to ignore or minimize the role of religion in history as the story gets closer to the present. It is no particular surprise to most historians to learn that while the average college text in European history devotes about 30 percent of its space to religious developments in the Middle Ages, only 2 percent or less of its space is taken up with specifically religious movements after about 1800.[13] There is no question that a glib unexamined assumption that "religion is through" is often behind this progressive neglect of religious factors as the textbook writers skim over the modern centuries. In any truly impartial search (if such were possible) for what made the nineteenth century tick, religion would bulk much larger than it does in most of our texts. But this is a matter for historians in general to settle with their scholarly consciences. Naturally a historian of Christian leanings will be interested in the religious factors in history and he will probably give them due space. But being human, he will be in constant danger of giving them *too much* space, of "dragging religion in," like the Marxian who distorts the historical picture by overweighting the economic factors. The plain fact is that specifically religious ideas, religious images, religious institutions, and religious influences in general were nowhere near so dominant in the Europe of 1800 as they were in the Europe of 1300, and any historian who blurs this fundamental fact is not being honest. There is no simple quantitative test of a Christian historian. His mark is not the quantity of

[13] *College Reading and Religion: A Survey of College Reading Materials sponsored by The Edward W. Hazen Foundation* . . . (Yale Univ. Press, 1948), pp. 209-211.

time he devotes to religious matters, but the quality of his whole treatment of his subject.

To follow out the example chosen, how will a Protestant Christian historian view the "secularization" of European society since the Middle Ages? How will his view differ, if at all, from the average textbook and classroom treatment? In terms of time and space devoted to religious movements it may differ very little, and yet I fancy there should be a profundity to it which is generally lacking in the ordinary treatment. "Secularization" is an extremely complex and subtle sort of historical process. In many ways people in the Middle Ages were as worldly and immoral as people in our own day, and considerably more brutal and insensitive in some respects. True, the Church dominated their daily existence, their whole culture became infused with Christian ideals, and there was no real alternative to Christianity as a system of ultimate truth. But when we ask whether the hold of Christianity upon their lives was more or less "totalitarian" than the hold of Naziism upon Germans under Hitler or of Marxism upon Russians under Stalin, the answer is that the hold was probably less total. Naziism and Communism are not religions, but they appeal to the religious emotions of men, they organize themselves along lines strikingly similar to the Medieval Church, and they make demands upon their followers that are best described as religious. If we grant that they are pseudo-religions, it could even be argued that we live in a more "religious" age than the Middle Ages. Christianity itself is more widely spread over the earth's surface than ever before, and even the economic and political philosophies of our day have to be given a "religious" dynamic in order to move great masses of men. This suggests that "religion," often in a bewildering variety of perverted and idolatrous forms, is still one of the major forces in the twentieth century world, as it was in the thirteenth. This is an exaggeration, of course, but it may serve to suggest dimensions of the problem of "secularization" which generally remain unseen by "secular" historians and which should be evident to those of Christian belief. The latter should be aware that the concept of secularization is only one of many—and a crude and clumsy one at that—which historians need to describe the historical change which has taken place since 1300. The Western world has become more "worldly" since Dante's day, but to anyone who knows the history of the "Dark Ages," the present battle of the Christian churches with "worldliness" is surely nothing new. The "secularization of society" is a far more subtle affair than it appears to be in most textbooks.

The Christian who is also a historian, then, will be known neither by any fully-rounded "philosophy of history" which is the necessary outcome of his Christian belief, nor by the amount of time he spends talking or writing about Christianity. He will be known by *his attitude toward history,* the quality of his concern about it, the sense of reverence and responsibility with which he approaches his subject. This attitude will of course be determined by the quality of his Christian faith and life. The intensity and character of Christian belief varies enormously. An indifferent Roman Catholic will differ a great deal in his attitude toward history from a recent convert, and a Calvinist will see things differently from a Quaker. But I believe it possible to sketch the characteristics of a sort of composite Christian historian, provided the reader remembers that the author of the sketch is a Protestant, and provided both remember that although it is given to all men to follow Christ in any profession, it is given to none to become like his Master.

The attitude of the Christian historian toward the past will be like that of the Christian toward his contemporary fellow beings. He may seldom mention the name of God, of Christ, or of the Church, but in every remark he makes in the classroom and in every paragraph he writes in his study there will be a certain reverence and respect for his material, a certain feeling for human tragedy and human triumph in history which is closely parallel to the Christian's respect for human personality in general. He will try to understand before he condemns, and he will condemn with a sense that he too, being human, is involved in any judgment he may make. He will not bleach the moral color out of history by steeping it in corrosive skepticism. Nor on the other hand will he use history as a storehouse from which deceptively simple moral lessons may be drawn at random. He will admire Lord Acton's unquenchable moral fervor in urging historians "to suffer no man and no cause to escape the undying penalty which history has the power to inflict on wrong," but he will not be impressed either by Acton's historical wisdom or by his Christian humility in this famous passage. He will have too lively a sense of his responsibility to his students, his community, and his society, too deep a sense of the urgency and crisis of his time, to dismiss the whole story of the past as a tale told by an idiot, signifying nothing. He will know that to see any meaning at all in history is an act of faith, not a result of studying documents, but he will not dodge the question for that reason. He will be aware that every man in his beliefs belongs to *some* school or party or church, and he will not be afraid to admit that his own beliefs have their source in a church. He will say that he thinks them to be far better beliefs than those which stem, for instance, from the school of skepticism or the Communist party.

At the same time he will remember that he is a teacher, not a preacher or a pastor; a layman rather than a clergyman. He will remember that as a layman and a historian he has no more right to pontificate about the ultimate meaning of history than his students or his friends. If he is a Protestant, he will not grant this right to any human being, whether priest or lay. Where materialists may see mere blind process, where rationalists may see evident progress, he will see providence—a divine *providing* in both the conscious decisions and the unintended results of history, a purpose partly revealed and partly concealed, a destiny which is religious in the deepest meaning of the word, in which human freedom and divine guidance complete each other in some mysterious way.

He will not blink the fact of evil in history. He will not be so naïve as to relegate it to a past which is progressively being left behind, or to an "environment" which can be changed merely by a little human goodwill, or to some convenient historical scapegoat such as a "bad" nation, an "inferior" race, or a "degenerate" class. But he will not leave his hearers or readers to wallow in masochistic enjoyment of history's folly and brutality. He will be sensitive to the unpredictable and sometimes unbelievable redemptive forces in history. He will not "know it all." He will neither sell his fellow human being short, nor will he over-rate them. Behind both the personal decisions and the vast impersonal forces of history he will see an inscrutable purpose. He will look for the working of God both in the whirlwinds and in the still small voices of history. He will give a sense of pondering and wondering more than of either dogmatizing or doubting. ". . . And if God's motives are hid, are they therefore unjust?"

There is a sense in which the Christian historian is justified by faith. No man can *know* the meaning of history, but his faith that there is meaning in history may perhaps be counted to him as knowledge in the same sense that faith is counted to the Protestant believer as righteousness. The Christian historian's faith may nourish, enrich, and deepen the faith of those about him for the very reason that it is *not* knowledge. Let us insist upon it again that it is *an attitude toward history* which is neither assurance nor doubt—*an understanding of history* which is something less than a philosophy but more than a mere frame of mind—it is these that are the marks of a Christian historian. In the last analysis, the attitude a Christian takes toward the history of which he himself is a living part will determine his attitude toward the history which is past.

This will not be enough to some—to an Orthodox Jew, for instance, to a Roman Catholic, or to a fundamentalist Protestant. To many others it will be too much. A professing Christian member of the historical profession will be constantly aware that he is fighting a two-front war, against non-Christians who think he believes too much and super-Christians who think he believes not enough. From the subjective point of view this consciousness that there is no wall for him to put his back to may be the ultimate mark of his calling. Deep within him will be the faith, counted to him perhaps as righteousness, that in spite of the conviction of Ranke with which we began, a man may be "first of all a Christian *and* a historian."

2 · THE "MEANING OF HISTORY"

AND THE

WRITING OF HISTORY*

I

S INCE the outbreak of the Second World War we have witnessed what may best be described as a "Renaissance of Christian Thought." Christian belief is more respectable among intellectuals than it was a generation ago. Philosophers, novelists, and poets who present the case for Christianity are widely read and taken seriously even by fellow-intellectuals who do not share their beliefs. Among the Christian intelligentsia there has been a striking rebirth of theology, and Christian theologians are read more widely outside clerical circles than they have been for perhaps a hundred years. The names of Barth, Brunner, Nygren, Maritain, Tillich, and Niebuhr are known at least vaguely to the same sort of people who could not have named a single theologian a generation ago. Both the quality and range of the revival are impressive. Christianity appears to be attracting first-rate minds, and Christian speculation is ranging all the way from social and political theory to ethics, philosophy, and history.[1]

* If there actually was a kind of Augustinian revival of interest in the meaning of history in the period between and after the wars, it should be possible to demonstrate it bibliographically and to estimate its effects. This essay was an attempt to survey and estimate the literature; it was read as a paper before a meeting of the American Historical Association in New York during December 1951, and published in *Church History*, June 1952. It is reprinted here by permission of the publishers.

[1] See e.g., "Religion and the Intellectuals: A Symposium," in *Partisan Review*, XVII (1950). The discussion runs through the numbers from February to June, and was separately published in 1951.

One of the most striking things about this "Christian Renaissance" is its concern about the "meaning of history." This is something relatively new. The rationalist onslaught on the theological interpretation of history was so devastating that for a century and a half after Voltaire got through with Bossuet no Christian thinker dared attempt anything like a reconstruction—unless it took the form of a doctrine of progressive evolution, mildly tinctured by Christian principles. History became "scientific," and the theologians either retreated in confusion or joined the enemy by becoming historians. In the past twenty years, however, something has happened to give the theologians new interest in the meaning of history and new courage to express themselves. During the 1930's, Berdyaev (a Russian), Tillich (a German), H. G. Wood and John Mac-Murray (Englishmen) published significant books on the Christian interpretation of history.[2] The American Catholic Historical Association devoted its major meeting of 1935 to consideration of "The Catholic Philosophy of History."[3] In 1937 the Oxford Conference of Protestant and Eastern Orthodox Christians devoted a significant portion of its time to the theme of "The Kingdom of God and History."[4] The Second World War accelerated the growth of interest. Reinhold Niebuhr, who had announced his interest in the problem of history in *Beyond Tragedy* (1937), became increasingly interested in it toward the close of *The Nature and Destiny of Man* (1941-1943), and finally devoted a volume to summarizing and elaborating

[2] N. Berdyaev, *The Meaning of History* (New York, 1936), first sketched in lectures of 1919-1920; Paul Tillich, *The Interpretation of History* (New York, 1936); H. G. Wood, *Christianity and the Nature of History* (New York, 1934); John MacMurray, *The Clue to History* (New York, 1939).

[3] See *The Catholic Philosophy of History*, ed. Peter Guilday (New York, 1936).

[4] See *The Kingdom of God and History*, ed. H. G. Wood (Chicago, 1938).

his thought in *Faith and History* (1949). The past ten years have seen the appearance of one essay after another on the meaning of history from the Christian standpoint, by theologians, philosophers, and historians.[5] And in 1948 the subject of the presidential address before the American Historical Association was "The Christian Understanding of History," the first avowedly Christian approach in any presidential address since the 1890's.[6] In other words, the era of the two world wars has produced a sizeable literature by Christian writers on the "meaning of history." This paper is an attempt to estimate the significance of this literature and to speculate upon what effects it may have upon historical writing.

II

What contemporary Christian theologians appear to be attempting is nothing less than the reconstruction of a biblical interpretation of history from the original sources. The venture is no mere revival of medieval historiography. It owes little if anything to Bossuet or Raleigh or Otto of Freising or Orosius. Rather it is an attempt to recreate a Christian understanding of history in modern terms, under the direct inspiration of Amos, Jeremiah, and the Second Isaiah—of Paul, Augustine, and Luther—in the face of historical catastrophe not unlike that which the prophets, the saints, and the reformers themselves faced.

[5] A few of the more significant are: E. C. Rust, *The Christian Understanding of History* (London, 1947); Karl Löwith, *Meaning in History* (Chicago, 1949); Herbert Butterfield, *Christianity and History* (New York, 1949); G. Thils, *Théologie des réalités terrestres: Vol.* II, *Théologie de l'histoire* (Bruges and Paris, 1949); Hans Urs von Balthasar, *Theologie der Geschichte* (Einsiedeln, 1951); John Baillie, *The Belief in Progress* (New York, 1951).

[6] With the possible exception of H. O. Taylor's address in 1926. See Herman Ausubel, *Historians and Their Craft* (New York, 1950), chaps. VI, VII. The address is printed in *American Historical Review*, LIV (Jan. 1949), 459-476.

At the center of this attempt is Protestant "Neo-Orthodoxy." Karl Barth's *Römerbrief* (1918) was the "95 Theses" of the New Orthodoxy, but its influence was not felt on this side of the water until about 1932, when Reinhold Niebuhr's *Moral Man and Immoral Society* appeared.[7] Neo-orthodoxy, with its emphasis upon the mystery and majesty of God, the total "otherness" of the divine, the depravity and helplessness of man, the necessity of grace, and the authority of biblical revelation, appears to supply much of the motivation for contemporary Christian speculation about history's meaning. Of course, it is not the whole story. There are differences of emphasis and nuance which stem from confessional, national, and temperamental peculiarities, as well as from contrasting attitudes which go far back in Christian history. H. Richard Niebuhr, for instance, in his recent essay on *Christ and Culture* (1951) distinguishes five major Christian attitudes toward secular culture (and so towards secular history) ranging from sharp rejection to willing acceptance, all of them rooted deep in the Christian past. But Neo-orthodoxy's pessimism about the nature of man, its skepticism about historical progress, its rejection of all utopianism, are typical of the writings of Christian thinkers as diverse in background as the Calvinist Brunner, the Anglican Temple, the Eastern Orthodox Berdyaev, and the Roman Catholic Louis Bouyer. It is in this sense that the new orthodoxy is at the center of the contemporary Christian concern with history's meaning: it is typical of the most influential attitudes.

This attempt to reconstruct a Christian understanding of history is obviously not yet a program for rewriting history on the working level. This fact helps to account for a certain paradoxical aspect of the new orthodoxy, namely that although it is peculiarly interested in the meaning of

[7] See W. M. Horton, in *Protestant Thought in the Twentieth Century*, ed. Arnold S. Nash (New York, 1951), pp. 113ff.

history, it is in some respects strongly "anti-historical" in the sense of being opposed to any doctrine of immanence or evolutionism or developmentalism or progress, such as has subtly dominated Western historical writing for over a century. Theology yielded her queenly throne in American seminaries to "scientific" church history sometime during the early 1900's, but recently she has reclaimed her rights and put the usurpers to rout. The result is, as one observer puts it, that "thanks to . . . the radical reconception of orthodox theology based upon a fresh examination of Reformation and hence Augustinian theology, American Protestants are paradoxically . . . more history-conscious than during the ascendancy of the historical method."[8] This is to say that the writers in question are like Isaiah and Augustine: most of them are prophetic commentators *on* the historical process rather than chroniclers *of* the process itself—closely interested in history but suspicious of any who see salvation in the historical process. In fact, the essence of the literature may be described as an attempt to attack secular utopianism in every form, all the way from the "American Dream" to the "Classless Society," without at the same time retreating into mystical rejection of all hope in historical effort. Reinhold Niebuhr puts it in a paradoxical nutshell: man cannot find salvation "either by an escape from history or by the historical process itself."[9]

The best point at which to demonstrate both the agreement and the differences of contemporary Christian writers on the meaning of history is their treatment of the question whether history reveals any pattern, particularly the pattern of progress. Three schools may be roughly distinguished: (1) a group of pessimistic extremists, heirs of the apocalyptic tradition, who reject all historical patterns,

[8] G. H. Williams, in *Protestant Thought*, ed. Nash, p. 167.
[9] *The Nature and Destiny of Man*, II, 320.

particularly that of progress; (2) a group of mediators, consciously devoted to finding a middle position between extremes; and (3) a group of optimists who cling to some modified form of the doctrine of progress. Arbitrary as such classification necessarily is, it points toward deep and genuine disagreements which cut across confessional lines and so are characteristic of the Christian world as a whole. Roman Catholicism has both its "eschatologists" and its "incarnationalists," just as Protestantism has its pessimists and progressivists. The one difference discernible between the two major divisions of Western Christendom is that because of Roman belief in the visible historical Church, the "incarnationalists" appear to represent the dominant current in Catholic thought, while the neo-orthodox appear to represent the major current in Protestant thought. It cannot be insisted too strongly, however, that the deeper differences have little to do with denominational distinctions.[10]

Consider a few examples of the first school. The Protestant philosopher-theologian Karl Löwith writes: "There never has been and never will be an immanent solution of the problem of history, for man's historical experience is one of steady failure. . . . History is, through all the ages, a

[10] See particularly the penetrating analysis of recent Catholic literature by L. Malavez, "Deux théologies catholiques de l'histoire," in *Bijdragen, uitgegeven door de philosophische en theologische Faculteiten der Noord- und Zuid-Nederlandse Jezuieten*, x (1949), 225-240. I do not know enough about contemporary Eastern Orthodoxy to determine whether the same broad divisions of thought are evident there too. There is material in the incarnational doctrine of the Greek Fathers for the development of both extreme views mentioned.

Further bibliographical surveys are to be found in R. Aubert, "Discussions récentes autour de la théologie de l'histoire," *Collectanea Mechliniensia*, xviii (1948), 139-149; and G. Thils, "La théologie de l'histoire: Note bibliographique," *Ephemerides Theologicae Lovanienses*, xxvi (1950), 87-95. The following journals are particularly apt to carry articles on the general subject: *Cross Currents, Dieu Vivant, Month, Revue Thomiste*.

story of action and suffering, of power and pride, of sin and death. . . . The importance of secular history decreases in direct proportion to the intensity of man's concern with God and himself. . . . A 'Christian history' is nonsense." Much the same note is evident in some Roman Catholic thought. Christopher Dawson writes: "In comparison with the optimism of liberalism the Christian view of life and the Christian interpretation of history are profoundly tragic. The true progress of history is a mystery which is fulfilled in failure and suffering and which will only be revealed at the end of time." Jacques Maritain, writing in the *Partisan Review's* symposium of 1950 on "Religion and the Intellectuals," says, "I am not much interested in the new turn toward religion among intellectuals. Nor even in any *new turn* or new *historic orientation* toward religion. What is of interest, from the point of view of faith, are the souls and their orientation toward eternity. In other terms, events which, by their very nature, do not take place in 'history,' but in what Berdyaev called 'metahistory.' " In such views as these, there is little meaning left in what secular historians would call "history." The real business is going on over one's head, upstairs.[11]

The mediating school is more consciously concerned with preserving the tension between "history" and "metahistory." Reinhold Niebuhr and the Jesuit Malavez among the theologians and Herbert Butterfield among the historians best represent this group. Niebuhr characteristically presents the problems as a paradox. On the one hand he recurs often to the baffling complexity of history. In a marvelously Niebuhrian passage he writes, "History is comprised of causalities and sequences, coherences and structures, which are not easily comprehended as meaningful.

[11] Löwith, *Meaning in History*, pp. 190-197; Dawson, in *The Kingdom of God and History*, ed. H. G. Wood (Chicago, 1938), p. 216; Maritain, in *Partisan Review*, XVII (1950), 233-327.

They are too varied and unique to fit into any simple pattern of meaning. . . . The meaning of history is more complex than conceived in even the profoundest philosophies of history. . . ." In other words, Niebuhr, using Christian presuppositions, is on the side of those secular historians who are suspicious of all simple historical patterns. He quotes the English historian E. L. Woodward to back up his point: "I can see evidence of design, but the pattern is on a scale beyond my comprehension." To Niebuhr, however, it is not enough to leave the matter thus. A "Christian philosophy of history" may be impossible, he says, but a "Christian theology of history" is not: "it 'makes sense' out of life and history." The "sense" is not self-evident, but it is there. There are genuine insights, he insists, even in the modern doctrine of progress which were obscured by medieval thought and should be preserved. "There is nothing incompatible between a biblical conception of a dynamic history and the modern view of historical development if the modern errors of regarding historical development as self-explanatory and of equating it with redemption are avoided." The biblical conception of history "begins with a sense of mystery embodying meaning, and moves to a sense of meaning in history which contains perplexity and ambiguity. . . . Mystery does not annul meaning but enriches it."[12] Or as Luther put it, God both *reveals* and *conceals* Himself in history.

The third group still preserves something of the optimistic nineteenth century reconciliation between Christianity and progress. Kenneth Scott Latourette, for instance, said in his presidential address of 1948 before the American Historical Association, "the Christian understanding of history does not necessarily deny progress. . . . As the centuries pass the evidence is accumulating that, measured by his

[12] Reinhold Niebuhr, *Faith and History*, pp. 56, 112, 136, 197, 144, 103. See also his *Nature and Destiny of Man*, Vol. ii, chap. x.

effect on history, Jesus is the most influential life ever lived on this planet. That influence appears to be mounting. . . . As the centuries pass the influence of Jesus grows rather than wanes. . . . [Efforts to combat disorder mount] and more and more make themselves felt through the earth. Increasingly they have a major source in Jesus."[13] The same sense of "increasingly," of "more and more," of a sort of Christian progress, is evident in Arnold Toynbee's essay on "Christianity and Civilization" (1940). There is, he says, "a *growing* fund of illumination and grace," an "*increasing* spiritual opportunity for souls . . . to come to know God better. . . . The Christian soul can attain, while still on earth, a *greater* measure of man's greatest good than can be attained by any pagan soul."[14] John Baillie, the Scottish theologian, in a discerning little essay on the idea of progress, shows that he is perfectly familiar with ancient and contemporary Christian criticism of the doctrine, but concludes that the core of the idea of progress is Christian. "The Christian faith *does* offer us a very confident hope for the future course of terrestrial history. It is a hope which has been too little represented in the Christian tradition, but to which we are now recalled. We must recover that sense of standing on the threshold of a new historical economy (or dispensation) . . . that confidence in ultimate victory of which the New Testament is so full. When the Church of today looks forward through the years, its vision of progress is not only of an increase in the number of Christian individuals but of the increasing Christianization of the whole life of the community."[15] Among Roman Catholics, the "incarnationalists" argue in much the same way that the best achievements of civilization "may be considered as the extension of the Incarnation, as the product

[13] *American Historical Review*, LIV (Jan. 1949), 272-276.

[14] *Civilization on Trial* (New York, 1948), pp. 234-252.

[15] John Baillie, *The Belief in Progress* (New York, 1951), pp. 220, 224.

of a grace which is gradually composing the climate necessary for its perfect flowering."[16]

Thus the intellectual and emotional fervor with which
the idea of progress is attacked varies considerably, from
the radical onslaught of writers like Löwith to the paradoxical attitude of Niebuhr and the cautious appreciation of
men like Baillie. Concern with the meaning of history is
almost universal among contemporary Christian thinkers,
but conclusions are by no means unanimous. Beneath all
the views we have considered, however, there runs a strong
undercurrent of doubt about progress, suspicion of historical pattern in general, caution about human ability to discern the rationale of history. Niebuhr set the tone fifteen
years ago when he prefaced *Beyond Tragedy* with the statement that "the idea of a meaningful history does not explain the actual content of meaning."

Something of the same disagreement-in-agreement—like
musical "variations on a traditional theme"—might be
traced out through other themes in the literature if there
were space. For instance, there is the theme of Christian
anthropology, or more precisely the reconstruction of a
biblical interpretation of human nature, to which Niebuhr
(among others) has made such a brilliant contribution in
his Gifford lectures.[17] Then there is the problem of moral
judgment in history, to which Herbert Butterfield among
secular historians has given such interesting thought.[18]
Finally there is the question of the nature and significance
of time, which has commanded the attention particularly
of Continental theologians.[19] Since Augustine these have

[16] L. Malavez, *loc.cit.* (note 10), p. 234.
[17] *The Nature and Destiny of Man*, particularly Vol. I, chaps. VI, VII.
[18] Both in his *Whig Interpretation of History* (1931) and his
Christianity and History (1949).
[19] Oscar Cullmann, *Christ and Time* (Philadelphia, 1950); also
Emil Brunner, and Jean Danièlou, in *Cross Currents*, I (1950), 24-34,
and 18-90; Reinhold Niebuhr, *Faith and History*, chap. III.

been the traditional problems of Christian theology of history: progress, human nature, divine judgment, and the meaning of time. Once more they are the object of probing and persistent inquiry, with the apparent end of accomplishing for the twentieth century through many lesser minds what one great mind was able to accomplish for the fifth.

III

If we ask what effect all this has had upon the actual writing of history, upon those who make their living by historical teaching and research, or what effect it may be expected to have upon them in the visible future, the answer may appear to be simply "none." The ordinary professional historian is usually a practicing positivist. If he has a philosophy of history, he feels uneasy about it, particularly in the presence of his colleagues. Carl Becker once wrote that he would "not willingly charge a reputable historian with a Philosophy of History"—and a Theology of History would probably be an even more heinous charge. But historians are remarkably sensitive to what goes on across academic fences. At one time or another they have owed much, both in the way of conceptual framework and of methodology, to Renaissance humanism, Newtonian physics, Darwinian biology, Freudian psychology, and recently, the social sciences. It is not beyond possibility at least that they may be influenced sooner or later by what transpires from the camp of the theologians. Assuming this possibility, it seems to me that four rather specific effects are already becoming clear.

In the first place, a new interest in the *history* of the Christian understanding of history is already evident and will probably continue to grow. The history of the Christian historical sense has yet to be written, but we may soon have the monographic basis if interest continues. We have a fine new study of New Testament ideas, for instance, in Cullmann's *Christ and Time*. Theodor Mommsen has given us a fresh approach to Augustine. There are a few recent studies on the historical thought of the High Middle Ages, but we need more. Hans Lilje has done a good monograph on Luther's historical ideas and there is a dissertation on the historical element in Reformation controversy, but much more remains to be done on the sixteenth and succeeding centuries. These are scattered instances only of what appears to be a fruitful and growing interest which may someday add a fresh chapter to the history of ideas.[20]

In the second place, the revival we have been considering has indirectly posed new problems and suggested new insights in the history of Christian thought and institutions. Eleven years ago Wilhelm Pauck felt that neo-orthodoxy had not contributed very directly to the "Luther Renaissance," but he suggested that the influence might grow.[21] The theological and the historical interests in Luther have certainly moved along hand-in-hand since then, and I think that, as Pauck suggested it might, the direct and mutual influence of one on the other has increased. Certainly the two excellent studies of Luther which have appeared in the past year show the influence of the contemporary revival of theology.[22] It is well not to press the point too far, but

[20] Theodor Mommsen, "St. Augustine and the Christian Idea of Progress," *Journal of the History of Ideas*, XII (June 1951), 346-374; Otto Herding, "Geschichtsschreibung und Geschichtsdenken im Mittelalter," *Theologische Quartalschrift*, no. 2 (1950); B.-M. Lacroix, "The Notion of History in Early Medieval Historians," *Medieval Studies*, X (1948), 219-223; Lynn White, Jr., "Christian Myth and Christian History," *Journal of the History of Ideas*, III (April 1942), 145-158; Hans Lilje, *Luthers Geschichtsanschauung* (Berlin, 1932); P. Polman, *L'élément historique dans la controverse religieuse au XVIe siècle* (Gembloux, 1932); the recent and excellent study by J. M. Headley, *Luther's View of Church History* (New Haven and London, 1963).

[21] *Church History*, IX (Dec. 1940), 313.

[22] Roland H. Bainton, *Here I Stand* (Nashville, 1950); and E. G. Schwiebert, *Luther and His Times* (St. Louis, 1950).

in the only field about which I can speak with any assurance, the Reformation, the current trend toward a revived Reformation theology has been a stimulating influence on historical scholarship.

Third, I think it can be shown that the treatment of Christianity by historians who are not believers is becoming somewhat more sympathetic than it was, say, a generation ago. The point cannot be proved, but one bit of what seems to me typical evidence may be offered. Since the First World War we have had three notable attempts to sketch the history of Western thought for the general reader in one volume: James Harvey Robinson's *Mind in the Making* (1921), J. H. Randall's *Making of the Modern Mind* (1929), and Crane Brinton's *Ideas and Men* (1950). Robinson had limitless faith in science and was coolly contemptuous of all religion. Randall had a genuine appreciation of Christianity, at least in its aesthetic and moral aspects, although his ultimate trust was in the scientific method. The atmosphere of Brinton's book is altogether different. The trust in science is chastened and disillusioned, and the treatment of Christianity begins significantly with a statement to the effect that although the writer is not a professing Christian, he will do his best to be fair. The change is probably something more than a difference of temperament between the three men concerned.

In the fourth place, I think it is quite evident that among historians who *are* professing Christians, the tendency to make Christian presuppositions more explicit is increasing. Again, the marshaling of evidence must be suggestive rather than exhaustive. The case of Arnold Toynbee is perhaps the most familiar. Toynbee began as a classical historian, much under the influence of Bergson and Spengler. Since then he has moved steadily in the direction of a more Christian and less classical interpretation of history, as both his writings and his conversation demonstrate. I have suggested elsewhere that his attempt to reconcile the cyclical and progressive views, to bridge time and eternity by the skillful use of the idea of the very, very long, is not altogether successful.[23] But there can be no question of the sincerity or of the increasing explicitness of his Christian assumptions, even though they are of a somewhat amorphous sort.

Even more interesting and somewhat less familiar is the case of Herbert Butterfield of Cambridge University. Butterfield is a professional historian who is proud of his belief in the importance of "microscopic research" and who is accepted by the profession in a way Toynbee is not. He has been a good Methodist all his life. Twenty years ago he wrote *The Whig Interpretation of History* (1931), a witty and devastating attack on Acton's Inaugural and its insistence on the historian's duty to pronounce magisterial moral judgments. "The most useless and unproductive of all forms of reflection," Butterfield wrote (p. 108), is "the dispensing of moral judgments upon people or upon actions in retrospect." The theme of the book was in the last sentence: "The understanding of the past is not so easy as it is sometimes made to appear." Three years after the close of World War II, Butterfield was asked to deliver a series of lectures at Cambridge on the theme of "Christianity and History," with the groping, disillusioned post-war undergraduate in mind. The lectures were so successful that they were later given on the Third Programme of the BBC and then published.[24] In them he tried to show "why I think that the general course of history is so shaped that a Christian is in the right relation with it." They make a discerning and mature little book, in which the author

[23] "The Problem of the Christian Historian: Arnold J. Toynbee," *Theology Today*, v (Oct. 1948), 388-405.
[24] *Christianity and History* (London, 1949; New York, 1950). Quotations below are from pp. 130, 59, 62, 52.

brings his Christian belief and his historical knowledge to interpenetrate each other. "There is a judgment embedded in the fabric of history," he concludes, but "this gives none of us the right to act as judges over others." Nazi Germany, for instance, undoubtedly fell under this judgment, but "it is a dangerous illusion to imagine that if Germany can be proved to have sinned those who were fighting against her may be assumed to have been righteous." In *Christianity and History*, in other words, as in his *History and Human Relations* (1951), Butterfield has followed the roots of his previous skepticism and humility about making moral judgments in historical writing down to their religious soil. When asked once if he felt that he had changed his basic beliefs in any way since writing *The Whig Interpretation*, he was quick to say no. The change of tone, which is so evident to any reader of the two books, lies in the fact that the Christian presuppositions which have to be inferred in the first book are quite explicit in the second. The change lies outside the author, I believe, in the audience and atmosphere of the late 1920's, and those of the late 1940's.

I have no idea whether the revival of a Christian understanding of history will have any more general effect on historical interpretation than the four specific results suggested: new interest in the history of the Christian interpretation, new insights into the history of Christian thought and institutions, a more sympathetic treatment of Christianity by non-Christian historians, and more explicit Christian presuppositions in the writings of historians who profess Christianity.[25] The revival may conceivably rein-

[25] This discussion has deliberately avoided the important but tangled question of textbook treatments. See the chapter on European History in *College Reading and Religion: A Survey of College Reading Materials sponsored by the Edward W. Hazen Foundation* . . . (Yale Univ. Press, 1948); and Lacey Baldwin Smith, "A Study of Textbooks on European History during the last Fifty Years." *Journal of Modern History*, XXIII (Sept. 1951), 250-256.

force the efforts of secular historians to write genuine "world history" rather than history warped by national or class bias. It may help to sensitize historians to moral and spiritual values in reaction against moral relativism. It may accomplish other things most of us would call "good." The literature we have been examining, however, *may* prove to be part of a general "anti-historical" movement, of which the "New Criticism" in literature, existentialism in philosophy, and the trend of thought about the nature of time in modern physics are other examples. The current interest in myth may be a straw in the wind. The "myth" of Christianity sometimes appears to be swallowing the historical element. The Christ of experience often seems to be absorbing the Jesus of history. Will we become so concerned with "the meaning of history" that, like some in the Dark Ages, we confuse what happened with what ought to have happened? G. G. Coulton, the medievalist, pokes fun (somewhat unfairly) at Agnellus, the ninth century Bishop of Ravenna who undertook to write a complete series of lives of his predecessors, and who tells us that wherever he was unable to find any materials whatever on one of his subjects—no documents, no monuments, not even any hearsay—he composed the life himself, "with the help of God and the prayers of the brethren."[26] Will we soon come to this sort of thing again?

This is surely to jump ahead too far and too fast with Sorokin and other prophets of the end of our sensate era. Actually what we are witnessing is a swing back of the pendulum which has not even yet reached dead center. Christian theologians and historians are once more frankly concerned, like Augustine, with the "why" of history. But, unlike the medieval chroniclers, they are imbued with considerable respect for the "when" and "how," and they are far more cautious and tentative than their medieval

[26] G. G. Coulton, *Medieval Panorama* (Cambridge, 1939), p. 439.

predecessors in answering the "why." It is hard to believe that a new Bossuet or Orosius is just around the corner. If Niebuhr and Butterfield are typical, the Christian historian of the future will probably err by concluding too little rather than too much. In fact it cannot be emphasized too strongly that although contemporary Christian writers insist upon the ultimate moral and spiritual meaning in history, most of them are just as suspicious as professional historians of vast philosophies of history, just as ready to search for secondary causes and accept hard fact over facile theory on the level of mundane history.

It has been the genius of Christianity at its best to value the historical but not to overvalue it. In the parable of the Last Judgment, as Niebuhr points out,[27] human beings are judged by what they have been and done in their historical existence. This is the Christian affirmation of the historical. But it is made clear that men can never know their own righteousness or the full meaning of their acts so long as they are in history. This is the limitation of the historical. It seems to be the object of contemporary Christian writers on the meaning of history to reassert the point of the parable. Whitehead once predicted "that that religion will conquer which can render clear to popular understanding some eternal greatness incarnate in the passage of temporal fact."[28] Twentieth century Christians hardly need to reassert their interest in "the passage of temporal fact," after two centuries of "historicism." Obviously, however, they feel that historians have well-nigh abandoned the search for any eternal greatness incarnate in events, and that such a search should be renewed. This is the heart of current Christian thinking about the "meaning of history." Whether it will appreciably affect the writing of history in the next generation may depend upon

[27] *The Nature and Destiny of Man,* II, 291ff.
[28] A. N. Whitehead, *Adventures of Ideas* (New York, 1933), p. 41.

[51]

the turn taken by world events. A tragic turn will almost certainly increase the numbers of those members of the historical profession who seek the meaning of tragedy in the Christian understanding of history.

3 · DIVINE PURPOSE AND
HUMAN HISTORY*

IS HISTORY in the hands of God—or of Man—or of Nature? The Odyssey of the Western mind in its search for the meaning of history could be written in terms of these three questions. Are we to view the development of societies and civilizations, the elaboration of technologies and cultures, the creative acts and crucial events of human history as the works of a personal divinity, or of man himself, or of natural process? Long before the birth of Christ, each of these three major conceptions of the character and meaning of history had been sketched out by Hebrew and Greek thinkers.

To the Hebrew prophets, history was the work of God. Time was the medium in which Jahweh worked out and revealed his will—choosing and guiding his people, comforting or chastising them, commanding, advising, warning, and saving them. As Hebrew thought matured, history as prophets and chroniclers saw it acquired direction and purpose through the refinement of three fundamental conceptions: Creation, the Covenant, and the Day of Judgment. By the time of the Exile, the vision of a universal history of all mankind, with a definite beginning and end, guided to its goal by a personal Deity who is both just and merciful, was fully outlined in the glowing poetry of Second Isaiah.

* Reinhold Niebuhr had argued eloquently that there is mystery as well as meaning in any Christian view of history. Judging by the reactions of committed Christians, I had fancied that I was closer to the Christian skeptic's role than to the Augustinian, but this essay belongs to a phase of assurance. Done as a paper for a conference of campus clergy at Montreat, N.C., it comes as close as I think I have ever come to finding unambiguous meaning in the historical process. It appeared in the *Christian Scholar* for December 1954, and is reprinted here by permission of that journal.

To the first great historians of ancient Athens in the following century, history was primarily the work of man. To be sure, the Greeks were always uneasily aware of divine intervention and natural forces in human history. But history to them was essentially the deeds of men, who were free within certain limits to create or destroy, progress or regress, as their own intelligence or ignorance, their own desire or indifference might dictate. Human behavior follows certain patterns, Thucydides believed; by the careful study of these patterns in all the richness of their concrete detail, men can learn from their own past how to conduct themselves in the future when similar situations recur—as they will. Men make their own history, and at the same time can learn from it.

Finally, some Greek thinkers were haunted by the thought that history is perhaps nothing more than blind, ineluctable, natural process, impervious to all wishful interference by God or man. This view lurks behind Herodotus' picture of the vast pendulum-like swing of political power from East to West and back again, behind the Greek dramatists' conception of Fate, and behind Stoic and Epicurean thought about history.

In other words, the three views that history is the work of God, the creation of man, or the movement of nature were each adumbrated during the millennium before Christ. There has hardly been a time in Western history when each of the three has not been a live alternative as a key to the meaning of history, and each is alive today. But as we think back over European history, it appears as if the three conceptions have succeeded each other chronologically as the dominant ways of understanding history, if we allow always for periods of mixture and overlapping.

I

From Augustine almost to Bossuet, the theological interpretation of history ruled men's minds. History was the record of divine providence in a very direct and literal sense. Against any theory of aimless and fortuitous coincidence of events on the one hand, or of iron determinism or regular cyclical recurrence on the other, Christian thinkers insisted that history is to be thought of as destiny, the purposeful providing and pre-destining of the God who had created the universe, who had incarnated Himself in a man at a particular time and place, and who would some day bring history to its appointed end in final judgment. There was a simplicity and grandeur about this sense of history as the drama of salvation which explains and justifies its hold on the European mind for over a thousand years. It is difficult to see how the struggling frontier society which succeeded the collapse of Roman society in the West would have had the heart to continue and eventually become the confident and dynamic civilization we call "Western" without the theology of history for which St. Augustine more than any other individual was responsible. For a good many generations before Augustine wrote the *City of God*, men had put their trust in the "Eternal City" of Rome. Even some Christians of Augustine's day had recently become convinced that the Hebrew prophecies of an age of peace and righteousness were being realized before their very eyes in the Christianized Rome of Constantine and his successors. And yet in A.D. 410 Eternal Rome, Christian Rome, was obviously disintegrating, a helpless victim of internal dissension and barbarian attack. It was at this moment that Augustine caught the imagination of Christians with a conception of history as the work not of man nor of nature, but of God. The end of Rome would not mean the end of history. The meaning of history was not *Romanitas*; the goal of history was not the *Pax romana*. What was really going on in history was the grim, mysterious struggle of two half-visible societies, the *civitas Dei* and the *civitas terrena*. This struggle would continue under God's providence until each "ran on and ran out to their separate proper and merited ends."[1]

The strength of Augustine's theology of history lay in its ambiguity. He was careful not to identify the *civitas Dei* with the Church and the *civitas terrena* with the State. So far as human judgment was concerned, these were invisible societies. But there was just enough ambiguity in the 22 books of the *City of God* to allow later thinkers to identify the *civitas Dei* with the medieval Church, the invisible company of the saints with the *respublica Christiana* of the medieval Popes. In his strictures on Roman virtues as simply "splendid vices," Augustine had come close to separating secular history and the history of salvation. By a kind of dynamic misinterpretation, the Middle Ages brought them together again, by historicizing the *civitas Dei* and identifying it with the Roman Church.

The cost of this misinterpretation was heavy, however. Augustine's theology of history was a healthy corrective to the excesses of a classical historiography which stopped short with man and nature in its search for meaning in history. But this Augustinian view was now enthusiastically taken over by a society which had lost much of the rich and concrete knowledge of man and nature which the Greeks had possessed. So far as empirical knowledge of man and his behavior is concerned, the average medieval chronicle or saint's life suffers terribly by comparison with Thucydides or Tacitus. The best of medieval theology has weathered well, but even the best of medieval historiography is unread today except by specialists. God is certainly lord of history in Gregory of Tours' *History of the Franks*, in the monastic chronicles, or in the saints' lives of the *Golden Legend*. But his lordship often appears to consist

[1] See T. E. Mommsen, "St. Augustine and the Christian Idea of Progress," *Journal of the History of Ideas*, XII (June 1951), 372 and *passim*.

in meaningless miracles, capricious interventions in human affairs, and acts of power whose meaning is exhausted in their relationship to the good of the visible Roman Church. The Reformation did something to restore the profundity and grandeur of Augustine's conception of history as the work of God, but as in the case of the Hebrew chroniclers, Protestant historians were never quite worthy of the prophetic insights upon which their religion was based. It has always been easier for theologians than for working historians to write convincingly of history as the work of God.

II

History as the work of man was the dominant conception in European historiography from Machiavelli to Gibbon. It was part protest against medieval historical writing, part return to the insights of the ancient historians, and part original creation. To Machiavelli man is alone in his world, his *virtu* pitted against a *fortuna* which appears variously as chance, caprice, and fate, but never as personal deity. Man is primarily a political animal, and history primarily the history of politics. Machiavelli was certainly no optimist about human nature, but he did believe that man could learn by studying the patterns of political behavior revealed by the past and could apply his learning to practical politics. Those who came after him grew far more optimistic. The historical philosophers of the Enlightenment pulled Augustine's Heavenly City down to earth and anchored it firmly in time and space. The spiritual progress from Creation to Last Judgment envisaged by Augustine was transformed into human progress, and man took God's place on the driver's seat of history. Past history appeared to Voltaire as simply the record of man's crimes and follies, now that man had discovered the clue to progress in the right use of reason in scientific method. Condorcet perfectly expressed the intoxicating enthusiasm and confidence in man of his generation: "No bounds have been fixed to the improvement of human faculties; the perfectibility of man is absolutely indefinite; the progress of this perfectibility, henceforth above the control of every power that would impede it, has no other limit than the duration of the globe—The course of this progress may be more or less rapid, but it can never be retrograde."

How strangely similar this absolute confidence in man is on the surface to Augustine's absolute confidence in God as the lord of history! In neither case is there any need for worry about the ultimate outcome, in Condorcet's case because history is in man's own hands, in Augustine's because history is in God's.

The historiography of the Renaissance and the Enlightenment probed and exploited the weaknesses of the theological interpretation of history. Machiavelli did not argue against Providence, he simply ignored it. He was interested only in human motives and this-worldly causes. "All armed prophets have conquered," he wrote laconically, "and unarmed ones have failed"; "men more easily forget the death of their father than the loss of their patrimony"; "men do not believe themselves sure of what they already possess except by acquiring still more"; "only those defences are good, certain, and durable, which depend on yourself alone and your own ability." The tone of these maxims suggests what medieval historiography had lacked: a shrewd, realistic, empirical knowledge of the workings of human nature in social and political relationships. The Enlightenment attacked the older theory of providence more directly. Bossuet's theological interpretation of world history up to Charlemagne was already considerably rationalized to conform to the temper of its age, but Voltaire mercilessly ridiculed even this rationalized version of the *civitas Dei*: what possible reason is there for us to believe that God "chose" that miserable people, the Jews, he asks;

or did God lead Alexander on to the conquest of the Near East simply to establish some Jewish second-hand dealers in Alexandria, as Dr. Pangloss insisted he did?

What I am suggesting is that we cannot count the overthrow of the Augustinian conception of history in the eighteenth century as pure loss, even from the Christian point of view. Surely we today can learn more about "divine purpose and human history" from Gibbon than from the *Golden Legend*—in spite of Gibbon's sardonic purpose of describing "the triumph of barbarism and religion" in the fall of his beloved Rome. In contrast with many other religions, Christianity is a profoundly "this-worldly" religion. When its conception of history loses touch with the world of man in all its concreteness and complexity, when the workings of God in history are reduced to miracle and caprice, then no fully adequate theory of divine purpose in human history can be developed.

III

The view of history as the work of man, which reached its climax in the late eighteenth or early nineteenth century, exaggerated the freedom and power of man not only with respect to God but also with respect to nature. Nowhere in Condorcet's view of history which we have quoted was there any understanding of the relentless pressure of natural forces on mankind, of the organic development of institutions, of the mysterious concatenation of events which so often appears automatic and utterly beyond the control of human purpose. Conscious of these deficiencies, historians of the next century developed views of the past which, in spite of differences, agreed in emphasizing evolutionary development, natural processes, and what were called "historical forces." Various sorts of determinisms became fashionable—geographical, biological, psychological, and economic. History, which had already slipped from the hand of God, now slipped from the grasp of man into the control of natural process. So long as belief in progress remained vigorous, there was no loss of optimism. What man no longer could do by himself, evolution would do for him. Carl Becker has wittily described this transition from providence to human progress to evolution in his essay on "Progress" in the *Encyclopedia of the Social Sciences*: the Bible says, and the Middle Ages agreed, that man cannot add a cubit to his stature by taking thought; the eighteenth century insisted that he could; the nineteenth maintained that cubits would be added to his stature whether he took thought or not.

In Marx's dialectical materialism, history is not shaped directly by natural environment but by a kind of intermediate environment created by man in his peculiar capacity as the one animal who produced his means of subsistence. This intermediate environment is created, but not really controlled by man. It develops and changes according to laws and forces which have only the most tenuous relation to human consciousness and intention— if they have any at all. "In the social production of their subsistence," Marx wrote in his *Critique of Political Economy*, "men enter into determined and necessary relations with each other which are independent of their wills. . . . The sum of these production-relations forms the economic structure of society, the real basis upon which a juridical and political superstructure arises, and to which definite social forms of consciousness correspond. The mode of production of the material subsistence conditions the social, political, and spiritual life-process in general. It is not the consciousness of men which determines their existence, but on the contrary it is their social existence which determines their consciousness."

Here again we encounter a boundless confidence and assurance in the outcome of history, but now it is because history is delivered from the control of either God or man into the powerful grip of "dialectical materialism." The *Communist Manifesto* moves relentlessly from its magisterial opening judgment that all history is the history of class struggles through what has happened, what is happening, and what is going to happen, with absolutely unruffled conviction. "The advance of industry," Marx writes, "whose involuntary promoter is the bourgeoisie, replaces the isolation of the laborers, due to competition, by their involuntary combination, due to association. The development of modern industry, therefore, cuts from under its feet the very foundation on which the bourgeoisie produces and appropriates products. What the bourgeoisie therefore produces, above all, are its own grave diggers. Its fall and the victory of the proletariat are equally inevitable." The Revolution then is a kind of Second Coming, the Classless Society a sort of millennium, the bourgeoisie are the ungodly, and the proletariat the righteous. The City of God is now a sure bet precisely because its advent depends neither on God nor on man, but on the historical dialectic itself. There is no hint whatever of personal significance or personal purpose, whether human or divine in the process. All is "involuntary," "inevitable." The greatest reproach Marx can throw up against rival socialist systems is their "total incapacity to comprehend the march of modern history," as he puts it—that relentless tramp of faceless feet marching blindly into utopia through no will of their own.

Again it is dangerous to say that the overthrow of Condorcet's optimism about history as the work of man by this sort of conception was unalloyed loss. The materialist view of history is of course a grotesque caricature of reality. But Marx's insistence upon the determining influence of methods of production upon social institutions and intellectual movements, his shrewd observation that all ideas are in some sense "ideologies," that is, rationalizations of class interest, his sense for the vast inertial forces and inevitabilities in the historical process—all these are valuable and integral parts of our twentieth century view of the past—and they are not incompatible with a Christian conception of human nature. Just as Bossuet's account of Rome seems naïve in comparison with Gibbon's, so Gibbon may seem naïve in comparison with Rostovtseff's work on the economic and social bases of Roman society, which owes a typical indirect debt to the economic interpretation of history. There is a sense—a very real sense— in which our understanding of the richness and complexity of the human past has expanded and deepened since Augustine wrote the *City of God*. We have lost much; but the loss is balanced by gain.

IV

It is only against such a background as this, I believe, that it is possible to understand the revival of interest in the Christian understanding of history which is such a striking mark of our present generation. The twentieth century literature on "Christianity and history" is already large, and it is still growing. It is obviously impossible to describe it here.[2] But we cannot avoid asking what its origins are and what its general significance may be.

Obviously the revival of Christian interpretations of history springs primarily from disillusionment with theories of history as the work of man or as the product of blind process. We have gone through two world wars of unprecedented violence and now cower in the shadow of a third, which may destroy every major city in the world. No wonder that the optimism of such views as those of Condorcet or Marx rings today on our ears with such hollow irony.

[2] See the brief survey in "The 'Meaning of History' and the Writing of History," Chapter 2 of this book.

No wonder that Augustine seems more intelligent and intelligible to us than he seemed to Gibbon. For the first time in several centuries, the meaning of history seems to be more comprehensible to those who take God seriously than to those who do not.

It cannot be emphasized too strongly, however, that this is no mere revival of the older theological interpretation of history. Renascences are always to some extent revolutions, born of the peculiar circumstances of the moment. It is impossible literally to revive the Augustinian conception of history because it is impossible to wipe from the historical slate the permanent achievements of later historiography and return to St. Augustine's thought-world. What the best of our contemporary Christian theologians and historical philosophers are trying to do, it seems to me, is to apply Christian insights to the understanding of history in the light of the varied and fascinating empirical knowledge of man and natural process which we have acquired since the Renaissance of the fifteenth century. Barth and Brunner, Berdyaev and Dawson, Toynbee and Butterfield, Tillich and Niebuhr, each in his own way, are trying to develop a modern Christian theory of providence which takes account of all that historical study has taught us about man and time in the past three or four centuries.

In this attempt, as each of them soon discloses, the central problem is the classical theological problem of God's revelation and concealment. To what extent is the divine purpose in history "totally other," and so totally unintelligible to man? To what extent, on the other hand, is God's will revealed in events? Even if we take seriously the Hebraic-Christian idea of a God who works in history—who chooses and chastises, suffers and redeems—we still must solve anew for ourselves the problem implicit in Luther's phrase *Die Verborgenheit Gottes,* the hiddenness of God. To what extent is God revealed, to what extent concealed, in events?

Events to a Christian must have a quality of uniqueness, of once-for-all-ness. Christ came "in the fullness of time," "died once for our sins, and rising again, dies no more." The Incarnation and Resurrection together constituted the central *Kairos* of history, but if this was a truly unique event, then all events are unique, and time is a straight line sequence of unrepeatable occurrences. *"Once* to everyman and nation comes the moment to decide . . . and that choice goes by forever. . . ."

From Amos to Reinhold Niebuhr, the prophets of the Hebraic-Christian tradition have attempted to read "the signs of the times," to discern the *Kairoi,* to sense the significance of the particular moment. That this tendency is authentically rooted in the New Testament, Oscar Cullmann has shown us in his brilliant essay, *Christ and Time.* The divine purpose to a Christian is not a generalized intent which can be reduced to a formula, a law, or a vision—as it might be to a Hindu, a Buddhist, or a Platonist. It is a *will revealed in persons and events.* "I hazard the prophecy," Whitehead once wrote, "that that religion will conquer which can render clear to popular understanding some eternal greatness in the passage of temporal fact."[3] But precisely what is the "eternal greatness" in any given historical fact, and what does it reveal of God's purpose? It is peculiarly difficult for the twentieth century Christian to discern the hand of God in the extraordinarily complex pattern of events and forces which three centuries of sophisticated historical study have revealed to us.

I think I have said enough to suggest that any Christian understanding must steer carefully between over-emphasizing the hiddenness of God and over-stressing the

[3] *Adventures of Ideas* (New York, 1933), p. 41.

revelation of God in events. Some contemporary theologies of history come close to saying that the divine will can never be revealed in any meaningful sense at all in specific secular events. Others come close to saying that the religious significance of certain historical events is as plain as the nose on your face. It is hard to say which is the more dangerous tendency. The first may lead to separation between the sacred and the secular so sharp as to preclude any discussion whatever of "divine purpose in human history" and end in despair. The second may lead to the facile identification of divine will and historical event superficially considered. The first is eloquently expressed by Karl Löwith when he writes, "There never has been and never will be an immanent solution of the problem of history, for man's historical experience is one of steady failure."[4] The second was coarsely expressed by Adolf Hitler the day he entered Vienna in the *coup d'état* of March 1938: "Within three days the Lord struck the former rulers of this country," he shouted to the crowds; "everything that has happened must have been pre-ordained by Divine Will."

It is obviously not enough simply to believe that history is in the hands of God. The content and quality of such a belief are the important things. There is often more reverence, more humility, and more profundity in the historical conceptions of some Machiavellians and Marxists than there is in the bloody providential theories of parts of the Old Testament and some medieval chronicles. Oliver Cromwell had a way of seeing divine dispensations in current events such as battles, but at this distance it is somewhat more difficult for us than for him to be sure that God was on the side of Independency and the New Model Army.

[4] *Meaning in History* (Chicago, 1949), pp. 190-197.

It is also not enough, however, to believe that God is dead and that history is in the hands of men or of natural forces. With all its faults and possibilities of perversion, the Hebraic-Christian tradition still offers mankind the profoundest and most satisfying understanding of history of all the alternatives offered thus far. Man never seems to rise to his fullest stature when he thinks of himself simply as man—or as animal. He comes into his own only when he thinks of himself as a creature of God and his history as the work of God.

More than any other in our generation, Herbert Butterfield, the Cambridge historian, seems to me to come close to reconstructing a truly Christian theory of providence, while doing justice at the same time to the views of history as in some real sense the work of man and the work of nature. Contemporary Protestant theology at its best has a way of taking account of the best in eighteenth century humanism and nineteenth century naturalism in formulating a theistic position, and this at least Butterfield tries to do, in simple, non-technical language. In all his writings he shows an extraordinarily sensitive feel for natural process, or, as he puts it, "that kind of history-making which goes on so to speak over our heads, now deflecting the results of our actions, now taking our purposes out of our hands, and now turning our endeavors to ends not realized."[5] This is the aspect of history upon which Marx and other determinists have cast so much light. But to Butterfield this aspect is an aspect of the work of providence, mysterious but still meaningful.

In the same way he shows a remarkable sensitivity to the aspect of history as human creativity and human free-will. In a striking figure he compares the human story to "a piece of orchestral music that we are playing over for the first time." You and I can only see and understand our

[5] *Christianity and History* (New York, 1949), p. 94.

own part as we play it—say, the second clarinet part. We cannot see the plan of the whole composition until we finish, although we can guess at it from what we have played. Any note we play gains meaning only as it sounds in harmony with those of the other players and continues melodic and harmonic lines already laid down. But "even this analogy is not sufficiently flexible," he says, "to do justice to the process of time; and to make the comparison more authentic we must imagine that the composer himself is only composing the music inch by inch as the orchestra is playing it; so that if you and I play wrong notes he changes his mind and gives a different turn to the bars that come immediately afterwards, as though saying to himself: 'We can only straighten out this piece of untidiness if we pass for a moment from the major into a minor key.' "[6] This is a striking figure, and I am not sure that it is not Pelagian heresy! But it is surely a profound and exciting attempt to reconcile free-will and predestination, history as the work of God, in a modern metaphor. Butterfield asks us "to think of history as though an intelligence were moving over the story, taking its bearings afresh after everything men do, and making its decisions as it goes along."[7]

He ends by insisting, as I have insisted, on the meaning which Christians must inevitably sense in concrete historical events. "Every instant is 'eschatological,' or, as one person has put it, like the point in the fairy-story where the clock is just about to strike twelve. On this view there can be no case of an absentee God leaving man at the mercy of chance in a universe blind, stark, and bleak. And a real drama—not a madman's nightmare or tissue of flimsy dreams—is being enacted on the stage of all human history—a real conflict between good and evil is taking

[6] *Ibid.*, pp. 94-95.
[7] *Ibid.*, p. 109.

place, events do matter, and something is being achieved irrespective of our apparent success or failure."[8] Whether "what is being achieved" is essentially a story of divine *power* working invincibly for the victory of righteousness, or of divine *love* suffering unendingly and drawing men freely, by "faith given freely" as Dostoievsky's Grand Inquisitor puts it—this is the central paradox of the Christian religion, and I must leave its solution to those who are better theologians than I.

[8] *Ibid.*, p. 121.

4 · THE AIMS AND HOPES OF MANKIND IN THE LIGHT OF ADVANCING SCIENCE: AN HISTORIAN'S VIEW*

THE HISTORIAN's job is to see things in the perspective of time, to describe human development, and to explain as best he can what change he observes. In a discussion such as this he *ought* to be able to establish how men's "aims and hopes" have changed, say, in the past thousand years, and precisely to what extent the changes have been the result of "advancing science" or of other factors. Some in his audience will probably expect him also to gaze steadily into the crystal ball and predict what is going to happen to human hopes and to science the week after next. Obviously all this is impossible to do in the time allowed—or in any length of time. What I propose to do is simply to show you an historian's mind at work on a very large, complex, and unanswerable problem. But before I begin I must warn you that historians are cantankerous people, given to skepticism and relativism, leery of eternal principles because they have seen so many of them change with time and place, and apt to minimize the contemporary sense of crisis by insinuating that, after all, things have always been in a mess and the plight of modern man is not so modern as it seems.

* In 1955, the late Arthur Compton, the physicist, convened a conference of people representing all the academic disciplines at Washington University, St. Louis, to discuss the place of science in modern culture. The paper which follows was planned for one of the sessions open to the general public. It appeared in the fall of 1955 in the *Journal of Public Law* published by Emory University Law School at Atlanta, Georgia, and reappears here by permission. The title was assigned.

Certainly the "aims and hopes of mankind" today are not exactly what they used to be, say, in the High Middle Ages. Let us take a few hasty soundings in the history of human aspirations in Western history. At the close of his *De Monarchia* Dante wrote: "Unutterable Providence, then, has set two ends before man to be contemplated by him: the blessedness of this life, which consists in the exercise of his proper power and is symbolized by the terrestrial paradise, and the blessedness of eternal life, which consists in the fruition of the divine aspect, to which his proper power may not ascend unless assisted by the divine light." Three centuries later John Calvin began his *Institutes of the Christian Religion* thus: "True and substantial wisdom principally consists of two parts, the knowledge of God, and the knowledge of ourselves. . . . The miserable ruin into which we have been plunged by the fall of the first man compels us to raise our eyes towards heaven, not only as hungry and famished, to seek thence a supply for our wants but aroused with fear to learn humility." Dante and Calvin are not so otherworldly as some we could select, but they are obviously convinced that human aspirations do not stop with this world. They are primarily interested in knowing God and attaining blessedness.

Compare Francis Bacon, writing less than a century after Calvin: "Now the true and lawful goal of the sciences is none other than this: that human life be endowed with new discoveries and powers." In his *New Atlantis* he described the purpose of Salomon's scientific foundation as "the knowledge of causes and secret motions of things, and the enlarging of the bounds of human empire, to the effecting of all things possible." Three centuries later Thomas Henry Huxley spoke for his century "On the Advisableness of Improving Natural Knowledge." Men blamed the Great Plague of 1666 on God and the Great Fire of the same year on the Papists, he recalls. Now when plague strikes, men do not flock to the churches, they look to the drains. "We have no reasons to believe that it is the improvement of our faith, nor that of our morals, which keeps the plague from our cities. . . . [I]t is the improvement of our natural knowledge." Something certainly has happened to modify the language of human aims and hopes between Dante and Huxley. Blessedness, knowledge of God, and humility are replaced by happiness, knowledge of nature, and self-confidence. The climate of aspiration has changed.

I think the majority of historians would agree with me in three things: first, that the development of modern science is the major explanation for this change; second, that it is not the only explanation; and, third, that the change itself should not be exaggerated.

There *was* a "scientific revolution" in the seventeenth century, and it was enormously influential. The preparation for it in Greek and Arabic science was long and slow, and there was no sharp breach of continuity about the year 1600 with men's previous efforts to know and to control the world of nature. But what happened in the seventeenth century in Western Europe—mainly in the 400-mile triangle between London, Paris, and Amsterdam—was something unique and decisive in the history of mankind: a close mating of controlled experiment and mathematical interpretation in the study of nature, and accelerated exchange of information leading to chain-discoveries, a fresh and overwhelming faith in the validity and utility of a new method of knowing. The result was a revolution which has continued to expand and accelerate down to our own day.

There is a naïve view of this "scientific revolution," still widespread though thoroughly discredited by historians, which sees it as the fortuitous work of a number of geniuses who happened to drop weights off towers and observe fall-

[71]

ing apples. This naïve view by-passes the real problem: why so many first-rate minds thought that observing falling bodies was important, and why they interpreted their observations mathematically. The answers to these questions have taken historians back into the history of everything from medieval scholasticism and technology to the rise of trade, the development of capitalism, the flowering of Gothic naturalism, and the spread of Renaissance humanism. Explaining the origins of modern science is actually a question of the same order of magnitude as determining the causes of Rome's fall. Let us say simply that most historians today view the "scientific revolution" as merely a phase—albeit a decisive one—of a very long and complex process, the secularization of Western society. Science came to full flower at a particular time and place—one is tempted to say, like Christianity, "in the fullness of time"—when all the economic, intellectual, and spiritual conditions were ripe. The belief that the natural world is interesting in itself, not merely as a storehouse of symbols of eternal truth, the thought that nature may be interpreted mathematically as well as symbolically, the faith that "nature always acts in the simplest ways," the respect for brute fact and immediate sense experience—all these had to come first before modern science could develop. "I generally observe," wrote a sixteenth century sage, "that when a matter is set before them, men are more ready to waste their time in seeking the reason of it than in seeking the truth of it. . . . They usually begin thus, 'How can that be?' They should say, 'But is it so?' " A perfect example of the scientific attitude, you say—yet this was Montaigne speaking—and Montaigne was no scientist. The emergence of the scientific attitude was an integral part of the whole development of Western society at a particular point of time.

Several features of the historian's understanding of this

scientific revolution have relevance to our problem. In the first place, historians look at the triumph of the scientific attitude in much the same way as they view the triumph of Christianity—incomparable as the two phenomena are. Both Christians and scientists have felt there was a certain finality in their own revelation or discovery of truth, yet historically speaking, the "scandal of particularity" attaches to both. Like Christianity, science "captured" the Western mind at a particular moment and spread beyond it, claiming to be the final answer to men's questionings, the fulfillment of their hopes. But the "Christian Civilization" of the High Middle Ages is dead, even though Christianity itself is still very much alive as a religion. The suggestion is inescapable that our modern "scientific civilization" may not necessarily last forever, even though the general method of science may prove to be a permanent acquisition of the race. We already have frightening hints in Naziism, Bolshevism, and even hysterical 100 percent-Americanism, of what may happen to science when the supporting social and intellectual conditions which gave it birth are withdrawn.

In the second place, one of the very conditions for the incredible success of science was its deliberate self-isolation in the seventeenth century from the methodology and whole intellectual temper of what we today would call the humanities and social studies. It was laid down in the charters of the first scientific academies that there was to be no discussion of theological, political, or moral problems. "All discourses of Divinity, of State Affairs, and of News" were barred. Final causes were to be ignored, and only such conclusions as could be "demonstrated invincibly" were to be admitted. No one today would deny that this rigid isolation from the vagaries of tradition and the hair-splitting of scholasticism was absolutely necessary to the establishment of an experimental, mathematical science. But the result was tragic. The long-standing contempt of early theologians and humanists for mere "natural" knowledge was repaid after 1700 by the contempt of scientists and positivists for theology and the humanist tradition. The final irony is the curious argument of some scientific enthusiasts in our own day that God is dead because a method of investigation which from the start excluded final causes has found no trace of the Living God.

In the third place, the circumstances of the origins of modern science help to explain the curious combination of diffidence and arrogance which sometimes characterizes the modern scientist's conception of his place in society. The scientist was a "new man" in late medieval and early modern society. There was no ready-made niche for him, and he had to carve his own. Naturally the most direct way was to insist that what he was doing was not self-interested magic, but for the glory of God and the public benefit. The theme of the "public weal" runs deep and strong through early modern scientific literature. Scientists were concerned to persuade others of what they were thoroughly persuaded themselves, that their work (in the words of the secretary of the Royal Society) was "All for the glory of God, the Honour and Advantage of these Kingdoms, and the Universal Good of Mankind." In fact, the late Edgar Zilsel has demonstrated brilliantly that the very concept of scientific progress—namely that knowledge grows cumulatively through the selfless contributions of individual scientists building on what their predecessors have contributed, and that the result is the "progress" of "civilization"—was first developed among the skilled artisans of the late Middle Ages and elaborated into a cultural concept by Francis Bacon and René Descartes.[1]

[1] Zilsel, "The Genesis of the Concept of Scientific Progress," *Journal of the History of Ideas*, VI (1945), 325.

There is no significant trace of it in the slave societies of the Orient and of classical times. But against the background of Christian respect for the person and the dignity of manual labor, it appeared among the gildsmen of Medieval Europe who knew they could not hope for individual fame (like a Renaissance painter or author) but were accustomed to think of contributing cooperatively to the commonweal and the glory of God by contributing their bit to the elaboration of a technique. This faith of the scientist is one of the really great ideas of the Western tradition, and its roots lie deep in Western social development. Its authors and modern supporters were and are deeply sincere. But this should not blind us to the fact that its advocates from Bacon and Descartes to Huxley and John Dewey have sometimes been naïve, particularly when they have argued that the extension of natural knowledge automatically and inevitably works for the public good and that science will some day save humanity. From the beginning scientists have been haunted by a bad conscience. Leonardo was afraid to give his submarine to such an evil race as man. The legend of Doctor Faustus was put on the English stage in the same generation which saw the appearance of Descartes's *Discourse on Method*. It is too much to suggest that scientists have often been too arrogant about the benefits of science to society because they were really too diffident deep down about the legitimacy of their calling. The wisdom of Pascal in this regard—convinced as he was of both the dignity and the limitations of the scientist's calling—outshines the uncritical enthusiasm of Bacon and Descartes at this distance.

Most historians I know would agree, I believe, if I should conclude that modern science is an amazingly recent nuance of the human mind; that it is an integral part of Western social and intellectual development; that it has accelerated the secularization of thought and aspiration wherever its influence has reached; and that human gains have been partly offset by striking losses in the process. The scientists and engineers who have built the material basis of our civilization have taught millions to look to the future rather than to the past; to think of the adjective "scientific" as a word of highest approval, as the word "pious" once was; to rely on sense experience and experiment; to measure, divide, and analyze; to quantify the qualitative and to interpret data mathematically wherever possible; to believe that nature can be controlled, that problems can be solved and ills remedied, and that something can be done about almost anything. Inevitably other human qualities and attitudes have suffered by competition: those of believing, trusting, and hoping; the sense of tradition and historical continuity; the reliance on intuition and a sense of the whole; the interest in quality and symbol; the impulse to accept, to appreciate, to wonder—yes, even to suffer—rather than to demand that something be done about everything within reach. This is, of course, an exaggerated list of the human attitudes and qualities which have tended either to burgeon or to atrophy under the influence of the enormous prestige of science. But I believe most historians would say it suggests the right point, that all gains in the development of "civilization" are bought at a price. Obviously modern science itself is moving in the direction of righting the balance with its recent sense of its own limitations, its consciousness of the symbolic character of its knowledge, its emphasis on "wholeness laws" and indeterminacy, its humility about how much can ultimately be known and done by scientists and engineers. But as almost any Oriental or man of the Middle Ages would insist, the price has been high.

This brings us to our final observation. What the science and technology of the past four centuries have done is to open up almost limitless possibilities either of realizing or of betraying the age-old aims and hopes of Western man—of peace, of freedom, of human dignity. The history of combustion is the classic example. When primitive man tamed fire, he found that he could use his new power either to cook his food or to destroy the hovel of his enemy. To-day we know that we can use atomic fission either to produce the power that will warm and enlighten the homes of men or to broil and char whole cities in an instant. The possibilities are more vast, but the problem is the same. It is dramatized vividly in Joseph Fletcher's *Morals and Medicine*.[2] The author asks all the tough questions: have we a right to know the truth from a doctor? have we the right to limit births, to sterilize the insane, to circumvent sterility in others, to grant death to the hopelessly ill? In every case medical science has opened up technical possibilities previously undreamt of. But the answers must come from our ultimate beliefs about man, his nature and his destiny, as they always have.

The danger is that we may think we have finally created beneficial possibilities too attractive to resist and other alternatives too horrible actually to try. Unfortunately the possibilities both for good and evil are increasingly remote from the concrete experience of the individual in peacetime. Slums multiply, or are replaced by modern housing, but the resident of suburbia knows of it only through his taxes, his charitable contributions, or his political contacts. The concrete immediacy of less civilized experience is gone. Good and evil are more remote, more complicated and impersonal. Think how proudly modern man may some day stand before his Maker and point out that he has not only fed the hungry but increased the average yield of the soil beyond belief and invented vitamin pills; that he has not only given drink to the thirsty but built reservoirs and inseminated rain-clouds; that he has built hotel chains

[2] Princeton University Press, 1954.

to entertain strangers, and synthesized dacron to clothe them; that he has cured, not merely cared for, the sick; and that he has rehabilitated the criminal, which is better than merely visiting him in prison. And yet all this has been done at a distance, the result of cumulative knowledge and elaborate cooperation. No wonder this same modern man is haunted by the thought that his science and technology have not saved him, or even made him any more acceptable, as he once thought they would. The possibilities before man are more golden—and more frightening—than ever before in his history. At least this is the way it looks to one historian.

5 · LIBERAL EDUCATION AND
CHRISTIAN EDUCATION*

M Y CONCERN in what follows is to state and try to answer a question of considerable importance to educators and Christians: can a liberal education be a Christian education—and (vice versa) can a Christian education be a liberal education? The question is centuries old, and I have no new answers. But it has become a live question on many of our school and college campuses in recent years, and because we have become confused about it, it seems worth while to review the main historical outlines of the problem and some of the most durable answers to it.

The relation of Christian faith to *liberal* education is still the crucial question, I believe, in spite of the steady decline during the last two generations in the relative number of American students devoting themselves mainly to the liberal arts in higher education. If we cannot come to some agreement about what bearing Christianity has upon that traditional education of all men for citizenship and enlightened living that we call "liberal," we will never agree on what bearing it has upon the technical and voca-

* In 1957 the Kent School celebrated its one hundredth anniversary with a conference on the "Christian Idea of Education." It was an unusual and distinguished gathering—Reinhold Niebuhr, Paul Tillich, Jacques Maritain, and Alan Paton were among those asked to participate. Within the theme of the conference, I was given complete freedom in choosing my subject, and chose the title indicated. It proved to be neither popular nor congenial as an approach to the subject, as the appended discussion suggests (I did not see the stenographic report before publication). To many Christians today, the word "liberal" is out of fashion and pejorative, unfortunately, and I found myself representing a minority point of view at a church-school. The address and discussion were printed, with amiable objectivity, by Edmund Fuller in *The Christian Idea of Education*, Yale University Press, 1957, from which it is reprinted by permission.

tional training which is mushrooming in such spectacular fashion in our society. The problem cuts across the line that divides secondary from higher education, and in this discussion I will largely ignore that line, although I am well aware that there are significant differences between the school and college settings of the question.

Let us consider first the idea of a liberal education. It is well to recall at the start that liberal education originated independently of Christianity, that it later developed in response to historical forces (such as the revival of the classics and the birth of modern science) which had nothing directly to do with Christianity, and that its main objectives have often appeared to be opposed to Christian ideals. Graeco-Roman society gradually came to agree on those "arts" which were peculiarly appropriate to the education of its ruling classes—that is, those who were legally freemen and did not have to work for a living with their hands. These were the "liberal arts": grammar, rhetoric, and dialectic; music, arithmetic, geometry, astronomy; the ancestors, in short, of what we call the "arts and sciences." The classic definition of them comes to us from the early Renaissance, from Peter Paul Vergerius: "We call those studies liberal which are worthy of a free man; those studies by which we attain and practice virtue and wisdom; that education which calls forth, trains and develops those highest gifts of body and of mind which ennoble men, and which are rightly judged to rank next in dignity to virtue only." Note the key words in this description: "liberal," "virtue," "wisdom," "ennoble." I think that on the surface of it we can say three things of this idea of a liberal education: it is on the whole, *secular,* deep-rooted in this-worldly concerns and aims. It is *aristocratic,* redolent of the ideals and standards of a ruling class. It is *uncommitted* to anything beyond an amorphous humanism as an explanation of the meaning of existence.

[80]

This is not the whole story, however. Like all great ideas, this idea managed to transcend its historical origins in a particular stratum of a particular society. Our dictionaries still preserve a significant ambiguity in the meaning of the word "liberal." Its aristocratic parentage is still evident in one group of synonyms: not servile or mean, unrestricted by pecuniary or utilitarian considerations, generous or bountiful. But out of this has grown another broad set of meanings, more culturally creative and more widely applicable: free, broad-minded, catholic, sensitive to new facts and open to new truths. Only at their very best have aristocracies actually incarnated these latter attitudes, but it is upon these broader meanings of the word that the best in the ideal of a liberal education has been founded.

The history of the Christian attitude toward the liberal arts is part of the larger history of the Christian attitude toward antique culture in general. Early Roman Christians were deeply suspicious of the secular schools to which they had to send their children to learn the three R's because they had no schools of their own. Virtue, wisdom, ennoblement of the mind—these were not characteristic Christian concepts—and the writings from which their children learned the rules of grammar were not Christian writings. Tertullian denied that Christianity had anything whatever to learn from classical culture, and even Jerome, humanist that he was and always remained, once dreamt that he was scourged before the Judgment Seat for being a Ciceronian rather than a Christian. It is important to remember that for the first thousand years of its existence Christianity developed no culture distinctly its own. Christians simply adopted classical culture—the liberal arts included—with various degrees of misgiving and enthusiasm. For a few brief centuries in the High Middle Ages, Christians tried to create a Christian civilization—and failed. Some twentieth century Christians nostalgically bemoan that failure, but Pope Pius XII was more realistic. In addressing an international congress of historians at Rome during the summer of 1955 he remarked: "One must not characterize the culture of the Middle Ages as *the* Catholic culture. . . . The Catholic Church does not identify itself with any culture; its essence forbids this." Even more outspokenly, the leading spokesmen of Protestantism have refused to identify Christianity with any form of culture, whether classical humanism or medieval ecclesiasticism or modern scientism. And so the liberal arts, although the basis of the curriculum in secondary and higher education from the Dark Ages to our own day, have never been considered bone of their bone and flesh of their flesh by Christians. (And properly so.) Except perhaps for one brief historical moment in the Middle Ages, there never has been a truly "Christian" culture.

The plain fact is, however, that Christianity and the liberal arts have grown up together. They have interpenetrated each other in ways too numerous to mention. Christians from Jerome and Augustine to Paul Tillich and Jacques Maritain have held aloft the ideal of a Christian scholarship based upon the liberal arts and applied to the Christian tradition itself. Augustine's *De Doctrina Christiana*, the classic text of Christian humanism, established the argument that for the committed Christian the liberal arts could be a means to deeper understanding of his faith, a steppingstone to profounder comprehension of Christian belief. Since Jerome and Augustine, there have always been powerful voices to proclaim that there is nothing inherently incompatible between Christianity and the liberal arts. Some Christian humanists have gone further and maintained that they stand and fall together.

The Middle Ages domesticated the liberal arts in Christian society. At the medieval University of Paris, theology was queen of the sciences, but theology was firmly based upon preliminary study of the liberal arts and the liberal arts faculty always far outnumbered the theological. The medieval Schoolmen were the first to work out a whole Christian theology and *speculum mundi* on the basis of the seven liberal arts, particularly logic. It was the Renaissance, however, that bequeathed to us the ideal of a *docta pietas* or *pietas literata*, a cultured devotion, compounded of the best in classical and Christian ideals. Perhaps it was best incarnated in the remarkable school that Vittorino da Feltre set up in Mantua early in the fifteenth century for children of the aristocracy and of his fellow intellectuals, but also of the poor and obscure as well. Vittorino believed that education should be a balance between three things: bodily exercise and athletic competition; rigorous training of the mind, particularly through study of the Greek and Latin classics; and instruction in Christian piety. He never saw any conflict between his enthusiasm for pagan literature and his devotion to Christianity. He set his students the example of regular confession, accompanied them to mass, and always took a personal part in their daily religious instruction. This, says a modern student, was "no nominal reconciliation between the new and the old. Christianity and humanism were [to him] the two coordinate factors necessary to the development of complete manhood."[1]

Vittorino was not alone. In the next century Christian humanism came to full flower in the north of Europe. Pietas literata, a Christian liberal education, was the ideal of Protestants and Catholics alike. "What profits all our learning, if our character be not correspondingly noble, all our industry without piety, all our knowing without love of our neighbor. . . ?" wrote Jacob Wimpfeling of Alsace.[2]

[1] W. H. Woodward, *Vittorino da Feltre and Other Humanist Educators* (Cambridge, 1905), p. 67.

[2] In F. P. Graves, *A History of Education* (3 vols., New York, 1909-1913), II, 149.

There was wide agreement that a balance between knowledge and devotion must somehow be worked out. "A wise and persuasive piety should be the aim of our studies," wrote Johann Sturm of Strasbourg. "But were all pious, then the student should be distinguished from him who is unlettered by scientific culture and the art of speaking."[3] John Colet founded St. Paul's School in London on these same principles, and tried unsuccessfully to persuade Erasmus, the prince of Christian humanists, to head it. Erasmus devoted his life to proving that Christianity needed the cleansing influence of liberal learning if it were ever to be restored to its primitive purity, and that the learning of his day needed to be Christianized if it were not to become dangerous. To those who asked what biblical scholarship had to do with salvation, he asked whether ignorance was any proof of holiness.

Luther disagreed sharply with Erasmus on a great many things, but on one thing they were agreed: the value to Christianity of liberal learning and honest scholarship. Luther knew that a preacher could not wait until the scholars reached agreement on the meaning of a text before he ventured to preach from it, but he maintained strongly that there must always be scholars in the Church who knew the three languages of Scripture: Hebrew, Greek, and Latin. "A saintly life and correct doctrine are not enough," he added. In urging the officials of German cities to establish schools, he incidentally expressed his regret that he had not had more of the liberal arts (particularly the ancient poets and historians) and less of theological sophistry in his own education.[4] Calvin helped establish the tradition of a learned ministry in the Reformed churches by basing the curriculum of his Academy at Geneva firmly upon the liberal arts. Jesuit higher education

[3] *Ibid.*, p. 159.
[4] *Works of Martin Luther* (Philadelphia, 1931), IV, 117, 123.

was no less clearly founded on the liberal arts and sciences. To Comenius, the great seventeenth century Christian educator, education had three main tasks: "Erudition which aims at man's reason, moral education which aims at man's character and independence, and piety which aims at his understanding of God."[5]

And so Christians down to the seventeenth century came to terms with the more literary and philosophical elements in the traditional liberal arts and accepted them as reconcilable with Christian belief—nay, even as aids to Christian self-understanding. In somewhat the same way Christians from the seventeenth century down to our own day have slowly come to accept the natural and social sciences, which have undergone such spectacular development during the last three centuries and now form two of the usual three "divisions" of liberal learning (natural sciences, social sciences, humanities). We sometimes forget that science is just as integral a part of a liberal education as art and literature, history and philosophy. The enormous quantitative expansion of scientific knowledge in modern times, together with the qualitative refinement of its methods, has tended to re-emphasize the contradictions between liberal learning and Christian belief. But it seems to me that we of the twentieth century are on the verge of a working reconciliation between science and Christianity not unlike that reconciliation between the humanities and Christianity which was the work of Christian humanism in Erasmus' day. At least the conviction is spreading that "science is not enough," much as the conviction spread among Erasmus' followers that the revival of classical learning by itself was not enough, no matter what its early enthusiasts claimed. And this may prove to be the beginning of a more intimate relation between Christianity and lib-

[5] Robert Ulich, *History of Educational Thought* (New York, 1945), p. 192.

eral education, of which science is now an integral if not a dominant element.

Perhaps one reason why liberal education and Christianity have never finally split apart in the West is that they have always shared one central belief and concern: belief in the dignity of personality and concern for its integrity. Christians of course cannot claim exclusive parentage of this belief for Christianity. It owes almost as much to Hellenic thought as to the Gospels. In other words, it is our joint heritage from Athens and from Jerusalem, a fusion of Graeco-Roman respect for man as something more than the beast and Judaeo-Christian respect for man as made in the image of God. Quintillian, for instance, was just as concerned as any Christian educator that the teacher should treat each pupil with respect as a person, each as capable of his own measure of growth. When Erasmus preached patience and understanding in the teacher and inveighed against the "hangman type" which "crushes into indifference many earnest, studious natures," he owed his inspiration as much to Quintillian as to Jesus. Perhaps you have heard of the dear old schoolmarm's advice to young teachers: "Whenever you uncover the spark of genius in a pupil —water it, water it!" Her intent, if not her actual program, is typical of the best in both classical and Christian pedagogy.

What is the answer then to the first half of our question: Can a liberal education be a Christian education? I believe the answer is a qualified yes. A liberal education can be, and often has been, illumined by Christian faith. Augustine was the spiritual father of a host of educated Christians who have believed that Christian insight casts a flood of light upon the knowledge that man has gained about himself and his world from other sources. To the Christian, no genuine learning can be really alien. In oft-quoted words Augustine said, "Let every good and true Christian understand that *wherever truth may be found, it belongs to his Master.*[6] Erasmus found Christ in Plato, and could even imagine saying "St. Socrates, pray for me." An important qualification is suggested by this case, however. Christians have often been too possessive about the truth discovered by the arts and sciences. Over and over they have been tempted to "Christianize" the liberal arts, to manipulate their data into Christian shape, to transform the liberal arts into Christian arts. Erasmus, it could be maintained, distorted Plato and misunderstood Christ in reading one into the other.

There is a certain integrity in the methods and results of the liberal arts which cannot be compromised with impunity by religious faith. This is why I believe that Christians should always be suspicious of attempts to devise a specifically "Christian curriculum," that is, presumably to develop a "Christian history," a "Christian sociology," a "Christian mathematics," and so on. I believe the historical experience suggests that a liberal education may be *illumined* by Christian belief and insight without affecting its "liberal" quality, but that the moment one tries to *transform* it into a "Christian curriculum" trouble begins. Then too often the classics must be cut and expurgated, indexes of prohibited books must be drafted, logic must be chopped to fit theology, and the dimensions of the universe must be remeasured to conform with Genesis.

With some misgivings I may suggest a modern analogy, that of radiation. A certain amount of radiation is beneficial to organic life on this planet; it fosters growth and may even check malignancies. Larger amounts of radiation are disintegrative and destructive of organisms. In somewhat the same way, a humble, inquiring, and penetrating Christianity may irradiate the liberal arts in a signally beneficial way. A possessive and imperialistic Christian

[6] *Ibid.*, p. 79.

[87]

ideology may destroy the integrity of liberal learning by the intensity of its radiation. I suppose the chief danger today is that the liberal arts are disintegrating into intellectual anarchy through the lack of beneficial irradiation of *any* sort, Christian or otherwise. Departmental provincialism, the isolation of scholars from each other and from society, intellectual irresponsibility—*these* are the most obvious dangers today in academic communities devoted to the liberal arts—not the imminent end of freedom of inquiry and research as the result of the resurgence of Christian belief, as some would maintain. But there is always the opposite danger, that Christians who are concerned about the plight of liberal education may try to repeat the mistakes of the Roman Church with respect to Galileo and the boners of Protestants with respect to Darwin—that is, to demand that liberal learning be made to fit the Procrustean bed of dogmatic Christianity. The cure for the divorce of liberal learning from Christianity is not "Christianization" of the content of the curriculum but more learned and committed Christians in liberal education shedding what light they can, in humility and devotion to truth, on the wider meaning of the subjects they teach.

This leads us to the second half of our question: can a Christian education be a liberal education? Here, of course, I am using the word "liberal" in the second broad meaning mentioned a short while ago: open-minded, above provincialism, receptive to new truth, eager for fresh perspectives. How can a *Christian* education, an education presumably beginning and ending in religious commitment, possibly be a *liberal* education in this sense?

The answer to this question of a great many Christians down through the centuries has been that it cannot. Open-mindedness and commitment, they point out, are logically incompatible. Genuine receptivity to new truth implies weakness of faith. The "liberal" belongs not among Christians but in the limbo Dante reserved for those who refused to take sides.

There is of course much historical and religious justification for this point of view. To the cultured, liberally educated Roman of the first few centuries after Christ, Christian belief was, in Paul's words, scandalous and absurd. The natural reaction of many early Christians was to insist upon a firmness and precision of belief which would resist all erosion by secular philosophy and the natural reason. From the early Church down to Presbyterians and Jesuits in the age of the Reformation, those Christians who took their faith seriously saw to it that no one was admitted to their company without careful instruction in the faith and strict examination to determine the results. *Catechesis* or religious instruction was recognized by the early Church as one of its major obligations, and the Church fathers devoted much time and energy to discussing how to teach the rudiments of Christian belief to children and other candidates for baptism.

About the time of the Reformation, this instruction regularly took on the form of question and answer, and "catechisms" in the modern sense began to pour from the new printing presses of Europe. To one carefully nurtured on this catechetical instruction, with neat answers to all major questions about his faith firmly implanted in his memory during childhood, it was—and still is—inconceivable that Christian education could be "liberal" in the sense we have suggested. A mind formed by the constant iteration and reiteration of set phrases is restless and disturbed in the presence of new truth. The idea that there is moral and spiritual value in openness to new truth can only appear subversive to such a mentality. At this distance it is difficult to say whether Protestants or Catholics were the worse offenders in the development of this authoritarian, catechetical Christianity. In the *Ratio Studiorum* of the Jesuit Order the authoritarian note is predominant: "Also in things which contain no danger for creed and faith, nobody shall introduce new questions on any important topic, nor an opinion, without sufficient authority or without permission of his superiors; nor shall any one teach anything against the doctrines of the Church Fathers and the commonly accepted system of school doctrines; but everybody shall follow the approved teachers and the doctrines accepted and taught in Catholic academies."[7] Such a statement could easily be matched by equally dogmatic expressions on the Protestant side of the fence.

It is apparent, I think, that catechetical teaching of this sort is inevitably dogmatic, domineering, and divisive. There is still too much of it around. It is a narrow sort of instruction-in-the-faith aimed mainly at perpetuating the particular beliefs of a particular community of Christians. It is not Christian *education* in any broad sense of the word. It pounds in, it does not draw out; it demands conformity, not free response; it is instruction, but not education. It will not carry the present generation of students very far, it seems to me, in this confused and tragic world of the twentieth century. Jesus seems to have had this kind of instruction in mind when he lashed out at the religious teachers of his day who made up heavy loads and laid them on men's shoulders but would not stir a finger to remove them, who shut the Realm of Heaven in men's faces and neither entered themselves nor let those enter who were on the point of entering, who filtered away the gnat and swallowed the camel.[8]

Not all Christian instruction has been of this sort, of course. Christianity would not be a living religion today if it had not been for the efforts of generations of selfless and

[7] In Graves, *A History of Education*, pp. 219-220.
[8] Matt. 23 (after Moffatt).

devoted parents and teachers in transmitting the faith in all its breadth and depth. To take but one notable example, the Brethren of the Common Life in their schools of the fifteenth century developed an amazingly effective way of inspiring a simple, undogmatic, and practical Christian piety in pupils learning their three R's. More than any other group, they were responsible for changing the meaning of *religio* from its medieval sense of denoting the particular devotion of a monk to its modern sense of describing the devotion of layman and cleric alike. Until the Jesuits, the Brethren's primary and secondary schools were the best in Europe. Out of them came no single type or sect, but rather a generation of Christian leaders who grew to spiritual maturity each in his own way. It is a striking fact that Erasmus, Luther, Loyola, and Calvin were all influenced more or less directly at critical points in their development by schools founded by the Brethren. Through the tragic fury of the religious upheaval of the sixteenth century, the influence of Thomas à Kempis' *Imitation of Christ*—the finest product of the Brethren's mystical piety —worked like leaven. Jansenist instruction and Quaker instruction had something of this same quality of religious warmth combined with ethical seriousness, and other examples could be cited.

Do we have any examples, however, of Christian educational theory and practice which we could say were clearly and consciously "liberal," that is, based upon some explicit theory of Christian liberty? The question immediately recalls figures like Erasmus and Comenius, Milton and Dostoievsky. Erasmus hated the little actual schoolteaching he had to do, but he wrote much on education and he probably had as much influence in the end on Christian education as either Luther or Loyola. Two things strike us at this distance about his attitude toward education: his insistence that a student's mind be treated with the respect due to a God-created thing, and his willingness to see any question of real human significance debated in the classroom, however controversial it might be. His *Colloquies*, begun as exercises for students learning their Latin, touched on most of the sensitive questions of his day in an effort to make the reader think. If Erasmus were a textbook writer today, I fear he would soon be out of a job and starving, thanks to the efforts of irate church groups, PTA's, and veterans' organizations.

Comenius was even more articulate than Erasmus about two ends of Christian education: that it must begin in individual freedom, and end in ecumenical-mindedness. Comenius was the first great ecumenical leader after the religious split of the sixteenth century, an apostle of a united Church and a league of nations as well. Through all his hazy idealism and his concern with the minutiae of pedagogy, there runs his dual faith in the unity of mankind and the freedom of individuals. "We must all have one and the same goal," he wrote, "the salvation of the human race." ". . . there is inborn in human nature a love of liberty—for liberty man's mind is convinced that it was made—and this love can by no means be driven out: so that, wherever and by whatever means it feels that it is being hemmed in and impeded, it cannot but seek a way out and declare its own liberty." Characteristically, it was the goal of his educational theory "to seek and find a method by which the teachers teach less and the learners learn more."[9]

The two classic statements of this kind of Christian liberty, however, were Milton's ringing appeal for freedom of thought in *Areopagitica* and the lofty irony of Dostoievsky's legend of the Grand Inquisitor. Both writers thought

[9] Robert Ulich, ed., *Three Thousand Years of Educational Wisdom. Selections from Great Documents* (Cambridge, 1947), pp. 340, 346. Cf. Ulich, *History of Educational Thought*, p. 198.

that God really meant man to be free in his response to truth and goodness. God, says Milton, takes no more delight in an unchallenged belief than in a cloistered and untested virtue. God deliberately refuses to compel man's response to his love, Dostoievsky seems to say through the various levels of meaning in the legend. Christ did not come down from the Cross when they shouted at him. "Thou didst not come down, for again Thou wouldst not enslave man by a miracle, and didst crave faith given freely, not based on miracle. Thou didst crave for free love and not the base raptures of the slave. . . ." In the Temptations, Christ rejected "miracle, mystery, and authority" as means to compel men's assent to divine truth. "Thou didst desire man's free love, that he should follow Thee freely, enticed and taken captive by Thee. In place of the rigid ancient law, man must hereafter with free heart decide for himself what is good and what is evil, having only Thy image before him as his guide."[10] Echoes of Milton and Dostoievsky still rang in "A Letter to the Christian People of America," adopted by the General Assembly of the National Council of Churches in December 1952: "In all education, and in culture as a whole, the interests of truth are dependent upon freedom of thought. . . . It is, in fact, good for truth to have to struggle with error. . . . Error must be met by truth in free and open encounter. The conscientious expression of ideas must not be dealt with by a dungeon, a boycott or an *Index*, nor by arbitrary governmental action, character assassination, nor by the application of unjust economic and social pressures."

Enough has been said, I think, to suggest that the history of Christian education is not merely the story of endless catechizing by authoritarian sects determined to preserve their own identity through all future time. A dis-

---

[10] *The Brothers Karamazov*, tr. Constance Garnett, Book v, chap. 5.

[93]

tressing amount of it has been just this, but the liberal note has never been utterly extinguished. Thus the answer to the second half of our question is again a qualified affirmative: a Christian education, under certain conditions and in certain times and places, *can* be a liberal education.

And now what conclusions can be drawn from this hasty historical survey? You will gather that I have chosen to be more interested in *what sort* of Christian education we are to have in our day than in *whether* or *why* we should have Christian education at all. The latter are perhaps prior questions, but the other, I think, is more proper to a historian. The *quality* of what we have and its relation to the liberal arts have been my theme. And my central thesis is that *a liberal education can be illumined by Christianity provided that the Christian education which complements it is liberal.* There can be no fruitful discussion of any significant relation between a thoroughly positivistic liberal arts curriculum and a narrow, highly dogmatic Christian instruction. But between a truly liberal education and a truly liberal Christianity there can be a relationship of unlimited creative possibilities.

It is the genius of Christianity that it sees the eternal significance in concrete events. From the turning points of Hebrew history to the Incarnation itself, God (to a Christian) has been manifesting Himself in the actual, concrete events of history. The event is not absorbed and engulfed in the significance as it is in more mystical religions; it remains an event, to be accepted in all its materiality. But it is not merely an occurrence without meaning. It is a manifestation of a divine Will working in events, a Will which both reveals and conceals itself in the events of nature and of history. Our knowledge of the events of astronomy and physics as of human history need be no less precise and objective for being illumined by faith in the God who works through these events. The goal of the liberal arts is to provide *hindsight* and *foresight* of varying degrees of exactness in this universe of things and events; the part of Christian belief is to provide *insight*. Since our hindsight is never complete and our foresight is never infallible, insight is of crucial significance for living. Religion, writes Mark Van Doren, "acknowledges objectivity, yet on such a scale that the nature of things becomes infinitely less wonderful than their existence. Science and philosophy must rest in nature; their inquiry is confined to what things are and how they are connected, in number, place, and time. Religion goes on into the darkness where intellect must grapple with the original fact that things are at all. This is an overwhelming fact, for it measures our ignorance. Religion is the art that teaches us what to do with our ignorance."[11]

But religious insight teaches us also what to do with our knowledge. Every fragment of man's hard-won knowledge of himself and his universe can take on deeper significance when considered in the mood of humble and childlike faith. This does not mean rejecting the sophistications of scientific method and returning to a Franciscan naïveté in understanding the world about us. Pascal is more helpful here to a twentieth century Christian than St. Francis. Pascal saw that there are three levels or orders of existence. A drop of water, he might have said, at the level of ordinary, everyday, commonsense experience, is a clear, globular bit of liquid matter, useful for many things from washing and cooking to cooling one's brow and slaking one's thirst. At the level of science, it is H_2O, a formula which implies a considerable amount of exact observation, sophisticated experiment, and mathematical analysis. At the level of religion, if it is something given in love to a

[11] Mark Van Doren, *Liberal Education* (New York, 1943), pp. 141-142.

thirsty human being, it may become a symbol of that love of neighbor which grows out of love of God. Pascal insisted that the three orders of body, mind, and spirit are incommensurable but related, and so they are. To view water as a symbol of baptism need not affect a single step of the reasoning that results in the conception of water as H_2O. It may nonetheless enrich the meaning of the material in question. In his *Varieties of Religious Experience* William James remarked upon "the difference between looking on a person without love, or upon the same person with love. . . . When we see all things in God, and refer all things to him, we read in common matters superior expressions of meaning."[12] And so in the case of events, their significance in the order of spirit should enhance, not annul, their significance in the order of intellect. ". . . that religion will conquer," Whitehead once wrote, "which can render clear to popular understanding some eternal greatness incarnate in the passage of temporal fact."[13]

Here is the essence of the relationship of Christian insight to the data of liberal education. In every concrete fact and temporal event there is potential meaning that beggars the imagination. A liberal education does not reach its *own* goal unless a student senses something of this meaning. Nor can a Christian education worthy of the name be satisfied to stop with general principles or intuitions and not push on to examine their incarnation in persons and events. Jesus never taught his listeners fishing or agriculture or housebuilding or "positive thinking," although he obviously knew quite a bit about each. Nor, on the other hand, did he ever teach his hearers systematic theology. His teaching was never purely practical—nor purely theoretical. Significantly he taught the people in parables

[12] (New York, 1902), p. 474.
[13] Alfred North Whitehead, *Adventures of Ideas* (New York, 1933), p. 41.

[96]

whenever he had something particularly profound to say
—and once he told his disciples why. He quoted Isaiah's
bitterly ironic meditation on the frustration of prophets:
"For this people has become coarse within; they have ears
that are hard of hearing, and they have shut their eyes,
lest one day they see with their eyes, hear with their ears,
understand in their hearts and be converted."[14] And he
went on to explain what anyone might *see* in the humble,
ordinary business of scattering seed on good ground and
bad, if only he had eyes to see.

In the most poignant moment of Thornton Wilder's
play, *Our Town*, Emily is allowed to return from the grave
for one brief moment, to relive her twelfth birthday. The
experience is too devastating to last for more than a few
short minutes. Emily can see her mother from the perspective of all that has been and is to be; but her mother is
too busy about the kitchen to stop and look and try to see
Emily in the same perspective, as Emily pathetically asks.
"It goes so fast," she says. "We don't have time to look at
one another. . . . Do any human beings ever realize life
while they live it—every, every minute?"[15] The answer
is of course no. If we did, we would see with our eyes, hear
with our ears, and be converted. And to pursue Isaiah's
irony, this would be a very unsettling thing on any school
or college campus. An Oxford don remarks, "On the face
of it, religion is a nuisance in a university, though not,
of course, anything like such a nuisance as cricket."[16]

Rather than suggest that Christianity should be a sort of
divine nuisance on the campus, however, I think I shall
stick by my earlier figures of illumination and insight.
The right kind of Christian faith can flood a liberal educa-

[14] Matt. 13:15, in *The Four Gospels*, tr. E. V. Rieu (Baltimore,
1953).

[15] (New York, 1938), pp. 124-125.

[16] Austin Farrar, in *The Twentieth Century*, Vol. 157 (June
1955), p. 490.

tion with meaning as light floods a Flemish painting and gives the scene coherence and significance. This right kind of faith will be an adventurous and inquiring faith, committed not so much to a particular church, a particular creed, or a particular ceremonial as to the person of Christ and to the Kingdom he proclaimed. It seems fair to say that the world is in too parlous a state, and this generation of students too dissatisfied with ready-made answers and half-measures, for anything less searching and demanding, anything less comprehensive and universal, to suffice.

PROFESSOR E. HARRIS HARBISON DISCUSSES
FURTHER THE THEMES OF LIBERAL AND
CHRISTIAN EDUCATION

FATHER WEED[1]: Professor Harbison pointed out how Christian faith permeates scientific theory, in other words, throws light on scientific achievement, but the fact is that science is still science. How is it changed? What effect does this light of Christianity have upon scientific theory? Is it really made any different?

PROFESSOR HARBISON: I tried to make it clear that there certainly is no change. If there is, it goes against everything I was trying to say about the integrity of the subject, and about a way of getting at truth that has been developed sometimes by very hard-won steps and a particular discipline, and often at the cost of rather obstructionist experience—I am speaking historically—from theologians.

Now, let's grant that and go on. What is the alternative? If what these particular disciplines have turned up in the way of what you call fact has no relation to Christian perspective, then we are dealing with two utterly watertight compartments. I just cannot believe that.

I am not a scientist. I would feel more at home if you asked me what does our knowledge of historical fact in-

[1] Paul C. Weed, Jr., St. Luke's School, New York City.

volve for a Christian, and there, of course, you are immediately faced with the obvious truth that Christianity is an
extremely historically minded religion which simply cannot avoid dealing with historical facts in some way or
other, and with the meaning of historical facts. Conversely,
what a secular historian turns up in the way of knowledge
of the past inevitably is going to be important to the Christian in the broadest sense.

Where you get into difficulties is if you say, "Yes, but
why should the Christian give himself any airs?" The
answer is, of course, that he should not. Does a Christian,
for instance, think more scientifically than a non-Christian?
I don't think we can claim that we do. On the other hand,
as Christians, the data must have for us dimensions, profundity, implications that they don't have for a nonbeliever.
I think that is obvious.

FATHER WEED: Would an application of what you mean
be found in the discovery of the atomic bomb and the
problem of a moral direction being given to the use of the
thing?

PROFESSOR HARBISON: That particular example, I suppose, has a very long history. Man's power to control his
environment always involved possibilities of good or of
evil. I suppose from the first discovery of fire, men discovered that they could either cook their food with it or
burn down the huts of their enemies.

The atomic bomb, it seems to me, is nothing new in
that sense at all. It may be that at the profounder level
the equivalence of mass and energy have implications for
Christian theology that I certainly would not be capable
of working out. I think there are possibilities in that range
and that the Christian intellectual may find them very
fruitful to work out.

For instance, the concept of efficiency in conservation of
energy and engineering sometimes fascinates me as being

an utterly non-Christian, if not anti-Christian, concept; and yet our whole material world depends on it—I mean, our whole technological society depends on it.

It may be that Christians have to come to terms with problems like that rather than with the more obvious and more ancient problems of the use of technology for good or for evil, for peace or for war. These have been with us for a long time.

VOICE: Would it be fair to say that in the world of today, scientists—I am thinking of people like those working on the Manhattan Project—having more social consciousness than those of us in the non-scientific world, know the implications of it? I am thinking of Dr. Compton, Dr. Urey, and so on. All those were closer to it. I don't think necessarily on a Christian level, but surely on an ethical and moral basis, they were more aware of the need for reconciling all the responsibility of the conservation of energy, if you please, on the Christian side.

PROFESSOR HARBISON: Yes, I think that is true, and I think maybe there are some reasons for it. One is that these men, at a certain stage in the discussion after 1945, were the only ones of us who knew the dimensions of the destructive power of atomic energy.

The second reason, I think, is that they came new to the social problem. I have often heard social scientists talk rather disparagingly about this sense of social conscience recently acquired by the atomic scientists, when perhaps the social scientist has been working all his life in a fairly long and steady tradition to understand how individuals and groups get into these tragic dilemmas that lead to war; whereas men like Urey, and Einstein himself, came to this kind of interest very late in their careers and in their collective history as scientists. This may not be entirely fair, but I think there is something in it, that the passion of the conviction of a man like Einstein is partly the result of horror and fear at suddenly being faced with destructive power that goes beyond the imagination.

VOICE: You mentioned a while ago that a historian, as a committed Christian, does not necessarily present the facts of history any differently than if he were not a committed Christian. How about the themes of judgment, providence, redemption, and so forth? If he is committed to the notion that the providence of God, the judgment of God, the love of God are all operative in history, does he write his history in such a way as to show how these themes are actually illustrated in history, or how these particular meanings are expressed through history?

PROFESSOR HARBISON: Do you know Butterfield's little book on *Christianity and History?*[2] I would follow him pretty closely, I would think, in answer to that. You see, granted that you have a historian who is also a Christian— let's start with a hypothetical case—there are two extremes possible. One is the extreme of the medieval chronicler who sees judgment all over the place: everything that happens is a kind of inscrutable judgment of God. If the enemy wins, well, that is chastisement of God of the "good guys," as our children call them, and if the "good guys" win, why, that is a vindication by God over the enemies.

At its most elementary, this is the Old Testament view before it becomes conscious of the complicated, individual profundities of the problem. That is a rather naïve view, we'd say today. It assumes that God's will is directly manifest in events which take place in history, that God reveals himself quite clearly.

The opposite view, and it is still a Christian view, is a kind of Christian agnosticism which might say that God's will is in history but no human being can possibly discern it. This is pretty close to Karl Barth's position. Naziism

2 Herbert Butterfield, *Christianity and History* (New York, 1950).

is apparently a very evil movement, but Barth's first position was that we don't know whether it is good or ill, and that this is none of our business; God is working his will out inscrutably in history. We cannot, as human beings, either condemn it or approve it. Of course, he changed that under the stress of the war years, but he still clung pretty closely to the position that God's will is inscrutable.

Between these two views—and I think they are both nicely balanced in Luther—between these two views, something like a Christian solution could be found. That is, that God both conceals himself and reveals himself in historical events; and both sides of that statement have to be emphasized, because if God completely revealed his will in historical events, there would be no place for faith. Luther says it would all be obvious. If God completely concealed his will in historical events we might as well take the position of anyone who says that this is chaos. We can't see any meaning in it whatever. Somewhere between those two the Christian has to find his own balance between concealment and revelation.

I would take another step here. I would say that we are talking in technical terms about a professional historian who is a writer and teacher, and I would say some things operate on the level of his own belief that need not operate and probably should not operate in everything that he writes as a professional historian and everything that he says day after day, week after week, in the classroom.

By this I mean that, as all of you know, what you say in perhaps one sentence which is forgotten by you immediately will be remembered by a student long after a half-hour lecture you have given on some point of judgment in history is forgotten. It may be that what you have worked out yourself and merely hint at in teaching or writing is more important than a very elaborate and documented and worked out defense of providence in history.

I sometimes think that to use the older theological terms like "providence" with students will cause more trouble than it is worth. With your conservatively brought up students it starts certain channels of thinking along older lines. With others it immediately sets up an antagonism. If you can say, "Is there meaning in this process to you?" and work from there, it is sometimes sounder teaching technique than if you start with providence.

Butterfield had a very interesting description of judgment. Of course, you remember that description of Naziism and judgment on Naziism. That is very ingenious, and I think it is pretty close to a good answer.

DR. PELL[3]: Your comments on dogma interested me very much. I think you said that education can be illuminated by Christianity if Christian education is liberal, that is, undogmatic. I wonder if you could expand that. Some of us have been thinking we see more dogma, not of the wrong kind, coming into Christianity, and a little stiffening up of doctrine and definiteness.

PROFESSOR HARBISON: Well, I saw a certain stiffening of the clergy as I went through that passage, and I expected it. I suppose we have to say what we think—what we believe.

Dogma to me is, in its real definition, the officially sanctioned teaching. This is not doctrine I am talking about; it is dogma. Once you are talking about dogma, you are talking about propositions—about Christianity, what Christianity is—which are promulgated by authority; and that means, of course, human authority.

I come of a tradition, the Presbyterian, which said in the sixteenth century in so many words, "You can have dogma

[3] Walden Pell, II, Headmaster, St. Andrew's School, Delaware.

that is not promulgated by any human authority; it comes directly from the Bible." That is what Calvin insisted; what John Knox insisted. In other words, both of them, all of the early Puritan tradition, insisted that this is not the work of man; this is drawn directly from Scripture, and Scripture is intelligible to the person whom God inspires. I think to a person of the twentieth century that is unsatisfactory. Immediately the question arises who is the interpreter of Scripture, who says that this is dogma. This was fought out between Calvin and Servetus, whom he burned.

In the case of a church like the Roman, which is quite clear in its definition of what is dogma and what is not dogma, you have a clean-cut choice. Then I should say to a Roman Catholic that dogmatic Christianity is something very important to defend. I respect that position, but I think that for me I have to confess that wherever a human authority—and that means a church in its this-worldly aspects—is your source of dogma, I am suspicious of it as a historian and as a Christian. I think that the tendency to reduce Christianity to a set of propositions, which is the dogmatic tendency, has generally been limiting of creation, growth, and profundity, rather than fostering them.

VOICE: It seems to me that some of the problems stem from the tendency in education today to emphasize the liberal spirit in all things, and this means that we praise broad-mindedness instead of narrow-mindedness; we praise tolerance instead of praising a dogmatic position; and we assume that effective teaching almost perforce calls upon us to commit ourselves to the position of the liberal. It appears to some of us that it is a contradiction to be a liberal and to be a conservative in religion, to commit oneself to a single political party or a single denomination and still be free to be teaching objectivity to our students. This, to me, poses the central problem. Is the ideal that Professor

Harbison set up representative of Christianity or of liberal Protestant Christianity?

PROFESSOR HARBISON: The answer to that is clear, isn't it? I can't claim to represent Christianity.

VOICE: Then automatically those Christians who have committed themselves to an inflexible denominationalism might have trouble agreeing with—

PROFESSOR HARBISON: Why, of course they would. Don't we disagree with each other? I disagree with them, but, my goodness, they have a right to their beliefs. Everything that I said this morning, I should think, would deny my right as a human being to say that I know they are wrong. Of course, I represent a liberal Protestant point of view. Let's say it is the one to which I am committed.

VOICE: That is why you were asked to be here.

PROFESSOR HARBISON: I presume so. We have all kinds of people represented on this program. We say what we believe.

VOICE: Would you like to comment on your notion of the relationship between liberal arts, liberal education, and liberalism as philosophy?

PROFESSOR HARBISON: I carefully avoided the word "liberalism." If you could be more specific about what liberalism means to you and what I am being asked to relate it to, I would know better. As a historian, I am uneasily aware that liberalism has changed its meaning radically in the last hundred years, that what a mid-nineteenth century person meant by it is not what a mid-twentieth century person means by it. It means one thing in politics, another thing in economics, another thing in education.

As close as I can get to it, the word has been associated, and I think rightly so, with the search for truth wherever it leads. I am willing to grant immediately that the search for truth depends upon certain presuppositions; there are certain commitments that all of us as human beings have to start with. But I still think, as a person in an academic profession, that the commitment to truth wherever it leads is an important ideal; and I think if we all right here in this room got down to our basic beliefs we would say that this is one of them, that it is possible, if you devote yourself to it wholeheartedly, to attain a certain measure of truth by devoting yourselves to it above all other things. This is very close to the meaning of liberalism in education, if you put the "ism" in.

That is why I deliberately used the much-quoted statement from St. Augustine. Afterward Dean Rose of General Seminary suggested two or three other very apt quotations he had run across recently all the way from Hugo to Simone Weil, all along the same idea, that truth wherever it is found cannot be alien to the Christian. Your hardboiled positivist on the college faculty will not admit the right of a Christian to even the title of being liberal or objective. I think it is fundamentally a fruitless kind of controversy.

Commitment doesn't necessarily destroy freedom. The commitment may be the beginning of a fruitful and openminded search for truth. The idea that the truth you find will somehow destroy your commitment is the thing I am terribly afraid of, and that is what I find over and over and over again when this argument about dogma comes up. It is the fear on the part of people that something they find out is going to destroy the dogma.

Now Simone Weil and others are close to the heart of this thing when they say that the truly committed Christian cannot be committed to any proposition that is not subject to analysis, to testing, to trial in the heat of experience; because we are only human beings. We can't get hold of this absolute truth and put it down in a set of propositions and say, "This is it."

VOICE: You would set liberal education in some context other than positivistic liberalism?

PROFESSOR HARBISON: I think the people who translate liberalism into positivism are abusing words. They haven't thought through the kind of words they use. Liberalism and positivism are not the same thing historically or philosophically.

The word "liberalism" has deteriorated in Christian circles. The reaction against liberal theology, against liberal Protestantism, has run very strongly indeed, and "liberal" has generally been the label put on anything we don't like if we are moving back in a neo-orthodox direction, or in a neo-classical direction. We have two kinds of fundamentalism: one a kind of scriptural fundamentalism and the other a kind of creedal fundamentalism. I have run into both on occasion with the people in college, but I think there is something in this current that is valuable.

FATHER WEED: You spoke in your paper of being aware of the difference between the elementary level and the college level and secondary level schools. Certainly that is true, and mostly my experience in teaching has been with the elementary level. I have used the catechetic method a great deal, and I think if used in the right way it need not be the hard and rigid type. I don't see how you can get away from something of the catechetic method. You have got to teach some facts, but if you do enough of them, one fact will offset another so that the child or the person learning is able out of the whole series to make his own free choice as to what this thing is. I don't see how you can get away from some type of catechetic method when you are teaching. Otherwise, you cannot convey anything.

PROFESSOR HARBISON: Yes, I wouldn't pretend to argue that at all. I have enormous respect for the people who have experience at the primary, elementary level and who have, through experience, worked out what can be done with that age level to sensitize children to religious values while not closing off their own search for what is to be theirs some day.

The thing I am afraid of, as you could probably gather, is the kind of pattern-making that I think goes on in some education in this country which is primarily concerned with duplicating the particular Christian community in perpetuity, with drawing the lines very early when it is ready to draw them, with imprinting a particular interpretation of Christianity.

MR. PERRY:[4] May I take just one minute on a thing which we have experimented with at Milton Academy—this is the second year now—which, in terms of a search for truth on the part of individual students seems to us to have been rewarding.

I got this idea from the headmaster of Millbrook School who said that some of his seniors used to come up to him and say, "We think we have exceptionally fine preachers in chapel here, but they come at us with everything from so many different angles that we are rather confused as to what the basic tenets of Christianity may be. Might we have one very good man and have him take four or five consecutive chapel services and then give us a chance to talk it over with him?"

I did that with Graham Baldwin of Andover a couple of years ago. We called it "the basis of Christianity," and then we made it an entirely optional affair. We said the man will take the subject of God or Christ or prayer or immortality—some large topic within the framework of Christian experience—and will preach on it in chapel for the customary fifteen to twenty minutes and then go to the library. What goes on after that I am not sure because we permit no adults, but because no adults are permitted, apparently the discussions are very lively and, I gather,

[4] Arthur B. Perry, Milton Academy.

[108]

rather fruitful. By starting with three or four major concepts, perhaps they manufacture for themselves, out of their own pursuit of truth at their age level, something that may be very rewarding to them. At least, they seem to have said so some years later.

PROFESSOR HARBISON: I think we have to remember one thing in this talk about dogma and education, and that is that an approach or an attitude which is appropriate in one kind of situation of human communication may not be appropriate in another. I suppose very few people who were arguing bitterly at lunch would think that I could believe in anything described as dogma. Actually, I do. I have had to sign a pretty mouth-filling statement as a trustee of Princeton Theological Seminary which certainly is classified as dogma. But the problem I was speaking about this morning is education.

There is a very important distinction, it seems to me. If you are preaching from a Christian pulpit, I don't think you can avoid certain dogmatic foundations in most of the major Christian denominational traditions; but preaching is not teaching. Teaching is something else, and I have respect for this aspect of the word "education," as I was trying to bring out this morning: that is, the aspect of it which is different from instruction. Instruction in the faith as it has traditionally been interpreted by the Christian Church is one thing, but I think some people tend to confuse instruction in the faith with education in the broadest sense, and most of us are in the business of education. We are educating people who are Christians, Jews, and sometimes of other faiths, or militant agnostics. I think that the problem I was talking about this morning is something which, whether we like it or not, we have to face, and something we have to puzzle out. My only concern is to make it more self-conscious with most of us, because I think perhaps the best that we can do, and what a great many of us are doing in the classroom, in the teaching situation, is to prepare the ground, so to speak, for Christian faith, to suggest the Christian faith, to hint at implications of a subject in the perspective of the Christian.

If you try to turn the classroom, so to speak, into a place for dogmatic instruction, I should say you are wrong in most institutions of higher education in this country that I know of. You are not going to accomplish your end, and you are going to destroy many of the values you are trying to save.

You know the wonderful phrase from Montaigne, where he quotes somebody—I don't know who it is—from the Greek period who said, "Just give me that philosopher's conclusions. I can supply my own reasons." There is too much of this going on: supplying the conclusions and not the reasons. I would rather supply a student with the reasons.

DR. PELL: I think you are lost in a classroom if you just lay it down in a dogmatic way, and yet it interests me to find that boys of secondary school age are a little more susceptible to a dogmatic approach. They seem to ask for it a little more than they did, say, twenty years ago; or when I started to teach sacred studies and religion. Certainly when I was being taught it myself, we were great skeptics. Everything had to be proved, explained away, or gotten out in some roundabout way; but the boys I get now rather want you to tell them something definite.

PROFESSOR HARBISON: Are you pleased by that?

DR. PELL: No, I am not particularly pleased. I was surprised by it, and it caught me off balance a little bit at first. But it's interesting that they seem more eager for something definite, almost dogmatic, than they used to be, say, twenty-five years ago.

FATHER WEED: Professor Harbison, you said that we should be suspicious of a specifically Christian curriculum of any kind. I don't know just exactly what you had in mind.

PROFESSOR HARBISON: Let's take the extreme example that I mentioned. Is there a Christian mathematics?

FATHER WEED: Obviously not.

PROFESSOR HARBISON: There was a Nazi mathematics, you remember. I mean that quite seriously. That was maintained by Nazi philosophers. There was a decadent Western mathematics. There is right now a Communist biology, as you know. The inheritance of acquired characteristics has been "proved" by Lysenko and the boys that were there. We haven't gone along with the evidence, but this is the kind of thing that has happened quite often in Christian history. That is what I am worried about.

Christian curriculum is an ambiguous term, and I am not sure that it has its place in a talk like this, because I find everyone has his own idea of what a Christian curriculum could be and what it means to him, and quite often it means what I was trying to commend and not trying to condemn. A Christian curriculum—well, if you take that in its literal sense, I am suspicious of it; but I suppose it could be interpreted to mean what all of you might be trying to build.

VOICE: I would like to ask: What is the scope of the expression "secular education"? Is it the absence of emphasis on teaching from a Christian viewpoint? That expression is used quite a bit by Dr. Pollard as though in all education today the emphasis were on the secular side.

PROFESSOR HARBISON: That is a big question. I think the development of the idea of what is secular, and what is secularism, is an immensely complicated thing. I would be prepared to maintain as a starter that Christianity is one of the most secular-minded religions in the world. Why? Because it has always insisted that its beliefs be carried out and rooted in this world. In the parable of the Last Judgment, we are judged by what we have done in this life, whether we have given a cup of water to a thirsty man, and so forth, and in almost concrete material terms.

This is quite strikingly different from Buddhism and Hinduism, so that when you say we live in a secularized world, a secularized society, it is, of course, literally true. A great deal of the Christian core has gone out of it; but at the same time I don't feel that this is as hopeless or as illogical historically as some people might feel.

I discern a feeling of hopeless resentment that back somewhere in Western history there was a Christian civilization, a Christian age. If we could only get back to that, we would be all right. Well, I know a little bit about that civilization, and I can see certain great advantages to it, and I can see certain great disadvantages to it, such as the arrogance of an institution which took unto itself to represent Christianity—not only to represent it but to build society, build culture around it. In some ways it is a magnificent, exciting ideal, and I would tell my students, and believe, that this came closer than any attempt ever to build a Christian culture.

This is the starting point for any talk about secularization; but you know, in many ways the work of a man like Latourette at Yale, in those great five volumes on the nineteenth century and the expansion of missions, is an eye-opener. It is a maintaining of the thesis that the nineteenth century, not the thirteenth century, is the great age of Christianity. Christianity spread further, faster, acquired more people as members, and brought more people in touch with itself than at any age of its previous history.

You can call the nineteenth century, if you like, the peak of secularization, but it was also a period in which the conscience of Europe was sensitized by Negro slavery, and about wage slavery, in ways pretty closely connected with Christian roots.

Yet secularized education, as the words are used by a great many clerical deplorers and viewers-with-alarm, is an authentic problem. Public education in this country is pretty thoroughly non-religious, and since it is non-religious, it naturally takes on aspects, in the minds of the students, of being anti-religious. This, I believe passionately, has got to be changed.

You may have noticed recently in the *New York Times* a teachers' manual that is being presented, suggesting moral and religious values which might well be a kind of code of ethics of the teacher. It has been backed now by Protestant and Catholic groups, interestingly enough. There has been a long history, a long battle, but Protestants have come to feel they can join the Catholics on this. I think until you get some kind of mention in our public schools of the fact that religion is important, a thing to be studied, a thing to be taken account of, a thing to be looked at exactly as other important human activities are, we are going to have an awful battle in our sabbath schools and right down to our seminaries to restore the religious view of life. I think it can be restored. I think religion can be taught in our public schools and is increasingly being taught. It is being taught in a cool, inquiring way that need not ruffle things.

DR. PELL: I have been reading quite a bit on the English religious training in the state schools there, and I am wading through one of those books now. It certainly is interesting how far they have gone and what very thorough outlines of Christian history and doctrine and the Bible they have, and what a thorough course it seems to be. They have worked it out, and are going along now doing it in all parts of England.

PROFESSOR HARBISON: The more thorough it is, the safer it is, on the whole. I mean, the more scholarly it is, the more substance there is, the safer it is for the teacher to handle.

FATHER WEED: A year ago I had to appear in court in the case of the custody of a child who had gone to the Higgins School, and the judge asked me why I thought that St. Luke's School was a good school to send this child to. I said, quite simply, "Because we teach Scripture there." He said, "Sir, do you mean to imply any criticism of our public school system? Don't you know that it is the foundation of American democracy, and democracy is the fruit of Christianity?"

PROFESSOR HARBISON: That is a good definition of secularism: teaching democracy and assuming you are teaching Christianity.

6 · THE PROBLEM OF THE
CHRISTIAN HISTORIAN: A CRITIQUE
OF ARNOLD J. TOYNBEE*

THE APPEARANCE of Arnold J. Toynbee's latest volume of essays[1] makes it still more clear than it has been that possibly the most interesting thing about him is his magisterial attempt to reconcile his two vocations as historian and as Christian. We have not had such a serious and comprehensive attempt since Bossuet, perhaps not since Augustine himself. On the whole, since the seventeenth century our greatest historians, from Gibbon and Ranke to Charles Beard and Carl Becker in our own day, have either been unbelievers or have laid their Christianity aside when they thought most deeply about the historical process. During the same period our seminal religious minds, from Wesley and Woolman to Kierkegaard and Schweitzer, have not been particularly interested in world history. One could mention minor exceptions from Bossuet to Sorokin, but I think it would remain true that within the past three centuries no first-rate historical mind has attacked the problem of Christian historiography so earnestly and on such a wide front as Toynbee.

This is certainly one of the many reasons for his amazing popularity in America today. There are others, of course.

* In the spring of 1948, Reinhold Niebuhr was in charge of program for a society of theologians which was holding its spring meeting in Princeton. At his suggestion, the subject of the paper he asked me to give was Toynbee. Although everyone at that time apparently had to write at least one article on Toynbee, the subject here was a bit off the track. The article was written, of course, before the last volumes of *A Study of History*, with their strong leaning toward Mahayana Buddhism, appeared. The critique appeared first in *Theology Today* for October 1948, and is reprinted here by permission.
[1] *Civilization on Trial* (New York, 1948).

The sweep of his historical vision, the unbelievable scope of his learning, and the sheer gallantry of his intellectual venture are certainly factors in the wide sale of Somervell's summary of the first six volumes. His key ideas—Challenge and Response, Withdrawal and Return, Schism and Palingenesis, Rout and Rally—have each of them the mark of all influential ideas: the man in the street can test their truth and workability to some extent in his own limited experience and find that they make sense. But there is more to it than this. Henry Luce may have sold Toynbee to the American public, but there has been remarkably little sales resistance. Here is a spiritual interpretation of history in an age of materialism, an alternative to Marxism. Here is an eloquent defence of freedom of the will in an age overwhelmed by various determinisms, an alternative to Spengler and his ilk. Most important, here is a strictly empirical "Study of History"—or so the author constantly describes his own work—which ends in the mystical vision of "a single figure" upon the farther shore of history, the figure of the Saviour who "rises from the flood and straightway fills the whole horizon."[2] "I like Mr. Toynbee," an older woman friend of mine remarked, *"because he is so hopeful."* "I read Toynbee," an undergraduate recently said to me, "because he has *the Christian answer* to so many of the questions you professors pose." From women's clubs to student honors programs, people are reading Toynbee as the Christian who possesses the key to history and to hope.

As becomes intellectuals, both the professional historians and the professional theologians have their reservations. Hardly one of them fails to admire the richness of Toynbee's learning, the penetration of his insights, the power and breadth of his historical imagination, and the sincerity of mind and spirit which is evident on every page.

[2] *A Study of History*, vi, 278; *Abridgement* (ed. Somervell), p. 547.

But historians have been wondering of late whether *A Study of History* is really history, and theologians are beginning to wonder whether what it preaches is really Christianity. In a recent number of the *Journal of the History of Ideas*, for example, Professor Geyl of the University of Utrecht subjects the *study* to the most penetrating criticism which I have yet seen from the side of the historians. After reading Toynbee, he writes, one feels inclined to exclaim, "C'est magnifique, mais ce n'est pas l'histoire." It is stimulating and it is inspiring, he says in so many words, but it is not necessarily so. It is not empirical and therefore strictly not history at all.[3] Most theologians have lagged behind in developing a frontal attack upon Toynbee's theological position,[4] perhaps because this position is not immediately evident and must be plotted by inference. The appearance of his latest volume, however, may very likely stimulate significant theological analysis and criticism. The reason is that if the one-volume summary made Toynbee's ideas seem more bald and dogmatic than they really are in the rich context of the major work, these latest essays make them seem even more naked and sharply-defined.

There are those, in other words, who are asking, "Is Toynbee a Christian?" (meaning "my kind of Christian"), and others who are asking, "Is he even a historian?" These questions are not really interesting except as possible indications that the most splendid attempt of the modern period to carry out a Christian philosophy of history into actual practice has been a failure. Are Toynbee's readers

[3] P. Geyl, "Toynbee's System of Civilizations," *Journal of the History of Ideas* (Jan. 1948), p. 111 and *passim*. Unlike the friend quoted above, Geyl sees a gloomy determinism behind Toynbee's professions of hope and insists that "we need not let ourselves be frightened by his darkness! . . . The future lies open before us . . ." (p. 124).

[4] James H. Nichols, however, contributed an analysis in the *Journal of Religion* (Apr. 1948), pp. 99-119.

really getting what they think they are getting: a sound reconciliation of Christianity and civilization, of theology and history? Has he solved, in a way satisfying to our day and generation, the problem of the Christian who is also a professional historian?

I

It is not easy to state the problem of Christian historiography in clear and simple terms. But let us say for purposes of discussion that the problem is twofold: first, to work out an interpretation in which man is *in* but not *of* history; and second, to define the movement of history in such a way as to do justice to both *recurrence* and *uniqueness*, both cycle and line.

The most brilliant exposition of the first aspect of the problem is to be found in the last chapter of *The Nature and Destiny of Man*. There Niebuhr remarks that man cannot find salvation "either by an escape from history or by the historical process itself. . . . The genius of the Christian faith makes it impossible either to view the trials and tumults of a civilization with detached and irresponsible equanimity nor yet to identify the meaning of life with the preservation of our culture and civilization."[5] In other words, the meaning of history is neither to be found wholly *within* history nor wholly *outside* of history. But the problem is to implement this insight in the actual practice of the historian's profession, to write history or "study" it in continuous consciousness of this truth. This is not easy. The prophetic interpretation of history is more convincing in the prophets, who never stopped to write actual history, than in the chroniclers, who did. It is easier to say that God acts constantly in history than to say precisely where and when. The conception of Jehovah as Creator and

[5] Reinhold Niebuhr, *The Nature and Destiny of Man* (New York, 1943), II, 320, and note, 307.

Redeemer, the God who acts in history, thus authenticating and at the same time transcending history—this profound conception is often reduced to a superficial and naïve level of interpretation in the Biblical chronicles. To the modern taste, the moral tensions of historical existence are too easily resolved in much Biblical narrative by subjective vision and dubious miracle. This is to say that the problem stated hardly existed in Biblical times because the Biblical writers had only an embryonic sense of "history" as anyone would use the term today. It was the Greeks who began that critical inquiry into what actually had happened in the past which came to be called "history," and who thus posed the problem for later Christian thought.

The second aspect of the problem—the reconciliation of recurrence and uniqueness in the historical process—is posed by the two limits of historical thinking in general and is not peculiar to the Christian historian. If there were no recurrence of any sort in history, no return of familiar situations, no parallelism or analogy, if all history were a succession of absolutely unique and unprecedented events, history would of course be unintelligible. If on the other hand there were no uniqueness in history, no unpredictability, nothing new under the sun, then historiography would theoretically be as exact a science of predictability as physics. Over-emphasis on the uniqueness in history may lead to one of many results: miraculous chronicle, a literalistic apocalypticism, crass predestinarianism, or a theory of automatic secular progress. Over-emphasis on the recurrence in history may lead to either a mystical or a rationalistic interpretation, in which perhaps the Buddhist cycle or the Western scientific "law" is the key to understanding the historical process. History is then reduced either to myth or to science. Ever since Augustine, Christianity has been more afraid of the cycle than of the line, more disturbed about history's being reduced to recurrence than about its being reduced to uniqueness. The reasons are familiar enough. The cornerstone of Christianity is the uniqueness of the Incarnation. History must be a straight-line succession of unique events in order to support the belief that God became man but once, at a certain time and a certain place. "For Christ died once for our sins, and rising again, dies no more," Augustine wrote in a famous passage, turning Paul's words in opposition to a theory which was certainly not in the apostle's mind when he wrote, the classical theory of cyclical recurrence.[6] There is no question that an essentially progressive interpretation of history is a necessary postulate for Christians, but the cycle has never been completely exorcised from their thinking because the phenomenon of recurrence simply cannot be ignored in human experience. In Christian history, for example, spiritual rebirth constantly recurs, in individuals and through them in social groups. And the secular cycles of classical thought are always close enough to being empirically verifiable to reappear over and over in the historical thought of times of trouble and to fascinate Christians from Luther to Toynbee.

The best way I have found to understand Toynbee's approach to these problems of Christianity and history is to reread two great predecessors of his, Augustine and Machiavelli. Augustine's *City of God*, Machiavelli's *Discourses on Livy*, and Toynbee's *Study of History* make interesting and often exciting parallel reading. Each book represents a search for wisdom through the study of history, stimulated by the belief at the back of each author's mind that his own age was one of crisis, disintegration, and decline. Each drew his primary data and even many of his basic

[6] *De Civitate Dei*, Book XII, chap. 13. Cf. Romans 6: 9-10 in Moffatt's translation: "For we know that Christ never dies after his resurrection from the dead—death has no more hold over him; *the death he died was for sin, once for all*, but the life he lives is for God."

ideas from the same civilization, the Greco-Roman. Each found in his search a kind of hope-within-despair. The first two were prophetic of the general attitude toward history which was to dominate succeeding centuries, Augustine of the medieval, Machiavelli of the modern; and there are those who believe that the mantle of prophecy has now passed to Toynbee.

The differences, however, are as striking as the similarities. Augustine found the merest fraction of history's meaning in history itself; the vast burden of this meaning he sought and found outside time and space in the soul and in God. Machiavelli found history a self-contained system and sought resolutely to find what meaning he could within this system. It may be that as he probed about this sealed container, he unwittingly poked a few holes through into the supra-historical with his idea of Fortune, but if so it was only to seal them hastily up again or to ignore the lowered atmospheric pressure within. Toynbee is steeped both in Augustine and in the classical conception of history which was Machiavelli's original inspiration. If anyone is equipped to combine or bridge the two views, surely he is the man.

II

Augustine's strength is in every case Machiavelli's weakness, and vice versa. His book begins with the sense of a "rotting and disintegrating world." Its subject, as announced in the opening sentence, is "that most glorious society and celestial city of God's faithful, which is partly seated in the course of *these declining times.*" "From all these miseries," he adds soon after, "[Christ] withdraws his flock and family by little and little out of all places of the declining world, to make of their company an eternal and celestial city."[7] And yet some fifteen years and twenty-two

[7] *De Civ. Dei,* Book I, chaps. 1, 31.

books later, he sketches a theory of progress which is the direct ancestor in the history of ideas of Condorcet's *Sketch of the Progress of the Human Race*.[8] The seven ages which he outlines from Adam to God's final Sabbath Day rest are certainly not much like Condorcet's nine ages, but the root idea of significant irreversible straight-line progress in time is the same. Augustine was born into a society which had idolized itself, which had decided (like England in the book entitled, *1066 and All That*) that when Rome became top-dog, "History came to a   ." For a variety of reasons which still puzzle historians, social growth had ceased, perhaps in some small part because of this underlying belief from the Augustan Age on that Rome's destiny was complete. Augustine saw that Roman society had inflicted mortal wounds on itself long before his own day, that most of its glory had always been hollow and over-rated, and that something far more important than the rise and fall of Rome was actually going on in history. This was the grim, obscure struggle between two half-hidden societies, the *civitas Dei* and the *civitas terrena*. Against a deterministic fate on the one hand and a capricious fortune on the other, he insisted that history was destiny, that the God who "in the fullness of time" had revealed himself in Jesus Christ was the author and predestinator of the course of human history. History then was more than flux, more than change, more even than growth. And it had not by any means come to a stop. In effect, Augustine helped to reveal to his own generation and his posterity a whole new dimension of historical growth, the dimension of the spirit. It is almost as if he had read Mr. Toynbee in a vision, had

[8] *De Civ. Dei*, Book XXII, chap. 30. This essay was completed before the appearance of the brilliant article of my then colleague, Theodor Mommsen, "St. Augustin and the Christian Idea of Progress," *Journal of the History of Ideas* (Vol. 12, 1951), pp. 346-374. See also my comments on pp. 8-18, Chapter 1 of this book.

noted the breakdown of Challenge-and-Response, seen the need for still further Etherialization, and prescribed Detachment and Transfiguration! It was a magnificent achievement. He helped give a new start to succeeding ages, and there must have been many who read him "because he was so hopeful."[9]

It was magnificent, but "was it history?" Did Augustine know enough or care enough about history really to face the problem of Christian historiography? I am inclined to think not. One has only to read Herodotus or Thucydides, Tacitus or even Polybius, then to read *The City of God*, to appreciate how far the grasp of historical reality, the sense for the great historical problems, had deteriorated by Augustine's day. His purview is limited to the Hebrew people, Assyria, and Rome; he rates the importance of Assyria above that of Athens because Assyria was bigger; his sense of relevance and significance is childish when he is relating the history of the *civitas terrena*; he shows no sense whatever for the organic development of societies; and many of the historical incidents which he culls from his second-rate sources are ludicrously misrepresented. Of course *The City of God* is not meant to be history and it is unfair to criticize it as such. It is an attempt to reread the universe in the light of one of the profoundest Christian conversion experiences of which we have record. But if we agree with enthusiasts that Augustine was the first to develop a "Christian philosophy of history," we must add with the critics that even by the standards of his own day, he was a third-rate historian. Except for his well-known flashes of insight when he is estimating the causes and character of Rome's greatness in Books v and xix, he leaves the

[9] On Augustine's historical thought, see particularly C. N. Cochrane, *Christianity and Classical Culture* (rev. ed., London and New York, 1944), chap. 12; and F. W. Loetscher's article in *Theology Today* (Oct. 1944).

grand theme of history as God's action in time for others to orchestrate. Even the brilliant insight into the importance of conflict as the dynamic factor in history he muddies over by his overemphasis on "peace" as the end of history and of all human effort. In fact, his very use of the word "history" betrays the fundamental ambiguity in his mind. At times he uses the term in the sense of the great Greek historians to describe what has been established by inquiry over against the legends and fables of "poetry"; at times he speaks of prophetic meaning as superior to "mere history"; and at times he talks of a "divine history" which includes the fall of Satan, the fall of Man, and the millennium.[10] In fine, he came dangerously close to reducing the tensions and relativities of secular history to "vain repetitions of the Gentiles" and limiting the application of the idea of significant progression to what we today would call supernatural history.

The faults of the Augustinian view of history were magnified many times in the popular piety of the Middle Ages. Striking examples of this magnification are to be found in the legends of the saints as they were pictured in stained glass and recounted in such collections as the *Golden Legend*. Here history has become a chain of marvelous and miraculous episodes. Emperors and kings, battles and treaties, sometimes even the ordinary life of getting and spending, all recede into a shadowy background. In the foreground is the saint, a kind of allegory of Gospel virtue, moving easily in and out of the next world through vision and miracle, and often as lacking in human virtues as in temporary interests and sense of humor. Anyone who is inclined to believe that a theology *of* history is enough, without the discipline of understanding how men have

[10] So at least in Book XVIII, the only point at which I have had occasion to check his use of the word. See especially chaps. 8, 16, 38, 40, 44.

actually lived and worked and striven in time and space, should read the *Golden Legend* and ponder.

III

It is only against such a background that the freshness of Machiavelli's realism can be appreciated. To move directly from the *Golden Legend* to the *Discourses* is to move from a gloomy Gothic-revival landscape to a brightly lighted Renaissance interior. Man is alone, and in spite of an uneasy feeling about what is outside the room, he is content to be so. Man is the product of history, and history the product of man's free will. Since human nature never varies, since the total quantity of good and evil in the world is always constant, and since the movement of history is cyclical, man can learn how to direct his own destiny by looking into history at any point and puzzling out the laws indicated by the events noted. "Whoever considers the past and present," he writes, "will readily observe that all cities and peoples are and ever have been animated by the same desires and the same passions; so that it is easy, by diligent study of the past, to foresee what is likely to happen in the future in any republic, and to apply those remedies that were used by the ancients, or, not finding any that were applied by them, to devise new ones from the similarity of events."[11] Having discovered the regularly recurring patterns or laws of history, man needs only the strength of will to apply his knowledge. Taken together, the two qualities of intelligence and will, or the cunning of the fox and the courage of the lion, constitute *virtù*, the quality *par excellence* of man as man. *Virtù* is pitted not unequally against *fortuna*, a difficult and fluid concept in Machiavelli's thought—now equivalent to blind chance, now compared to a woman, fickle but conquerable by bold-

[11] Machiavelli, *The Prince and the Discourses* (New York, 1940), p. 216. Cf. p. 530.

ness, now pictured as a kind of providence which brings men and peoples "to their ruin or their greatness by some great occasion" deliberately offered to test and challenge their mettle. Here Machiavelli is specific where Augustine is general. Fortune, for example, saw to it that the Senate and people of Rome quarreled, and this quarrel was "the very origin of their liberty." As a result Rome emerged with a mixed government compounded equally of monarchical, aristocratic, and democratic elements, "which rendered the constitution perfect" and accounted for the amazing longevity of the Roman state. At times the author pauses to discuss such things as the effects of rigorous environmental conditions and of self-imposed rigor in the law as typical factors evoking the response of *virtù*.[12] In many passages Machiavelli, like his classical historical models, uses the concept, if not the exact phraseology of Challenge-and-Response. He is at every point passionately interested in "secondary" or immediate causes, and in the relative part played by virtue and fortune in each class of events.

What is the measure of historical significance with Machiavelli? With Augustine the measure of the temporal is always the eternal, of the spatial, the infinite. This is beautifully exemplified in his criticism of Cicero's definition of a commonwealth as rooted in "justice." What sort of justice was it, he asks, which did not first render to God his due?—significantly forgetting to emphasize immediately, as did the original Hebrew covenant, that to render to God his due inevitably demands rendering to men their due.[13] Machiavelli has rejected the eternal and the infinite for a closed space-time system. And so his test of historical

[12] *Ibid.*, pp. 91-94, 116, 119, 274, 277-281, 500, 504, and particularly 380-383.

[13] *De Civ. Dei*, Book XIX, chap. 21. Toynbee goes beyond Augustine here in insisting that "Seeking God is itself a social act" (*Civilization on Trial*, p. 246).

significance is always *duration* and *extension*, longevity and size. How can a society best cheat the cycle? How can a state acquire stability and strength in flux? How have past peoples resisted corruption from within and conquest from abroad? Such questions lead him to an examination of Sparta and Rome, of France and the Ottoman Empire, but above all of Rome. At one very interesting point he hints that there may be a conflict between duration and extension, that a people may burn itself out in time in the effort to expand in space.[14] But there is no wavering on the essential point that the ultimate test of policy as of religious and moral codes is duration in time and extension in space. In many ways Machiavelli was just as poor a historian as Augustine in his one-sided belief in the sameness of human nature and the repetitiveness of history. But he saw far more deeply into the mechanisms and regularities of history, the continuities of immoral man and his still more immoral society, than his predecessor. Furthermore at times in his treatment of *fortuna* he seems to have accomplished what Augustine failed to accomplish, a circumstantial account of how God actually acts in history— without believing in the existence of God!

This brief and inevitably distorted discussion of Augustine and Machiavelli may serve at least to point up the two extreme errors into which Christian historiography may fall: a *theology* of history which never makes significant contact with the complex development of societies in time and space and which loses itself in history of the disembodied spirit; and a *science* of history which elaborates a self-contained system of regular recurrences and finds no meaningful place for the unique event, the freely creative act.

[14] Machiavelli, *The Prince and the Discourses*, pp. 127-128. Cf. pp. 115, 121.

IV

Against this background it may be possible to estimate the character and significance of Toynbee's attempt to solve the problem of Christian historiography: to bridge the eternal and temporal and to align the cycle. In practice, this attempt takes the concrete form of accomplishing once more the perennial task of Western society—the reconciliation of the Christian and the classical traditions. It is impossible to say whether Toynbee is more soaked in the Bible or in the classics, but it is possible to speculate upon how far the process of osmosis has proceeded.

Toynbee's starting-point, as one illuminating commentator tells us,[15] was an almost mystical experience in Crete during 1911 in which the "philosophical contemporaneity of civilizations" was overwhelmingly borne in upon him. This insight was further deepened and confirmed in 1914 while he was expounding Thucydides to undergraduates at Balliol: "Thucydides, it now appeared," he writes, "had been over this ground before." When the first three volumes of the *Study* appeared in 1933, the author was to speak sharply of "the illusion of progress as a movement that proceeds in a straight line" and to state his conviction that civilizations are to be regarded not only as "philosophically contemporaneous" in time, but also as "philosophically equivalent" in value, types of a species hardly yet firmly established but far enough along the road to stability for their individual representatives to be compared with each other.[16]

The central idea in Toynbee's original scheme was that of repetition. Perhaps the reason for this was that he was trained in the history of a civilization which had already completed a cycle of birth, growth, breakdown, and dis-

---

[15] Tangye Lean, "A Study of Toynbee," *Horizon* (Jan. 1947), pp. 24-55; cf. Toynbee, *Civilization on Trial*, pp. 7-8.
[16] *A Study of History*, I, 172-181; *Abridgement*, pp. 41-43.

integration, a civilization furthermore which itself believed in the cycle. Perhaps the reason was a psychological one, the need Toynbee has felt all his life for undermining the "egocentric illusion," the "parochialism" of his own society. At any rate, as he saw it, history was to borrow from science on the one hand and from fiction on the other, and to lay bare the repetitive patterns evident in the history of civilizations. These patterns would partake both of the quality of scientific law and of myth (the immediate source of the most famous of them all, Challenge and Response, was the myth of Mephistopheles in Goethe's *Faust*, for instance).[17] They would be tested by rigidly empirical methods, but, given the end in view, the chief method would be that of parallel and analogy. No historian of our generation has used parallel and analogy more brilliantly—and more dangerously—than Toynbee. The classic examples are the illustrations he offers of Withdrawal and Return, drawn as they are from the disparate scales of individual biography, national history, and the history of whole civilizations, in fantastically contrasting contexts of time and space. The most striking example in his new volume is the analogy of the battle of St. John Chrysostom *vs.* the Empress Eudoxia—and that of Trotsky *vs.* Stalin.[18] How all-pervasive the idea of repetition is in his thinking may be gauged from the fact that he is not afraid in this to compare history with biology, although elsewhere he rejects Spengler's organic interpretation of societies. "The works of creation are apt to occur in bunches," he writes. The Creator, then, multiplies civilizations presumably as he multiplies men or rabbits, in a kind of "process of trial

---

[17] *Study*, I, 441-464; *Abridgement*, pp. 43-47; *Civilization on Trial*, pp. 11-12.

[18] *Civilization on Trial*, p. 182. Cf. *ibid.*, pp. 58, 136, 164, for other examples. See Geyl, "Toynbee's System of Civilization," p. 121, for criticism of Toynbee's use of analogy.

and error." As men learn through suffering, so man learns through the repetition of civilizations. (The rabbits are my addition to Toynbee's thought.)

There has been remarkably little change in the architectonic structure of Toynbee's thinking as the years have gone by, but a certain shift of emphasis is noticeable with the appearance of the second three volumes of the *Study* in 1939. Here the famous figures of the wheeled vehicle and the growing web appear. The wheels give movement in a straight line to the vehicle of history; the shuttle of Time moves back and forth, but the tapestry grows continuously. We note a "harmony of two diverse movements—a major irreversible movement which is borne on the wings of a minor repetitive movement." "Thus the detection of periodic repetitive movements in our analysis of the process of civilization does not imply that the process itself is of the same cyclic order as they are. . . . This is a message of encouragement for us children of the Western Civilization. . . ."[19]

The point Toynbee was trying to make became clearer in the most brilliant essay he ever wrote, "Christianity and Civilization," the Burge Memorial Lecture for 1940. Here the famous theory "that the successive rises and falls of civilizations may be subsidiary to the growth of religion," barely adumbrated at the close of volume six of the *Study*, was sketched in exciting outline. "If religion is a chariot," he wrote, "it looks as if the wheels on which it mounts to Heaven may be the periodic downfalls of civilizations on Earth."[20] As in this case, all the key sentences are introduced by "if" and there is a liberal use of subjunctive verb-forms, but the general intention is clear. It is not only to guarantee the freedom of the will and to provide

[19] *Study*, IV, 33-35; *Abridgement*, pp. 253-254.
[20] *Civilization on Trial*, p. 235. The essay is republished as it was written in 1940.

"encouragement"; it is also to suggest, if not to establish the uniqueness of Christianity. If we can change our historical viewpoint, he suggests, if we can come to look on the rise and fall of civilizations including our own merely as "vain repetitions of the Gentiles," then we shall see that "the greatest new event in the history of mankind" was and still is the Crucifixion. The decline of Western civilization need not necessarily mean the birth of a *new* religion. Christianity may be left as "the spiritual heir of all the other higher religions." In fact, after "primitive societies" and "civilizations," the Christian Church may even become the third species of human society. In any case, the spiritual progress of individual souls in cumulative. There is "a growing fund of illumination and grace," an "increasing spiritual opportunity for souls . . . to come to know God better and to love him more nearly in His own way." If it be asked why Christianity is any more final among religions than Western society among civilizations, the answer is: "The Christian soul can attain, while still on Earth, a *greater* measure of man's greatest good than can be attained by any pagan soul. . . ."[21]

V

If this brief summary is faithful to the broad development of Toynbee's thought, I believe it is evident that he has become increasingly concerned to subordinate the cycle, to develop a theory of "spiritual progress," and thus to approach a position from which the uniqueness and finality of Christianity can be contemplated. As his historical vision has widened, his Christian faith has deepened.

Has he finally bridged the gulf between Machiavelli and Augustine, reconciled classicism and Christianity, and solved the riddle of the cycle which is really a line? There

[21] *Civilization on Trial*, pp. 234-252. (Italics added.) Cf. pp. 262-263.

are two ways of attempting an answer to this question: first, by drawing up a sort of balance-sheet of classical and Christian influences upon his key ideas; and second, by critically examining his method of reconciliation. The first approach leads to suggestions only, the second to more positive conclusions.

Examples could be multiplied of Toynbee's debt to the tradition of which Machiavelli is a part. "Challenge and Response" owes as much to classical thought on the workings of Virtue and Fortune as it does to Bergson and modern psychology. Typically Greek again (as well as Bergsonian) is his faith that history has much to borrow from both science and myth. What often seems to be an exaggerated emphasis on the importance of individuals and minorities is a characteristic trait of classical and Renaissance historical thought. And most striking of all, Toynbee often makes conscious and effective use of the tests of extension and duration as criteria of historical significance, even though what he is interested in is the lasting and diffusive qualities of a whole culture rather than merely of a political society, as is the case with Machiavelli.[22]

Toynbee's debt to Christianity, or better the particular quality of his Christianity, is more difficult to describe. But it can be plotted by certain intellectual intersections. The decisive effects of violence are minimized in this thinking. Societies are never merely murdered, they commit suicide. Physical expansion by war is a sign of inner decadence, not of vigorous growth; that is, *mere* size and *mere* endurance are no test of vitality. Religion is ultimately more important than politics, and politics more important than economics and technology. The tragedy of man's existence is the "sensational inequality" of his achievement in these three spheres. He has been "relatively good" in dealing

[22] See, e.g., *Civilization on Trial*, pp. 5, 65, 88-91, 158, 161-163, 214-216, 242.

with non-human nature, "bad" in dealing with human nature, and "very bad indeed at getting into the right relation with God."[23] Specifically biblical roots appear time without number in such ideas as Withdrawal and Return, Learning through Suffering, and the choice of the stone rejected by the builders (Toynbee uses the American translation of this, the myth of the Dark Horse). Even the spirit diffusing the whole *Study*, a kind of cosmic historical humility, is in a sense a Christian virtue.

It is dangerous to type such an undogmatic and unsystematic Christianity, but it is perfectly evident that it belongs to the Pelagian-Erasmian stream rather than to the Augustinian-Lutheran. If we ask, for instance, whether the central actor on the stage of Toynbee's history is Augustine's God or Machiavelli's man, the answer lies perhaps in the delightfully British caution of the following sentence: "With God's help, man is master of his own destiny, at least to some extent in some respects."[24] And the tone and temper of this sentence lead us to our final observation.

The method by which Toynbee attempts to solve the fundamental problem of Christian historiography, that is, to bridge the temporal and the eternal, the finite and the infinite, is, I have come to believe, *the interposition of the very long and the very great.* The Fathers like Augustine made a sharp, clean distinction between this world and the next, then moved between one and the other almost at will by vision, prophecy, and miracle. The men of Machiavelli's day saw the weaknesses of this method and did their best to reject the next world (just as their medieval predecessors had sometimes tried to reject this world). Toynbee

[23] *Civilization on Trial*, p. 262. On Toynbee's hierarchy of religion —politics—economics, see *ibid.*, pp. 5, 91, 94, 127, 130, 135, 143, 156, 216-220. Machiavelli's order of importance appears to be religion— politics—war—culture (*The Prince and the Discourses*, p. 141).

[24] *Civilization on Trial*, p. 30.

would lead us from this world to the next by regular stages, by forcing us constantly to enlarge our perspective, by continually changing the point of observation and the scale of measurement to force us to think in longer and longer periods of time, in larger and larger units of space, until *perhaps—maybe—if* we make the final effort, we may arrive at the universal point of perspective, the eternal and the infinite. I do not profess to know how conscious a process this is with him, but I am sure the process goes on. We are told that he has always been fascinated by maps and time-tables.[25] Any reader knows how brilliant he can be with geography, as for instance when he is comparing the desert with the sea. The geologists' time-scale is almost an obsession with him.[26] It is crucially important to his illustration both of the cycle and of the line. On the "true time scale" of earth history, he says in his latest volume, events of ancient history are *"virtually* contemporary with our own lifetime."[27] Thus the reader is led up to "philosophical contemporaneity" by way of "virtual contemporaneity." On the same scale, the Crucifixion, he says, is "a very recent event—perhaps *the most recent significant event* in history."[28] What does this mean—that the Crucifixion is likewise the most *significant recent* event of history? In the confusion of thought here there seems to be a half-expressed belief that to reduce the apparent interval of time between an event and the observer is to enhance the significance of the event. Perhaps Toynbee means that if we could move far *enough* away from A.D. 33 and A.D. 1948, we should see that they are "philosophically contemporary"—or in religious language, that Christ is cruci-

[25] Lean, "A Study of Toynbee," p. 28.
[26] There are five important and typical references to it in *Civilization on Trial*: pp. 36, 151, 163, 216, 237.
[27] *Civilization on Trial*, p. 37.
[28] *Civilization on Trial*, p. 238. (Italics added.)

fied in us. This means, I suppose, that in the last analysis there is continuity, not discontinuity, between time and eternity—that at the vanishing-point of perspective, differences do actually merge into unity, and that a curve which approaches infinity may get there after all.

VI

Unlike Augustine, Toynbee is a practicing historian; unlike Machiavelli, he is a practicing Christian. One cannot help admire him for the very thing that many of his critics on both sides dislike: his refusal to separate his historical writing and his Christianity, his unwillingness to say (as so many are willing), "Over here is my professional study of history and over there is my faith; they don't agree, but history is one thing, theology another; a spiritual interpretation of history is childish and a historical interpretation of Christianity is presumptuous." Toynbee refuses to separate his vocation as historian and his vocation as Christian.

It need not seriously qualify this judgment to add immediately that there seem to be grave faults in his integration of the two callings. Toynbee dislikes paradox. He prefers to state one good common-sense truth in one place, and then to state another good contradictory truth in another, several pages, several thousand words, or several years later. Has Western civilization really "broken down"? In this case, as Toynbee himself insists, the inevitabilities of the historic process are enormously increased and we must be slipping rapidly to our doom. Or have we still a real chance to reinvigorate our secular society? In this case we should bestir ourselves, repent, and rebuild our spiritual foundations, as he urges us over and over. Would he look upon the final disintegration of our civilization with the equanimity of an Augustine or the passionate despair of a Machiavelli? One could quote passages from his most recent volume to prove either view. Can we find exact analogies to our present situation in the histories of other civilizations, or are there unique elements in the present position of the West, such as the apparently decisive triumph of our technology and culture in competition with the four other remaining societies? Again the answer is yes to both questions. When Toynbee writes as a student of contemporary international affairs (and he is a profound one), he emphasizes uniqueness; when he writes as a historian of civilizations, he emphasizes recurrence.[29] What he refuses to do is to bring together these antinomies and to write nice, crisp sentences like "Man can find salvation neither by an escape from history nor by the historical process itself."

Beside soft spots, he also has his blind spots. He underemphasizes what might be called the anonymous forces of history—the technological and economic. He tends to underestimate the undeserved evil which falls impartially upon just and unjust. In the end he comes close to saying that men and societies get about what they deserve. And for the taste of anyone brought up in the Reformed tradition, he lacks too often the sense for the critical importance of the unique event as an integral part of the self-revelation of the hidden God of history, for what the prophets called "signs of the times" and Cromwell called "dispensations."

Each generation of Christians must attack anew the problem of understanding and writing history in the light of its own particular historical situation. In an age which has almost forgotten the supernatural and the suprahistorical in its fascination for evolutionary modes of thought, Toynbee sets himself to bridge the gulf between time and eternity by the *very, very, very* long view. This may be as

[29] Cf., e.g., chaps. 5 and 12 in *Civilization on Trial*.

fallacious from the point of view of Christianity as it is from that of mathematical theory. But it is undeniably a mode of thinking thoroughly intelligible to our age. One sometimes wishes that Toynbee had more of Augustine's ever-present sense of spiritual significance in historical events, or more of Machiavelli's shrewd and disillusioned secular understanding of these events. But Toynbee's readers no longer move in Augustine's world of prophecy and miracle or in Machiavelli's world of *virtù* and *fortuna*. We are saturated in continuity and probability, in "field theory" and "wholeness laws," all the way from our atomic theory to our Gestalt psychology. Toynbee speaks in this idiom when he writes in the revealing preface to his latest volume, "The universe becomes intelligible to the extent of our ability to apprehend it *as a whole*." We must see beyond nations, beyond civilizations, even beyond religions, to "a Kingdom of Heaven of which this world is one province. So history passes over into theology."[30] The mood of this passage is ancient, the application modern. When one considers this Kingdom, what are nations and civilizations that God is mindful of them? Toynbee's conclusion is not unlike the psalmist's. A civilization which truly knows itself and repents may be saved; if it collapses, its death-throes may give birth to a new religion or communicate new vitality to an old. The cycle may either be prolonged or completed in order to thrust forward the line. In either case, it is the long view which enables us to think more broadly and to act more humbly. There is "a growing fund of illumination and grace," "an increasing spiritual opportunity." History is not transformed by divinity, it "passes over" into theology.

[30] *Civilization on Trial*, p. v. (Italics added.) Cf. *Study*, IV, Preface, p. ix.

II

CHRISTIANITY IN HISTORY:
THE PROTESTANT
REFORMATION

7 · THE PROTESTANT REFORMATION*

THE PROTESTANT Reformation was a vastly complex religious upheaval within Western Christendom which began in 1517 with Martin Luther's protest against the abuse of indulgences. It reached the climax of its creative and destructive power in European society within the next century and a half. Now after four centuries the force of this revolutionary movement is largely spent, but Protestants can never entirely forget that they are heirs of a revolutionary tradition.

It is well to be humble about any attempt to understand such a movement. Like a river, placid on the surface, but fed by countless unseen springs and rivulets, the Reformation is a simple historical movement only to those who are content to look at the surface and ignore the myriad crosscurrents beneath. Too many Protestants today, for instance, think of the Reformation as simply a revolt of intelligent and long-suffering people against obvious and intolerable "abuses" in the Roman Church, on the analogy of their grammar-school picture of the American Revolution. "The movements of the human spirit, its sudden flashes, its expansions and its pauses, must ever remain a mystery to our eyes, since we can but know this or that of the forces at work in it, never all of them together." So a very great historian, Leopold von Ranke, wrote a hundred years ago of the Reformation—and we know of some complications today of which even he was ignorant.

* In 1957, a friend of mine on the faculty of Princeton Theological Seminary, Hugh Thomson Kerr, Jr., had the task of lining up visiting lecturers for a course primarily for church-school teachers on the history of the Church. He asked if I thought I could sum up my thought about the Reformation in about 5,000 words. I have forgotten why it sounded so easy at the time that I said yes, but this was the result: the Reformation in one easy lesson.

The idea of the Reformation and what it meant in the history of Christendom has a four-century history of its own. The earliest Protestants saw the movement of which they were a part as a direct intervention of God in history to chastise the Roman Anti-Christ and confound Satan. Their Romanist opponents naturally saw it as a diabolical rebellion against divine authority motivated by pride, greed, and heretical bigotry. Liberals and romantics of a later age saw in the Reformation mainly a vast upsurge of freedom, of protest against obscurantism and release from clerical bondage. To followers of Karl Marx it became a mere readjustment, on the level of religion, to deep underlying economic changes. At one time or another, the Reformation has been all things to all men.

Historians are agreed by now, however, on the general nature of the historical forces which Luther unwittingly released. It was these forces which gave the Reformation the momentum without which even so great a leader as Luther could never have overcome the inertia which had confronted religious radicals for years. First of all, the Reformation was intimately related to *the economic revival* of the later Middle Ages. The expansion of commerce and industry, the opening up of trade routes to the New World, the accumulation of wealth, the development of a "middle class" of enterprising businessmen, the appearance of something like the modern business cycle of boom and depression—all this made for new and half-understood stresses and strains in European society. To the new classes in the European economy, the medieval Church appeared to be inordinately wealthy, corrupt, grasping, and reactionary in its economic doctrines. It is far too simple to jump from this fact to the conclusion that the Reformation was simply the result of the greed of laymen for Church wealth. But there is no doubt that economic instability and economic change were in a sense the seed-bed of religious revolution.

So too in the case of political change. The steady *development of a sense of nationality*, together with the centralization of power in the states of Western Europe, were striking features of Luther's age. In Luther's own country, the growing Germanic patriotism was exacerbated by the political decentralization of Germany and focused with great intensity upon the greed of a "foreign" papacy at Rome. The Reformation was not a mere "national" revolt against a supranational papacy, but the national and local tensions of the age certainly had much to do with its spread.

Finally, the Reformation was related in a subtle way to *the intellectual quickening* which we call "the Renaissance." Very few of the scholars and teachers and artists whom we associate with the Renaissance joined the Protestant movement, but the critical spirit which they developed from their study of the classics carried over into their attacks on medieval philosophy and on clerical dominance of the life of the laity. And this critical attitude had its effect on the Protestant movement.

It is well to remember, however, that the Reformation was first and foremost *a religious movement*, not primarily an economic, political, or intellectual movement. However obviously it may be related to economics, politics, and the history of thought, it cannot be "explained" from these points of view. Whether we view it from Rome and call it a "revolution," or from Wittenberg and call it a "reformation," the Protestant movement was an upheaval in the religious life of European society at a time when religion occupied a far more central place in the consciousness of men than it does today.

Perhaps the best brief description of Protestantism is that offered by the German scholar, Troeltsch, who describes it as "a modification of Catholicism, in which the Catholic formulation of problems was retained, while a different answer was given to them." The problems—four in particular—were old, all reaching back to the very beginnings of Christianity. (1) What must a man do to be saved? (2) Where should one turn for religious authority? (3) What is the nature of the Church? (4) And how must a Christian live in this world? But the answers were relatively fresh and new. A man is saved by "faith alone," said the first Protestants; his authority is "the Word"; the Church is a company of the faithful, the "priesthood of all believers"; and the Christian life is "serving God in one's calling." Since the eighteenth century, all but the last of these questions have become irrelevant for masses of nominal Christians. But they were the central questions of the Reformation, and if we must try to simplify a complex movement, it is well to understand the original Protestant answers to them.

Two difficulties face us at the outset: all Protestants did not agree on their answers; and they insisted that they were advocating nothing "new."

Sixteenth century Protestantism took four major forms: the Lutheran, the Anglican, the Calvinist, and the Anabaptist (this last including a number of different radical groups). These forms are still reflected more or less clearly today in the major types or groupings of Protestant churches. The general nature of each may perhaps be suggested by saying that the religious genius of Lutheranism was best exemplified in Luther's hymns, that of Anglicanism in Cranmer's Prayer Book, that of Calvinism in its founder's *Institutes,* and that of Anabaptism in the idea of a purely voluntary church of converted believers. The Lutheran's warm inner piety and sense of being in, but not of this world; the Anglican's good sense and moderation in all things; the Calvinist's zest for theology and moral discipline; the Anabaptist's naïve enthusiasm for the literal imitation of Christ—these are startlingly distinct spiritual colors in the spectrum of Protestant piety. It is well not to blur them. In the sixteenth century a great deal of the richness and diversity of medieval Christianity, its wide range of Christian thought and feeling, passed directly into the Protestant movement, while the Roman Church closed its ranks at the Council of Trent (1545-1563) and became a far more monolithic type of Christianity than it had ever been before. Lutherans broke with Calvinists, both argued with Anglicans, and all three burned Anabaptists because of differences on the proper answers to the four questions already mentioned.

There was a real measure of agreement among Protestants, however, especially when seen from the perspective of contemporary Rome. The area of this agreement may be roughly indicated by two words: *Bible* and *conscience*. In *all* the four major forms of Protestantism, the Bible and the individual conscience came to occupy the central position in Christian faith and life in a way which was never true of medieval Roman Christianity. So it is possible to insist that Protestants differed, and at the same time to insist that they had something in common: a renewed sense of Scripture and a heightened sense of the meaning of Christian conscience.

As to the second difficulty—the conscious conservatism of most of the early Reformers—historical progress is often the result of attempts to turn the clock back. Luther never meant to be a revolutionary. He never once thought of himself as breaking off from the "Catholic Church," though he rejected the Roman papacy. He thought of his mission as one of restoration, not of revolution; purification, not destruction. But to restore the Church of the Apostles in the 1520's was a task which called for revolutionary effort, as Luther himself discovered. Calvinists felt that Luther had stopped short too soon in this effort; Anabaptists were convinced that both Luther and Calvin had betrayed the forward movement. To the Romanists, all were equally revolutionaries. But we need not stop over such historical quarrels. The point is that while none of the answers offered by Protestants was really new—all went back in one way or another to St. Paul and the Gospels—these answers were new enough for their own day to touch off a religious revolution. The Christian who tries seriously to "restore" apostolic Christianity is always a revolutionary in any age.

(1) To the first question—the question of salvation— all early Protestants except the Anabaptist groups and the Socinians (or Unitarians) answered that man is justified by faith alone, rather than by "good works." The root of this view was to be found, of course, in Paul's arguments against salvation by "works" of the Law. The view that God saves men through their sheer faith in Christ as Lord and Redeemer, not through their sacramental participation or moral effort, was always a natural response in the history of Christianity to threats of legalism, moralism, sacramental magic, and ritualism. It had been a prominent element in the thought of St. Augustine and St. Bernard, to mention only two between Paul and Luther. But it was Luther's personality and his frustrated search for peace in the monastery which gave the doctrine the point and poignancy it has always had in the main stream of Protestantism. Out of the depths of a frantic striving to merit forgiveness by good works—and they were the highest and holiest good works recognized in his day, the ascetic practices of a monk, came the revelation that forgiveness is a gift of sheer grace, that it can never be bought, bargained for, earned, or even deserved. The initiative, incredibly enough, is God's, not man's. Faith in a God who through Christ freely forgives the undeserving sinner is the faith which is

counted to a man as righteousness, since as a sinner he can never *attain* to righteousness. This faith, Luther wrote after his experience of it, "has appeared to many an easy thing; nay, not a few even reckon it among the social virtues, as it were; and this they do because they have not made proof of it experimentally. [But] it is not possible for any man to write well about it, or to understand what is rightly written, who has not at some time tasted of its spirit under the pressure of tribulation."

It is easy to see how this doctrine became a kind of surgeon's knife in the hands of the Reformers. If man is saved by his faith alone, they asked, of what use then are all these penances and pilgrimages, these saints and relics, these sacraments and ceremonies, these priests and popes? If the truly contrite heart is forgiven already, what need is there of indulgences—and absolution—and a priest? Actually, none but some of the radical groups ever pushed the argument quite this far to its logical conclusion— and these groups were apt to argue that a man is not saved by his faith so much as by his love. But the startlingly direct connection which Luther made between the Divine Grace and the individual sinner did much to short-circuit the whole, elaborate medieval system for *mediating* this grace through priest and sacrament.

It is more difficult to measure the height and depth of Luther's insight in our own secular age. At the heart of the Reformation was a profound pessimism about human nature, combined with a corresponding trust in God's power and goodness through Christ. We seldom stop to think how radically different this early Protestant view is from all the varieties of optimism about human nature which permeate modern Protestantism, especially in America. Salvation by "good works" has reappeared, in bewildering varieties: psychiatry and self-improvement now offer a way to "peace of mind" as confidently as monastic practices once promised peace of soul in Luther's day. But our half-century of war and revolution, of alternate apathy and fanaticism, have shaken our complacency and driven many Protestants to the despair and humility which enable Christians once more to understand the doctrine of salvation by faith. After four centuries of criticism of the doctrine from both the religious right and left, Protestants should be well aware of its dangers: an intolerant emphasis on belief and an underemphasis on the works of a sensitive conscience, a divorce of inner piety from the zeal for service. But it remains true that Luther recaptured the central truth of the Christian experience of God, that His Grace is utterly free and undeserved, overwhelming in the compelling power of its love.

(2) For authority Protestants turned from the visible Church of Rome to *the Word of God* embodied in the Old and New Testaments. Luther's experience of God was a biblical experience, and this fact proved to be of signal importance in the history of Protestantism. The conversion of many other great Christians had come through vision or trance, through sacramental or mystical rapture. But to Luther, a professor of Bible, it came apparently as he was pondering the meaning of Romans 1:17 while preparing lectures for his seminary students. This was a symbol of what the Bible came to mean to later Protestants of all varieties. As an English historian once said of the Puritans, Protestants became "People of the Book." Against the authority of Rome they erected the authority of the Word, and the Word came in time to permeate their whole spiritual life, their thought and speech, their theories about Church and State, industry and war, art and diversion. It is almost impossible today to imagine the impact of the first vernacular translations of the Bible, whether read aloud from the pulpit or scanned in private, upon a generation which knew nothing of newspapers, movies, radios, or

television. After the saints' lives which had hitherto been the pabulum of the lower classes, and the "commentaries on commentaries" on Scripture, which had been the intellectual fare of the clergy, the effect of bringing the biblical text itself within the reach of both clergy and laity was revolutionary. Within a generation of Luther's and Tyndale's translations, the Devil could find thousands upon thousands in Europe who could quote Scripture as well as he.

It is too simple to say that "for an infallible Pope the Protestants substituted an infallible Book." But the epigram serves to emphasize a fact which is difficult for us to grasp today. The early Protestants considered the Bible as an *objective authority*. Practically none of our historical doubts and queries about divine inspiration and copyists' errors had arisen to trouble them. If God had not founded His Church upon the Bishop of Rome, He had certainly not left it without authority: He had given men His Word in written form. To Luther this Word was *in* the Bible, though not necessarily in every part of it; to Calvin it *was* the Bible, all of it; and to some later Protestant literalists it even included the Hebrew vowel-points of the original text. But all Protestants agreed, however much they might differ on such points, that God had revealed Himself in Scripture, that He meant this revelation to be authoritative, and that He would naturally find means of impressing its authority upon men. The meaning of revelation depended thus not upon human interpretation but upon God Himself.

The dangers in this concept of Christian authority were perfectly evident before the sixteenth century reached its close. Romanists were quick to point out that the Church came before the New Testament manuscripts and the canon; lesser Protestant scholars were soon busily at work elaborating the stupid literalism which has been the peculiar curse of the Protestant attitude toward the Bible; and Anabaptist visionaries were soon demonstrating the capricious vagaries to which "dim-witted saints" (as William James called them) may come in their interpretation of Scripture. After the seventeenth century Protestantism acquired a deeper respect for reason and tradition in Scriptural interpretation, and by the twentieth century it had come to terms with "the Higher Criticism." But it is not too much to say that the authority of the Word is still the rock upon which Protestantism is founded. Whenever pressed for their final authority, Protestants are still "People of the Book."

(3) The doctrine of *the priesthood of all believers* was the answer of the Reformers to the third great question of their day, the question of the true nature of the Church. The Medieval Roman Church had come perilously close to saying that the Church was the clergy. The priest was a man, but as priest he was more than man in that his human nature did not affect the validity of the sacraments he performed. The stamp placed upon him at ordination was indelible. His position was a high one since outside the Church and its sacraments there could be no salvation, and he alone could administer the sacraments. But what if a man is justified by faith alone? What then became of the need of priests? Luther's answer was that there is still need of priests, but not of a separate priestly caste; we are all priests, each one to the other. "A cobbler, a smith, a peasant," he wrote, "every man has the office and function of his calling, and yet all alike are consecrated priests and bishops, and every man in his office must be useful and beneficial to the rest, that so many kinds of work may all be united into one community: just as the members of the body all serve one another." Thus the distinction between priest and layman becomes purely functional, and the Church becomes the company of the faithful. This com-

pany has its ministers, but every member is truly priest to his neighbor.

The principle of the priesthood of all believers played a varying role in the different forms of Protestantism. Anglicans clung to an almost Roman idea of the priesthood. Calvinists developed a lofty view of the clergy's place in the Church, but insisted upon moral and intellectual leadership, not magical power, as its foundation. Some Baptists and Quakers erased all real distinction between clergy and laity. Undeniably, however, there was a deep-rooted anti-clericalism at the heart of primitive Protestantism. The ancient fear which the ordinary man has always had of a celibate priesthood undoubtedly played its part here, together with the fear of spiritual tyranny as the Protestants saw it exercised by a clerical caste in the Middle Ages. The dangers in their attack on clericalism became evident soon enough in the relaxation of moral discipline, the multiplication of sects, and the breach in historical continuity which were such striking features of the early Protestant movement in general. It is always easier to attack priests than to be a priest to one's neighbor. But Protestants have maintained stoutly—and rightly—that self-discipline is preferable in the long run to priestly discipline, congregational autonomy and voluntary membership to hierarchical and established churches, and spiritual renewal to the preservation of tradition. If a "high" view of the Church inevitably entails a "high" view of the clergy, then the Reformers unwittingly undermined the foundations of the Church by preaching the priesthood of all believers. But their own belief was that the Church of their day would be strengthened, not weakened, by bringing it closer to the model of the Apostolic Church.

What Tillich calls "the Protestant principle" may serve to summarize this third answer and lead on to the fourth. It is the principle of protest against any human attempt to limit or circumscribe or define the will of God. Against the dogma that God had founded His Church upon Peter, that Peter was thus the Head of the Apostles, and that the Bishops of Rome were Peter's successors as Vicars of Christ, Luther protested that "to reduce the Christian Church to one man" was "a devilish and damnable heresy." He might have said that God gives no blank checks either to human individuals or to human institutions. Even the Church itself stands under His judgment, as do all human institutions—and judgment may come in unexpected ways. "Balaam's ass was wiser than the prophet," Luther noted: "If God spoke by an ass against a prophet, why should He not speak by a pious man against the Pope?" Unfortunately, it has always been easier for Protestants to see this principle exemplified in the Pope of Rome than it has been to see it incarnated also in their own churches. The "Protestant principle" must apply even to Protestantism.

(4) The fourth answer of the Reformation followed inevitably from the other three. If salvation is by faith alone, if authority lies in the Word, and if there is no qualitative distinction between priest and layman, then it follows that the Christian life is the inevitable overflow of faith in Christ as he is revealed in Scripture, in whatever occupation, clerical or lay, to which a man is called. In other words, the Christian life is *to serve God in one's calling*— as priest or potentate, banker or farmer, artisan or peasant, soldier or public hangman.

Medieval Christendom had developed a sort of division of spiritual labor. There were those to work (the peasants); those to fight (the nobility); those to administer the sacraments (the secular clergy); and those to pray (the monks). In theory, the Reformation abolished this division of labor at a stroke. To Luther there were no higher and lower callings, no higher and lower ways to salvation (such as those of the monk and the layman). A housewife may serve

God in her calling as well—nay better—than a nun. A shoemaker is as true a Christian as a monk. A soldier—even the public hangman—must somehow love as he slays. There are no exemptions from the service of God, whatever position in life one may occupy.

This was the most active and seminal principle in Protestantism. It was no more entirely new than the other Protestant answers, but it underwent a startling expansion in Protestant Europe during the sixteenth and seventeenth centuries. *Vocatio* was already a significantly ambiguous term meaning either a spiritual "call" (like that which came to Samuel) or a secular occupation (such as Paul's trade, at which he worked conscientiously to support himself). What many Protestant groups did was to take the ascetic ideals of the monastery out of the cloister and inject them into the life of serving God in a secular "calling." They rejected utterly the belief that God calls men to renounce the world and enter a cloister. And so it was natural to believe that God calls men to serve Him in their worldly vocations. From this it was only a step to saying that a Christian serves God not only *in*, but actually *through*, his calling. Shoes well-made, a business well-run, a marriage well-lived, a public office conscientiously filled —were not these evidences of Christian service and stewardship? When Martin Luther, a priest, married Catherine von Bora, a nun, the act was a symbol of his belief that marriage was a high calling, not a second-best way of life for laymen. The marriage—a happy one—has always been a scandal to Roman Catholics and a sermon to Protestants.

It is hard to say exactly how the doctrine of serving God in one's calling was related to the two most important historical developments of the age of the Reformation, the vast economic expansion and the rise of the modern state. Historians have argued long and hard about the relationship, and they are still arguing. New and more exciting economic callings were opening up in each succeeding generation; new and more responsible administrative posts were being created in the rapidly expanding governments of the day. Whereas the Church had once been the only institution which offered a career open to the talents, business and government now offered quicker roads to fame and fortune than a moribund ecclesiastical organization which was increasingly on the defensive. The older religious ethic which upheld the monastic life as the highest ideal rapidly lost its hold over men in such an age. The conception of serving God in one's calling was thus not merely a compromise with the world—it was that, of course —it was actually a very significant means of disciplining and Christianizing the secular pursuits which were now so much more rewarding and socially influential than they had been a few centuries earlier.

The fact that Puritans and some radical Protestant groups looked on the whole world of secular pursuits as a vast potential field for the direct service of God was undoubtedly a very important factor in the expansion of economic activity and the development of modern governments in Europe and later on in America. But historians cannot measure such influences, nor can they be sure what was cause and what effect. The ideal of the God-fearing business man, austere in his personal living, diligent to the point of self-exhaustion, honest in his dealings, and generous in his charities—this ideal certainly was a product of the Reformation. So too, though somewhat more obscurely, the ideal of the Christian citizen or public servant, accepting the duties of citizenship, the burdens of office, and given perhaps the task of military service as a religious trust, comes in part from the Reformation. Certainly neither the so-called "bourgeois virtues" of industry, frugality, honesty, and sobriety, nor the civic virtues of loyalty, prudence, and courage are necessarily Christian. But the

belief that God is to be served through one's secular vocation led to a peculiarly stable amalgam in Protestantism
between these virtues and the Christian virtues of faith,
hope, and charity. The dangers of such an amalgam were
evident enough. If the Christian element melts away, what
is left is either a purely materialistic ethic of acquisition or
a purely secular devotion to the state which is the seed-bed
of totalitarianism. But at its best, the Protestant ethic of
the secular calling has bent the world to its ideal, rather
than conformed its ideal to the world.

Across the top of the splendid Reformation Monument
at Geneva is written the motto which Protestant tradition
has come to associate with the Reformation: *Post Tenebras
Lux* ("after darkness, light"). These words have captured
something of the Reformers' conviction that God was intervening again in history before their eyes, cleansing His
Church, and bringing light out of darkness. Below, on the
same monument the spirit of the age is still more vividly
suggested in a contemporary description of John Knox's
prophetic activities in Scotland: "The voice of one single
man is able to put more life in us in one hour than the
blast of five hundred clarions sounding without cease in
our ears." Perhaps the medieval shadows were not so dark
as the early Protestants pictured them. Perhaps the Reformers exaggerated their own light. Perhaps they were too
little concerned by the prospect that the darkness might
close in again, on their own churches and followers. But
however much we may discount the zeal of those who first
felt compelled to break with the Roman papacy, it remains true that the Protestant Reformation was one of the
few really decisive revolutions in the history of Christianity. Wherever Christians the world over are really concerned about the problems of salvation, authority, the
nature of the Church, and the character of the Christian

life, they must inevitably reckon seriously with the Protestant answers of the primacy of faith, the authority of the Word, the priesthood of all believers, and the service of God in one's calling.

8 · FREEDOM IN WESTERN THOUGHT*

ALMOST a hundred years ago in one of the dark moments of our Civil War, Abraham Lincoln remarked, "The world has never had a good definition of the word liberty, and the American people just now are much in want of one." This was 1864, and we are still in want of one today —all over the world. One of the commonest phrases on our lips these days is "the free world." We think we know what it means: free from totalitarian slavery. And yet our "free world" includes some pretty tough and dictatorial regimes, all the way from Franco's Spain to South America, the Middle East, and Formosa. A cynical reporter wrote not so long ago from Buenos Aires that he had finally discovered a good definition of democracy: "that form of government with which the State Department is on friendly terms." One reason that the free world is sometimes confused about its freedom is that the Communists have often stolen the word for their own uses. Freedom means one thing in East Berlin, another in West Berlin; one thing in Budapest, another in Vienna. You have to define the political frame of reference before you know what a man means when he talks about the "freedom" of Poland, or of Korea, or of Egypt. A free man in one corner of our bewildering world becomes a slave if he moves to another, and a slave who escapes from his bondage in one place is a hero and free man in a different society. Even in our own nation, we differ—often violently—about freedom. The

* The essay that follows is based upon the Stearns lecture at Phillips Academy, Andover, for 1956. For many reasons it seemed appropriate to choose the theme indicated and to introduce into its treatment some of the main ideas worked out over the years in the cooperative Humanities course, 201-2, started during the war and originally called "Man and his Freedom in the Western Tradition." The essay has not been previously published.

word means one thing to a conservative, middle-western Republican, quite another to an eastern New Dealer. It means one thing to a Negro parent applying for his child's admission to a white school and quite another to a member of a white citizen's council in the same town. There seems to be a frightening relativity that spreads like dry rot in any definition of freedom that we propose these days. In other words, when freedom is the subject of discussion, there are always a lot of people ready to confuse the argument—like the political opponents whom Harry S. Truman once accused picturesquely of "dredging up dead horses to obscure the issue."

The one thing that seems certain is that Greeks and Europeans and Americans, through their long history, have been enormously *concerned* about freedom—more so than the members of any other of Mr. Toynbee's twenty-odd civilizations. The West has done an enormous amount of thinking, planning, and arguing about freedom. Its leaders have talked and written about it, seemingly with unflagging interest and energy. One has to admit immediately that Western society has devised some very ingenious and brutal ways to enslave the bodies and minds of men—from the Medieval Inquisition and *lettres de cachet* to Negro slavery and the modern police state. But always there has been protest and revolt against these systems and devices. And the protest has left behind a literature, a body of thought, about the problem of freedom, which has hardly any parallel in other civilizations. I have heard President Lowry of Wooster College say that "in judging men as in judging churches, it is not the reasons they give for things, but the things they give reasons for, that are important." Western writers have given a lot of reasons for something they call liberty or freedom. With this obvious *concern* about the problem we can at least make a start here.

Is there any way of defining, simply and clearly, what

Western thinkers have had in mind when they have talked about freedom? Unfortunately there is not, and dictionary definitions do not help much. Here is one "On the negative side, [freedom is] the absence of restraint; . . . on the positive, the organization of opportunities for the exercise of a continuous initiative."[1] This is hardly what my students would call the "cold dope." Perhaps we had better admit at the outset that life itself is not simple, and so we have no right to expect simple and clear definitions of its problems.

I suggest that we spend our time thinking about the three major *settings* in which the problem of freedom arises in Western thought: the natural setting, the social setting, and the psychic setting. The problem, it seems to me, always appears in one of these three settings: in man's relations to nature, his relation to society, or his relation to himself. These are the stage-settings of the drama of freedom, let us say. Let us look at each of them in turn, try to see what the relation of freedom in one setting is to freedom in the others. They are not the same. In fact, the historian will tell you that he is constantly struck by the fact that freedom in one setting is often won at the expense of freedom in one or both of the others. Along the way we will take time now and then to look briefly at some great writer who speaks eloquently for the view of freedom we are discussing. And at the end, I hope you will have some foundation on which to build your *own* conception of what Western thought on freedom is all about.

I

Freedom in the natural setting means, of course, freedom from hunger, cold, disease, and natural disaster. In our comfortable, steam-heated, sanitary existence, we some-

[1] Harold J. Laski, in *Encyclopedia of the Social Sciences* (New York, 1925).

times forget that this has been the main preoccupation of man throughout his career, and that it is still the main concern of most of the human race, particularly in Asia and Africa. Every living creature on this planet is bound by iron laws to the particular environmental conditions that enable it to survive—that is, every creature but man. In very recent times man has developed a marvelous ability to manipulate his natural environment so as to expand his freedom of movement and of growth far beyond that of any other creature. His science and technology have given him knowledge of the processes of nature and control over them, which he has used to clothe, shelter, and feed himself like a king, to fly at break-neck speeds all over the globe, to communicate instantaneously with his fellows everywhere, and to destroy whatever gets in his way, including other people. A civilized society is apt to become blasé about the slowly and painfully acquired knowledge and techniques that underlie its social institutions and culture. We either take these things for granted or else we become inordinately proud of them as our own generation's achievement. We are apt to tell more backward societies that what they need is democracy, the two-party system, and the Australian ballot if they are to become free—when what they really need is agricultural technique, industrial know-how, and medical science. We forget that men who are cold, emaciated, and disease-ridden have more basic freedoms to win in their natural environment before they can get really excited about political and social freedom.

If you want to recapture the enthusiasm that swept over our men of science when they first discovered a method that promised to win almost limitless quantities of this basic sort of freedom for man in his natural environment, read René Descartes's *Discourse on Method* (1637). The full title of the book is "Discourse on the Method of Rightly Conducting the Reason and Seeking Truth in the Sciences," and the main idea was that if everyone simply learned to use the brains that God gave him *in the right way,* by the right "method," useful knowledge would accumulate and mankind could vastly improve its condition on earth. Descartes tells us how he came to this conclusion. As a schoolboy he studied about the same subjects we do. But he quickly became fed up on languages, literature, poetry, history, philosophy, and theology, because there were no certain conclusions in any of them, nothing you could put your finger on. No two philosophers agreed an anything, he complained. He liked mathematics for this reason, "on account of the certitude and evidence of their reasonings," he said. And so in the end, he came to discover and admire a method that led to "useful" discoveries and that was subject to none of the doubts and disputes of what we would call the "humanities" today.

Descartes thought he had found a "practical philosophy" that would render men "lords and possessors of nature," as he put it. He saw that he and his fellow-scientists had uncovered a cumulative sort of knowledge, based not on revelation but on human intelligence and cooperation, which would loosen those strings that bind man to his physical environment and give him a freedom from hunger and disease he had never known before so long as he had accepted suffering as irremediable. Two centuries later Thomas Henry Huxley crossed the i's and dotted the t's of Descartes's enthusiasm for science. He was sure that "improving natural knowledge" was the only way to human happiness and freedom. "We have no reason to believe," he remarked, "that it is the improvement of our faith, nor that of our morals, which keeps the plague from our city; . . . it is the improvement of our natural knowledge." When plague strikes, men no longer flock to the churches, he remarked, they look to the sewers. All the pride of generations of scientific benefactors and emancipators of mankind breathes through these words—and in what his grandson, Julian Huxley, writes today.

How much freedom has Western man actually won in the natural setting? Almost from the beginning, the dangerous and demonic possibilities in this sort of emancipation from environmental restrictions haunted the mythmakers and poets and prophets. The myths of Prometheus and the Tower of Babel, together with the legend of Faust, contain the record of Western man's feelings of guilt about usurping God's creative power, his uneasy suspicion that control over nature may lead as directly to slavery as to freedom. Prometheus was pinioned to a rock for bringing down fire from heaven to benefit man; the builders of the Tower of Babel were thrown into the confusion of unintelligible tongues for their presumption in constructing a stairway to heaven; Faust paid for his thirst for knowledge and power with his soul.

But all this must not blind us to the almost incredible freedom that modern man has won for himself through his science and technology in his natural environment. To take but a single familiar example: medical science has not only freed us from the thralldom of countless diseases, it has actually widened the spectrum of moral choices open to us. The savage has little or no control over conception, disease, and death. But thanks to modern medicine, civilized man can prevent conception or produce it artificially, sterilize or stimulate the organs of generation, prolong life or terminate it by euthanasia. Every one of these physical possibilities implies new moral dilemmas and new moral possibilities. And where there is expanded moral choice, there is expanded freedom. At the very simplest level, it is clear that a man who is warm, well-fed, well-clothed, and in good health is free to do a great many more things than his less fortunate primitive ancestor. When the destructive power of modern warfare strikes civilized populations and city dwellers are forced overnight to grub for food, clothing, and shelter, men can suddenly discover how much of their freedom to move about, work, and act like civilized human beings depends upon the machines and devices which we have developed over the course of long years. This sort of freedom then, like all freedom, is a bit like good health—we never really know what it is until we have lost it. Freedom in the natural setting is the basic freedom, the freedom for which man has fought longest, hardest, and—in Western history at least—most successfully.

II

This leads us to the second setting of freedom: the social. This is the most familiar setting, the one any American naturally thinks of first when he glances at the word "Liberty" inscribed on the coin in his pocket. "Liberty" to an American means first of all national independence in a world of sovereign states. Second, it means a certain order within the nation, a certain freedom for religious, social, and economic groups within the state, a political structure encouraging and guaranteeing a high degree of individual freedom of choice and action. "A free church in a free state," "civil rights," "free enterprise"—these are the phrases that come most readily to mind when an American thinks of freedom. And behind them is a long tradition of Western thought about freedom in the social setting.

It is the strength of Western thinking at its best that it conceives of freedom as something more than a feeling, something more than a state of mind. It is an objective set of conditions, capable of being tested—a social state. Of course a man's *feeling* that he is free is infinitely important. I like Robert Frost's simple and provoking thought that "freedom is feeling easy in your harness." We are

[163]

"sociable" beings, as Dante says, echoing Aristotle, and this means that we are all under the harness of living in sociable relationships with our fellow human beings. "Feeling easy" in these relationships is not a bad definition of freedom in the social setting. But this freedom must be more than a "feeling." What if someone looks at us and remarks (as the Communists do) that we are really slaves and that our feeling of freedom is only a pathetic illusion? Our answer must be that freedom is a set of conditions that can be objectively defined and tested. A great Polish anthropologist (Malinowski) defines freedom as "those cultural conditions under which human beings can mature their purposes, execute them efficiently, and reap the benefits of their labor." This is considerably more prosaic than Robert Frost's definition, but just as important in its own way. What it says is that a free society should be capable of being described from the outside. Let us say that the members of a certain society tell us that they are free men. We can take them at their word, but if we are true to the best in our tradition we will ask certain searching questions about their society: Is it at peace, and not under the compulsion to go to war to solve internal tensions? Can people move freely across its borders? Can they move freely up and down the social scale? Can they combine and organize to accomplish their peaceful purposes? Can new ideas penetrate the society from outside? Are the higher gifts of culture available to all? Are individuals left free to think and feel and aspire, with none but the most necessary social restraints? Such an examination is based on the premises that freedom is a *context* as well as a *conviction*.

Before we go any further, it is important to notice that freedom in the social setting is conditioned in a strange and complicated way by freedom in the natural setting. Any advance in man's control over his natural environment may make possible an advance in social freedom. The grip of tyrants or slave-masters has been loosened more than once in history by the introduction of some invention or technique which has undermined the whole social system. But it may work the other way. A gain in man's freedom from the bondage of natural conditions may result in increasing his social bondage. The transition from hunting to agriculture in any society, for instance, seems to result in the growth of despotic monarchies and empires. In more recent times the transition from agriculture to industry has usually been accompanied by severe social strains that may end in war, revolution, or totalitarian despotism. It seems to be a truism that our science and technology pile people up in cities, as Thomas Jefferson feared they would. The resulting industrialization and urbanization pose possibilities of *both* freedom and slavery that were unknown in simpler agricultural societies. The American political boss, the *Gauleiter*, the Commissar—these are symbols of enslavement possible only in an urban, industrial economy. As the need for organization, discipline, and law grows with the industrialization of society, the social setting of the problem of freedom is constantly changing.

This suggests the important observation that liberty is always somehow related to law. Freedom and restraint are not so much opposites as complementary concepts. If one of our great cities were utterly without law for even a day, there would be no "liberty" in any civilized sense of the word for anyone before the day was over. The development of any skill, whether it is playing the piano or hitting a golf ball, requires strict discipline and obedience to certain laws. The freedom of movement that results from acquiring a skill is the consequence of following certain rules of the game. This has led some extremists down through the history of the West to conclude that freedom is simply perfect obedience to perfect law. Stoics, Calvinists, eighteenth century philosophers, and nineteenth century Marxists differed sharply on what they meant by law—to some it was divine, to some moral, to some natural—but they all agreed that man becomes free by submission to this law. In contrast, there have always been extremists on the other side—from Renaissance humanists and nineteenth century romanticists to followers of Nietzsche and Hitler—who have insisted upon the limitlessness of human powers, the lack of predetermined limits to what a hero or a Fuehrer may accomplish if he has the will. To the legalists, freedom is conformity to law; to the voluntarists, or apostles of will, it is boundless creativity and anarchic activity. In the twentieth century the Communist dialectic is the harshest example of the first, Nazi ideology, the nastiest example of the second. But whether you reach a totalitarian end by obeying the inexorable historical laws which govern universal history and are bringing in the proletarian paradise, or whether you reach it by playing up the *Wille und Macht* (will and power) of a heroic Herrenvolk which recognizes no law that extends over all mankind, the results are the same. Both extremes are wrong. There is an element both of autonomy and of obedience to law in any sound theory of freedom. The two are complementary, not contradictory.

It has been the genius of Western thought about political freedom to develop both sides of this apparent paradox and at the same time to preserve a sort of working balance between the two extremes. The best examples of the two different approaches to political liberty are what we might call Anglo-Saxon constitutionalism as expressed by John Locke and Continental European democracy as conceived by Jean Jacques Rousseau.

Locke's basic principle was that liberty is rooted in law. It was the great achievement of the English people to work out in their history the principle that government is grounded in law, that both the rulers and the ruled are equally subject to the law, and that the very purpose of government is to preserve certain rights vested by natural law in individuals. Locke had no doubt whatever of the existence of such a "natural law." He said it was "as intelligible and plain to a rational creature and a studier of that law as the positive laws of commonwealths, nay, possibly plainer." But because natural law was a bit vague and because some were apt to ignore it, men formed societies with governments, to attain a higher, civilized sort of liberty. The essence of this liberty was consent to live under law. Freedom under government, he said, was "to have a standing rule to live by, common to every one of that society, and made by the legislative power erected in it . . . not to be subject to the inconstant, uncertain, unknown, arbitrary will of another man." The essence of the Anglo-Saxon idea of political liberty is that the individual is free only in a society whose government obeys the law of nature and the constitutional law of the land.

Over against this English theory of constitutionalism, the French developed the theory of democracy. To Rousseau it did not matter so much whether government obeyed natural law and constitutional principles so long as it was truly popular. If the people are really sovereign, if their general will is directly expressed in the acts of government, then (said Rousseau) there are and should be no limits on what government may do—because government *is* the people. Freedom, then, consists in a kind of collective independence of all cramping or hindering influences, whether of law or of anything else. Freedom, said Rousseau, is obedience to a law that I myself, as an integral element in a completely democratic society, have had a share in making. Freedom lies in the feeling that the general will of a perfect democracy is *my* will.

Logically, I suppose that these two conceptions of political freedom are quite incompatible. One sets up a limited sovereign, fearful of individual rights. The other sets up an unlimited sovereign power, confident that all will be well if the people really control that power. Actually our American concept of political liberty is a nice, illogical, but very successful blend of these two ideas—of constitutionalism and democracy. It is not a thoroughbred born of either one of the two, but a hybrid of both. Occasionally the two clash, as they did in 1937 when Franklin D. Roosevelt, with an overwhelming majority of the Congress and the popular vote backing him, stood for democracy and Rousseau, while a solid majority of the Supreme Court stood for constitutionalism and John Locke. The compromise that resulted was in the best tradition of American political practice.

Notice that most of this classical Western thought about political freedom was focused upon the problem of something called the individual versus the State. There is no denying the radical individualism of much of European thought about Church, State, and society since the end of the Middle Ages. Respect for the unique, free-standing individual is a striking characteristic of modern political and social thought, and it has its roots deep in stoicism and in Christianity. The Chinese Communists knew what they were about several years ago when they invited the parents of imprisoned American airmen to come over and see the suffering of their sons. They knew there was no better way to influence the policy of a nation long imbued with a sensitive respect for the dignity of individuals.

But I wonder if this highly individualistic phase of Western thinking about freedom is not about through. At its peak it lasted from about 1500 to about 1900. Before 1500, medieval European thinkers were not so individualistic. When they thought and wrote about freedom, it was always the freedom of *groups* they had in mind—the freedom of the Church from dictation by the State, the freedom of a monastery from the control of a bishop, the freedom of a gild of stone-masons, for instance, to regulate their trade, and so on. Freedom was elbow-room in which groups could move about within society, and this was typical of all the earliest arguments about freedom about which we have any historical record. They were arguments that concerned groups, not individuals.

The pendulum swung very far toward individualistic interpretations of freedom in the four centuries after 1500, but I think it has begun to swing back toward center these days. Our crucial arguments as often concern groups as they do individuals. In the face of Big Business, Big Labor, and Big Government, our struggles to preserve some measure of freedom for the individual take the form of efforts to protect small businesses, weak labor unions, and local governments. Our social sciences and psychology have impressed upon us the fact that we can never understand the individual apart from his social context, and our religion has become more socially minded since the nineteenth century. The earliest Christians never made the mistake of succumbing either to a radical individualism or to totalitarianism. St. Paul was infinitely concerned about individual souls, but he also talked about Christians as "the body of Christ," in which the suffering of one member is immediately transmitted to all. Perhaps we are beginning to recover the early Christian insight that freedom and community are not opposites, but complementary terms, as liberty and law are. Our keenest minds today are aware that the problem of freedom involves not only the individual versus society, but groups versus society, and groups versus groups within society. The balancing of power between groups within what we call a free state has come to be the outstanding modern problem in the preservation of freedom. The trouble is, of course, that our popular myths and our political propaganda lag behind our best insights and our finest achievements. We still talk the language of rugged individualism and laissez-faire, but to the outside world it is our corporate and cooperative achievements that are most characteristic of us. If we would emphasize our cooperative achievements, our federal form of government and our TVA, for example, rather than "free competition" and "individual rights," in our propaganda directed toward Asia today, we would win more friends, influence more people, and also perhaps be closer to the facts of our particular national genius. Asians can understand the freedom gained by cooperative effort; they have difficulty understanding our highly individualistic vocabulary.

III

So much for the second setting of freedom, the social. What if a man finds himself in a free society, in command of scientific techniques that give him a large measure of freedom in nature, and yet discovers that he is a slave to himself? What if a man gains the whole world, as the New Testament puts it, and loses his own soul? There is obviously a third dimension of freedom here, a third setting of the problem: the psychic setting. I suppose it is theoretically possible to imagine a slave society in which there are nevertheless many free minds and free souls—as there must be in Communist Russia and China today. I suppose it is also possible to imagine a free society in which the natural desire to conform limits the development of truly free minds—let us hope this is not true of our own society. A free society and a free mind are not *necessarily* the same thing. But I suppose we can say that in the long run freedom of the mind will flourish only where there is actual freedom to inquire, to communicate the results of inquiry to others, and to persuade others of the truth that inquiry discovers. And free souls will multiply only where there is freedom to believe as you must, to worship as you wish, and to witness to the religious truth you have found. Social freedom and psychic freedom are not the same thing, but they affect and support each other. They are related, as freedom in nature and freedom in society are, in subtle and complex ways.

I use the word "psychic" to describe this third kind of freedom for a reason. The Greek word *psyche* is ambiguous: it can be translated either "mind" or "spirit." And so it is a good word to suggest something very important about the Western tradition: namely that although mind and spirit have often been sharply separated by Western writers—sometimes disastrously separated—they have never been permanently divorced. The Greeks were more interested in freedom of the mind. The passionate quest of some of their greatest intellects was to free man's mind from superstition, dogmatism, and prejudice. Christians, on the other hand, have been more interested in freedom of the spirit. To free the soul from sin, to release captive spirits—this has been the task of Christianity as of all the great world religions. Some of the most important thinkers who have shaped our ideas belong more to the Greek tradition: Montaigne, Descartes, Voltaire, Thomas Huxley, and John Dewey, for instance. Some belong more to the Christian: Augustine, Luther, Pascal, John Wesley, and Reinhold Niebuhr today. But from St. Augustine to Sigmund Freud the profoundest thinkers in our tradition have realized that the mind is not independent of the spirit, nor the spirit of the mind. The way we think is intimately related to the way we feel and believe. Error is not the same thing as sin, and sin is not error, but the two have a way of getting mixed up with each other. Emancipation of the mind from ignorance and misconception, emancipation of the soul from the sins of pride and sensuality—these are the two main interrelated themes of Western thinkers when they have wrestled with the problem of freedom in the psychic setting.

What is a free mind? What are its marks and how may we recognize it? Several years ago Mr. Blackmur and I and some others had a lot of fun trying to put on paper the marks of a "liberally educated man." We have taken quite a licking on the monstrous paragon of perfection that we described,[2] but I think we would stick by most of what we wrote. The liberally educated man, we said, "thinks of his business or profession, his family life, and his avocations as parts of a larger whole. . . . Whether making a professional or personal decision, he acts with [a] perspective which comes ultimately from his knowledge of other persons, other problems, other times and places." The most obvious mark of a free mind, I think, is that it is impatient of boundaries, both temporal and spatial.

Our ability to do this sort of thing is a hard-won privilege, and we sometimes forget the price that has been paid for it by all those who have fought for freedom of thought down through Western history. There have always been those who have cried that broadening our horizons and stretching our imaginations in this way is dangerous—immoral—blasphemous—perhaps even "un-American." The assumption of these people is that all knowledge is a dangerous thing: read Karl Marx's *Communist Manifesto* and you will become a Red, they say; read Myrdal's *American Dilemma* and you will become a "nigger-lover"; read the UNESCO literature forbidden in Los Angeles city schools and you will fall for "globaloney."

If we want to see what Western thinkers at their best

[2] *General Education in School and College* (Cambridge, 1952), p. 20.

have done with this problem of freedom of the mind, we can go back to the greatest fifty pages ever written on the subject: John Milton's *Areopagitica,* published illegally in 1644. Milton's argument against censorship of the press was written not against his political opponents but against his own political party, which had climbed into power in the name of freedom, then had restored the censorship when the going got tough. This is one reason for its greatness. It is easy for us to tell the Russians how to treat the satellites, but if we came into control of Hungary tomorrow and if our troops set up a reign of terror against the former rulers, I wonder how many American Miltons would protest? In other words, Milton defended freedom the hard way—against his and freedom's friends. And he did it in English cadences that are impossible to forget once you have heard them: "I cannot praise a fugitive and cloistered virtue, unexercised and unbreathed" . . . "God sure esteems the growth and completing of one virtuous person more than the restraint of ten vicious" . . . "The State shall be my governors, but not my critics" . . . "Let [Truth] and Falsehood grapple; who ever knew Truth put to the worse in a free and open encounter" . . . "Give me the liberty to know, to utter, and to argue freely according to conscience, above all liberties." There is an echo of this in one of our greatest jurists, Oliver Wendell Holmes: "The best test of truth is the power of the thought to get itself accepted in the competition of the market." Prosy and American—but still good.

If we ask what are the marks of a free spirit, the answer is more difficult. I suppose the one thing we could agree on is that a truly free spirit has no fear. This characteristic would link together canonized saints like Francis and Thomas More, and uncanonized like Abraham Lincoln and Albert Schweitzer. Not that such men never faced fear, but rather that they came through the abyss with a fearlessness and strength that sometimes seems almost terrifying. But I think the truest mark of a free spirit is the willingness to accept responsibility—the responsibility that goes with all freedom. Anyone who has read Erich Fromm's psychological analysis of Naziism called *Escape from Freedom* knows how tempting it is for the masses in modern nations to run away from the demands and burdens of freedom into the comforting clutches of a political dictator. What has been true in politics has been equally true in religion. In order to dodge the insecurity of real spiritual freedom, men have thrown themselves over and over again into the arms of an authorition Church, or sheltered themselves behind an authoritative creed, or bolstered their sense of security by burning heretics alive at the stake. Somehow it makes some people feel better if they can put an Inquisitor in charge and shift onto him the heavy choice of what is right and wrong, true and false.

There are a good many eloquent pleas for religious liberty in the history of Western thought, all the way from Martin Luther and Sir Thomas More to Voltaire, Jefferson, and more modern writers. But you have to go to a famous chapter in one of Dostoievsky's novels to realize the full profundity of the problem of spiritual freedom. It is the legend of the Grand Inquisitor as it is told ironically by Ivan to his brother Alyosha in *The Brothers Karamazov*. Christ is imagined as returning to earth. He appears before the cathedral in sixteenth century Seville, where a hundred heretics had been burnt "to the greater glory of God" the day before by the Grand Inquisitor. Christ raises a dead child from her coffin—and is immediately led away to prison by the Inquisitor. A strange conversation follows, in which the Prisoner never speaks, the Inquisitor doing all the talking. Why had Christ dared to return to earth, the Inquisitor asks, after He had clearly given the Pope and the clergy full powers to act in His name? Christ had put an intolerable burden of freedom on mankind. He had resisted the Devil's three temptations in the wilderness. He had refused to abolish human hunger by turning stones into bread. He had refused to make people sure of God's existence by performing the miracle of casting himself down from the temple without hurt. He had refused to accept Satan's terms for organizing mankind into one single universal state and so abolishing wars and conflicts. And so he had made men miserable instead of happy. Men would always be in doubt about whether or not Christianity was really true, always oppressed by the necessity of *choosing freely* whether or not to bet on its truth. The Church, said the Inquisitor, had been "correcting" all this. She had assumed this fearful burden of freedom herself and was making people happy in a way Christ had refused to make them, by offering them what they really wanted: "Miracle, mystery, and authority." And so it was the Church that really loved mankind because it made them happy, not Christ, who not only refused to diminish man's freedom but actually increased it to the point where it became a nightmarish burden. God wanted man's *free* love, not belief compelled by "miracle, mystery, or authority"; but, said the Inquisitor, this was expecting far too much of human beings. It is a frightful thing, he might have said, to be faced with the riddle of a universe that may or may not have a meaning—then be given utter freedom to puzzle the riddle out and to take the consequences.

Now it is dangerous to take this famous story out of its context in the novel, but I think it is plain that Dostoievsky was measuring the depth of the idea that *God really meant men to be free.* Milton had said the same thing in *Areopagitica*, and wrote *Paradise Lost* to dramatize it. At its best, the Western tradition has taken with utter seriousness the idea that man is endowed with a real intellectual and spiritual freedom and that he must be worthy of it.

9 · WILL VERSUS REASON: THE DILEMMA OF THE REFORMATION IN HISTORICAL PERSPECTIVE*

THE DILEMMA of contemporary Protestantism is the dilemma of Western society in general. Rooted historically in the concept of freedom, Protestantism is no longer free.

Four centuries ago almost half the Christians in Europe cut themselves off from the medieval Church in the name of Christian freedom, and for four centuries they have been struggling to give that freedom moral effectiveness and theological significance. Within the past generation the crisis appears to have been reached. The freedoms of the past—whether they be those of economic, political, or religious liberalism—have somehow brought forth the slaveries of the present, and we are told by the leaders of totalitarian states that bondage is "freedom," that the liberty of Western cultural tradition is the true bondage of our day. The most striking characteristic of the new "freedom" preached in Central Europe is that it is a voluntaristic, not a rational freedom—a freedom from all objective, universal norms and standards, rather than a freedom within such norms. To men who believe in this dynamic freedom of the will, the "liberties" of the West

* The first part of this essay owes much to the brilliant mind of Lynn White, Jr., now of UCLA, and once my colleague at Princeton University, although he should not have to take responsibility for what became of some of his ideas of many years ago. I confess that Protestant voluntarism does not seem so dangerous a tendency as it did in 1941 under the shadow of Naziism. The paper was meant to rouse discussion at a meeting of the National Council on Religion in Higher Education during the summer of 1941, and was published by the *Journal of Bible and Religion* in November 1941. It is reprinted by permission.

appear coldly rationalistic, decadent, incapable of inspiring historical action. It is more than coincidence that religious liberalism, more deeply rooted in Protestantism than in any other religious group, has been subjected to the same attack. Apparently Luther's "Christian Liberty" has finally ended in theological division, sectarian strife, and moral relativism.

The antinomy of will versus reason is a very old one, and it can be contended that our contemporary dilemma—particularly that of Protestantism—was rooted in the sixteenth century itself. To Luther and Calvin the will of God was too free, too sovereign and transcendent, to be embodied in the Church of Rome. Was it then too free to be embodied in *any* relative human institution or idea? Was the will of God so unconditioned as to be irrelevant to all the orders and regularities in nature and man which were both apparent and fairly intelligible to human reason? If so the question of how to translate the will of God into temporal and finite terms was insoluble—and yet that will must be done. Apparently the Protestant was doomed to waver forever between waiting upon God and hurrying on ahead of Him, between a reverent but purposeless quietism and an idolatrous but purposeful activism.[1]

It is the primary assumption of this essay that there is both *continuity* and *parallel* between the problems of the sixteenth and twentieth centuries. The current revival of Reformation theology is partly an attempt to restore to

[1] For a few recent discussions of the Protestant dilemma from various points of view, see Paul Tillich, "The End of the Protestant Era," *Student World*, xxx (1937), 49-57; Paul Lehmann, "Barth and Brunner: The Dilemma of the Protestant Mind," *Journal of Religion*, xx (April 1940), 124-140; Reinhold Niebuhr, *The Nature and Destiny of Man: Human Nature* (New York, 1941), pp. 60-61, 219-227, 283-285, 299-300; and Peter Drucker, *The End of Economic Man* (New York, 1939), pp. 85-111.

contemporary Protestantism the sense of historical continuity between past and present, partly a tacit recognition of the fact that the Reformers lived in an age much like our own, that they faced problems reminiscent of our problems, and that their solutions are therefore historically relevant today. The Reformation lies *behind* us in time, but it also lies *beside* us in a sense. If the thirteenth and eighteenth centuries have been called ages of reason, it is because we see them today through the perspective of an age of will. And if Luther is any more intelligible today than he was to the eighteenth century, it is because the contemporary cult of *Wille und Macht* has led us to sense the similarities between the voluntarism of his day and the voluntarism of our own.[2] Historians are justly suspicious of the concept of parallel as an instrument of historical thinking because it is so susceptible of abuse, but it is precisely the tension between uniqueness and parallel which gives history meaning. It is because the Reformers' situation was very much like our own, yet not exactly the same, that Reformation theology holds such profound interest for Protestants today.

On the assumption that this is so, it is the purpose of the present paper to inquire whether a voluntaristic theology is a *cure* for the ills of a voluntaristic age, or rather a mere *symptom* of these ills. Was Calvin's God the master or merely the reflection of Machiavelli's Prince? Is Karl Barth's theology the answer to or the product of totalitarian ideology? Is "existential thinking" a bulwark against voluntaristic fanaticism or a stimulus to it? On the other hand, can a rationalistic theology ever meet the needs of

---

[2] "Voluntarism" is often used in the technical sense of a doctrine of salvation which emphasizes merit and "good works." For lack of a better word, it is used throughout this essay in its more general sense of a doctrine, whether of God, man, or the nature of reality in general, which is based upon the primacy of will.

an age which has lost all instinctive confidence in reason? Was thirteenth century scholasticism even relevant to the needs of the sixteenth century? Can the tide of contemporary voluntarism be stemmed by the Thomists of Toronto and the "peeping Thomists" of Chicago?

I

To us—and in some degree to the men of the Renaissance—the most striking characteristic of medieval thought was its sense of the *givenness* of things. The law was not made; it was found. Institutions, whether ecclesiastical or secular, were not "instituted"; they were accepted as already constituted by providence. Moral standards were not a subject of inquiry in the ordinary sense because they were already implicit in the mind of God and the mind of man. Truth was not discovery; rather it was recovery. This meant that in theory man could attain worldly success or spiritual salvation only by *conformity* to standards already given. The ordinary man did not need to search for an economic ethic because he already had one in the Bible. The king did not make the law; the law made the king. The Church did not discover new religious truth—only heretics did that; the Church conformed itself to a truth already given in revelation.

Understanding of and conformity to standards already given was not only *necessary* (this the Reformers also believed), it was also *possible* (here the Reformers would have grown doubtful). The universe was somehow intelligible because it was orderly. The *summae* of the schoolmen, the poetry of Dante, the sermons in stone which were the Gothic cathedrals—each in its own way reflected the hard-won and lofty conviction that God was both intelligible and good, that revelation was reasonable, and that truth was ultimately one. "The prime author and mover of the universe is intelligence," wrote Aquinas; "it is impossible for the truth of faith to be contrary to principles known by the natural reason." Ultimately, of course, God's will was inscrutable, and even Aquinas insisted upon the limits of "natural reason," both in understanding the universe and in directing the will. But the striking thing is how far both Dante and Aquinas were able to go in demonstrating the rationality and intelligibility of providence, how deep was their sense of the dignity of man's reason. When men thought seriously in the thirteenth century, they tended to think in terms of givenness, conformity, and intelligibility—and were generally believed by their contemporaries.

A second and correlative characteristic of medieval thinking was its sense of the *mediacy* of things. This is to say that thirteenth century man thought in terms of organism and hierarchy whenever he thought profoundly. Salvation was not a matter of the immediate relationship between the isolated individual and his God. "The way of religion," wrote Boniface VIII in *Unam Sanctam*, "is to lead the things which are lower to the things which are higher through the things which are intermediate. According to the law of the universe, all things are not reduced to order equally and immediately; but the lowest through the intermediate, the intermediate through the higher." Thus there was not only a mediating priesthood between the individual and God. There were mediating secular callings and institutions, mediating saints, and mediating symbols. Authority and obedience, whether in matters of religion or of temporal affairs, were usually indirect, not immediate. The prince's authority was ultimately of God, but it came through the law—some said also through the Vicar of Christ; obedience was always conditioned by the ideas of custom and contract. The sense of mediacy—of hierarchy and organism—permeated all of medieval society.

In fine, a philosopher might say that the thirteenth century thought primarily in terms of Being rather than of Becoming—and that in this respect the eighteenth century was much like the thirteenth. The universe was rational and intelligible because it was conceived of primarily in terms of form rather than of vitality (to borrow Reinhold Niebuhr's categories). Because economic and social conditions at least allowed of such an interpretation—if they did not actually dictate it—it was a "satisfying idea" in Dante's day to think of the universe in terms of givenness, conformity, intelligibility, and mediacy.

II

The debacle of this way of thinking in the fourteenth and fifteenth centuries is far too complicated a subject to enter into here in any detail. The important fact for us in this transition is a psychological fact: the contemporary conviction that the past was dead, but that in its dying—contrary to all analogies in nature—it had not produced the seeds of the future. "The old order of things was not good," wrote Machiavelli, speaking of the art of war, "and none of us has known how to find a new."[3] Readers of Drucker's *End of Economic Man* will recall how this sentiment reappears in twentieth century European thought. "The old orders have broken down," he writes, "and no new order can be contrived from the old foundations. . . . If you are caught between the flood of a past, through which you cannot retrace your steps, and an apparently unscalable wall in front of you, it is only by magic and miracles that you can hope to escape. *Credo quia absurdum* . . . is

[3] *The Prince* (Everyman ed.), chap. XXVI.

[181]

heard again for the first time in many a century."[4] Those
who know Huizinga's *Waning of the Middle Ages* will feel
themselves on familiar ground when Drucker speaks of
the masses in totalitarian countries living in "the happiness
of the dream," and when he adds that since there can be no
solution abroad "within the realm of reason, it must be
found in that of mysticism."[5]

It cannot be too strongly emphasized that the fourteenth
century was one of the most disastrous and neurotic centuries in the Christian era. War, famine, and plague took
their toll of men's lives while the breakdown of government
and the papal schism darkened their spirits. In the black-
ness and despair of the Hundred Years War the *danse ma-
cabre* was born, and a century after the Black Death had
consumed men's bodies, the witchcraft mania began to in-
fect their minds. How could the universe be so orderly, so
intelligible, so benevolent as cloistered thirteenth century
scholars had said it was? How could the sense of mediacy
be maintained when the stable governments of the last
century were crumbling, the papacy divided against itself,
and society in general apparently dissolving into atoms?
How could one believe in the givenness of things and the
virtue of conformity to objective standards when all of life
appeared to have taken on the horror and unpredictability
of a nightmare?

The answer to these questions had a certain inevitability.
If law—divine, natural, or human—was no longer *given*,
it could perhaps be *made*. Instead of conformity, creation;
instead of *coûtume* (the ancient French word for law),
ordonnance, an act of sovereign power; instead of reason,
will. If standards could no longer be found, they could
perhaps be created by an heroic act of will—whether of

[4] Drucker, *The End of Economic Man*, p. 22. See also pp. 20, 54,
57-58, 77, 82, 226, 234, 236, 238ff.
[5] *Ibid.*, pp. 228-229.

God or man. If men could no longer comprehend the universe in terms of Being, they could at least try to apprehend it in terms of Becoming. If the why of things, their ultimate significance, was beyond the grasp of man's reason, man could at least observe how things worked—and perhaps he could learn how to work them himself.

To state the answer in these terms is, of course, to exaggerate. During the past generation we have learned that there was far more continuity between medieval and early modern times than we had thought. But there was difference enough within the continuity. Economic historians have traced out the subtle change in economic ethics between Aquinas and the Puritans. Historians of political theory have shown how unmedieval was Bodin's definition of sovereignty as *legem dare*, no matter how thoroughly embedded it was in typically medieval concepts. And with all our recent and salutary qualifications, the Renaissance view of man was not that of the schoolmen. Machiavelli's *virtù* was not the *virtus* of the schoolmen, nor was Luther's God the God of Aquinas.

The best barometers of fourteenth and fifteenth century "climates of opinion" are nominalism, mysticism, humanism, and nationalism. With all their differences, they had one thing in common: a profound concern with the problem of will.

The nominalists limited the area of "natural theology" so narrowly as almost to destroy it, in a genuinely religious attempt to restore mystery to revelation and freedom to God. They agreed with Tertullian (who lived in an age much like their own) that "it is more worthy to believe that God is the free author even of evil things than to believe that He is a slave; power of whatever sort better becomes Him than pusillanimity." Half-consciously they argued in theology as princes were soon to argue in politics: law without sanction is anarchy; enforcement is obviously as important, perhaps more important, than what is enforced. Once the problem had been: how far can rational man understand a God whose essence is "intelligence"? To the nominalist the problem was: how far can the will of man be reconciled with the will of God? There were apparently only two answers to this question: merit and grace. Each was to appear to be increasingly exclusive of the other.

At first glance, the mystics do not appear to have been concerned with will at all. But in trying so desperately to annihilate the will, the fourteenth century mystics betrayed their social and psychological background. It is only against the background of strenuous and futile "willing to do good works," which was fostered by one school of later nominalists, that such statements as this from Meister Eckhardt are intelligible: "The poor man is not he who wants to do the will of God but he who lives in such a way as to be free of his own will and from the will of God even as he was when he was not."[6] It was no accident that the fourteenth and fifteenth centuries saw the "Flowering of Mysticism."

It is a commonplace that the humanists thought highly of human reason, but their definition of reason was not that of the thirteenth century. The further one probes, the more apparent it is that their real concern (as Niebuhr suggests) was to establish the autonomy and dignity of man's will (guided of course by reason, in the sense of "intelligence") in contradistinction to the will of God.[7] While the mystics were trying to annihilate will, the humanists tried to apotheosize it. Machiavelli's definition of *virtù* in terms of the virtues of the lion and the fox, strength and shrewdness, is perhaps a good barometer of how far both

[6] Quoted by Niebuhr, *Nature and Destiny of Man*, p. 58
[7] Cf. *ibid.*, pp. 21, 64.

will and reason had changed their meaning since the days of the schoolmen.[8]

If nominalists, mystics, and humanists were concerned primarily with the individual will, there were others who were concerned with the collective will. The history of the medieval origins of modern nationalism has yet to be written, but the historians who eventually accomplish the task will undoubtedly be struck by the parallelism between the growth of individualistic voluntarism and the spread of collective voluntarism. Just as German Romanticism later moved easily and naturally from worship of the unconditioned individual to worship of the unconditioned *Volk*, so Machiavelli's amoral Prince became the living symbol of what was to be the sovereign national state. To Sir Thomas More and others, the concept of the national will implied in Henry VIII's statutes was in striking contrast with the rational and universal norms which were the basis of the medieval *respublica christiana*.

To be sure, one can search the Renaissance in vain for any purely Nietzschean conception of the universe in terms of naked and unqualified will-to-power. Even Machiavelli believed that there was a "spirit of the times" to which princes and peoples must conform, which could be grasped partly by intuition, partly by rational analysis of history. Men still believed in objective norms at the dawn of the Reformation, if only because it was too difficult for them to cut themselves off irrevocably from their medieval past. But the problem of sanction and power—in short, the problem of will—was always involved in every discussion of politics and religion as it had never been before during that past. What was the use of a norm, men asked, if it could not be realized? In political theory and practice law as custom was giving ground to law as legislation. The mark of the same process in intellectual history was the contemporary

[8] See *The Prince*, chap. XVIII.

fascination with the problem of free-will versus predestination. Dr. Johnson once remarked, "All argument shows that our wills are bound, but we know that we are free and that settles the matter." That did *not* settle the matter, however, for Manetti, Pomponazzi, Lorenzo Valla, Erasmus, Luther, Calvin, and a host of lesser men who wrote interminably on the subject at the turn of the fifteenth and sixteenth centuries. Which leads us to the observation that the real difference is not between those who believe in predestination and those who believe in free will, but between those who think the question is important and those who (like Dr. Johnson) think it is not worth bothering about. And this last appears to be the fundamental difference between those who live in an age of will and those who live in an age of reason.

To summarize, when belief in the rationality and intelligibility of old institutions and ideals began to crumble at the end of the medieval period, no new order appeared to take the place of the old. Men grasped at new, or rather far older authorities, and fell back upon intuition; but beneath all their search for certainty was the sense of the ultimate reality of will—of creation rather than of conformity, of effort rather than of attainment, of discovery as well as of recovery.[9]

III

Enough has been said to indicate something of the mental and spiritual limits within which the Protestant Reformation was bound to move. The nominalism which Luther absorbed at Erfurt taught him to think of God and man primarily in terms of will—an observation which has be-

[9] For striking nineteenth century parallels to what has been said of the fourteenth and fifteenth centuries, see Eugene N. Anderson's article, "German Romanticism as an Ideology of Cultural Crisis," *Journal of the History of Ideas*, II (June 1941), pp. 301-317.

come something of a historical truism in the past two generations. It was in terms of his own will versus that of God that his personal problem presented itself. The influence upon him of mysticism, humanism, and eventually of nationalism gave deeper meaning to his religious problem, but did nothing to change its essential nature. His familiar strictures upon the power of human reason are indicative of his deep conviction that only the free and sovereign will of God could justify individuals and cleanse the Church. It is difficult to escape the impression that to Luther the religious question was primarily a question of power rather than one of understanding.

The crux of our problem still remains, however. Granting that the Reformers were compelled by the temper of their times to think of the religious question primarily in terms of will, how far is it true to say that they merely submitted to the dominant voluntarism of their day without transcending it? To what extent, for instance, was Calvin's God merely the "ideal type" of the Renaissance monarch? Is it true that "the *Leviathan* of Hobbes [we might add the Fuehrer of *Mein Kampf*] owed more of his non-moral attributes than the author knew to the ideas of God which had been present ever since the last days of nominalism?"[10] And if it is true that the Reformers did transcend the extreme voluntarism of their day, which form of Protestantism—Lutheranism, Calvinism, or Anabaptism—right-wing, center, or left-wing—best preserved the balance between will and reason and best met the religious need of its time? The relevance of this question for Protestants today is obvious, once the parallelism suggested between the sixteenth and twentieth centuries has been granted.

The answer which I propose to maintain is this: first, that all forms of Protestantism were radically infected by a

[10] J. N. Figgis in *Cambridge Modern History*, III, 745-747.

"pathological" form of theological voluntarism (which is not to say that an extreme rationalism cannot be just as "pathological" in theological history); and, second, that the form of Protestantism which most successfully transcended the prevailing voluntarism—which most successfully met the needs of its day while preserving the best in its past—was Calvinism. How unpopular such an answer is today, I am well aware. But if one grants the validity of our statement of the sixteenth century problem and the relevance of our approach to it, the answer appears to be inescapable. Much depends upon interpretation of the Reformers' doctrines of the nature of man and the nature of God. What to Luther and Calvin was the relation between reason and will in both man and God?

At first glance it would appear that there is nothing of significance for the present inquiry in the Reformers' doctrine of man. To Luther and Calvin, as to Machiavelli and the humanists, man was a compound of two qualities in roughly equal quantities: reason and will. The analysis of man in terms of understanding and impulse, mind and heart, was traditional and fairly stable in both the philosophical and theological traditions, despite numerous minor differences and refinements from Plato to Aquinas. It is his possession of *both* reason and will which distinguishes man from the brute. To Luther sin is rooted "not in the 'flesh,' that is . . . 'the inferior and grosser affections,' but in the most exalted and most noble powers of man . . . that is, in the reason and in the will."[11] Calvin analyzes the anthropology of the philosophers and fathers, and concludes "that the human soul has two faculties . . . , the understanding and the will"; or, as he puts it in another place, "the faculties of the soul consist in the mind and the heart." The Greeks, he notes, distinguished intellect from

[11] Luther, *The Bondage of the Will*, trans. Henry Cole (Grand Rapids and London, 1931), p. 334; also p. 377.

appetite, and then divided appetite into will (governed by intellect) and concupiscence (governed by sense); but he adds significantly, "Instead of the word 'appetite' . . . , I use the word 'will,' which is more common."[12]

The question of the freedom or bondage of man's will was not, strictly speaking, a question of the will alone—on this both Protestants and humanists like Erasmus were in agreement. It was a question of the freedom or bondage of *both* will and reason. "The power of free choice," writes Calvin, "is not to be contemplated in that kind of appetite which proceeds rather from the inclination of the nature than from the deliberation of the mind. For even the schoolmen confess that there is no action of free choice but when reason sees and considers the rival objects presented to it; meaning that the object of appetite must be such as is the subject of choice, and that deliberation precedes and introduces choice."[13] The original ambiguity of the word *arbitrium*—thinking and choosing—is still deeply rooted, in other words, in the free-will controversy of Reformation times.[14]

The apparent equality of reason and will in Reformation anthropology is still more evident in the familiar doctrine that *both* are corrupt since the Fall. If man's reason is "blind and ignorant," as Luther puts it, his will is "evil and impotent."[15] "Everything in man, the understanding and will, the soul and body, is polluted," says Calvin; Paul removes all doubt on the subject by insisting upon "the

[12] Calvin, *Institutes*, Book I, chap. 16, pars. 6, 7; Book II, chap. 2, par. 2. In the latter place, Calvin's words are "appetite, or will—which appellation is now more commonly used." The most significant chapters of the *Institutes* for Calvin's anthropology are Book I, chaps. 15-17, and Book II, chaps. 1-5.

[13] *Institutes*, Book II, chap. 2, par. 26.

[14] See Luther, *Bondage*, pp. 128, 335; Calvin, *Institutes*, Book II, chap. 2, par. 4. Luther censures Erasmus (without grounds) for confining "free will" to the will alone (*op.cit.*, pp. 128-129).

[15] *Bondage*, p. 335.

blindness of the mind and the depravity of the heart."[16] Man can neither know the truth nor will the good without grace, hence there is a kind of equality of insignificance between reason and will in man's nature.

But there is a subtle difference of approach between the elder and the younger Reformer, a difference impossible to illustrate by short quotations but evident to anyone who compares two of the most significant texts, Luther's *Bondage of the Will* and Calvin's *Institutes*. It can be suggested by saying that while Luther is primarily concerned about disciplining man's reason, Calvin is primarily concerned about disciplining his will.

Luther is more profoundly suspicious of the pride of intellect than Calvin, more willing, for instance, to dispense with every pagan philosopher and a great many of the fathers in his inquiry as to how the truth of grace had been preserved in history. Erasmus might appear to have the weight even of religious scholarship on the side of "free will," Luther admitted, but those who *thought* and *wrote* free will generally *lived* by grace; and "men, good as well as bad, are to be judged of more from what they feel than from what they say."[17] Unlike Dr. Johnson, Luther says that while ratiocination will generally end in a belief in free will, common sense, feeling, and experience will always end in the sense of predestination. If Luther had to choose between the primacy of will or of reason in man, would he not choose will, the non-reflective activity by which the ordinary person lives most of the time?

The primacy of will is still more evident in the familiar Lutheran doctrine that while man's will is bound in the realm of grace, it is free in the realm of nature. Significantly, this "free will" which Lutheran man exercises in nature is compounded more of power than of intelligence. In view

[16] *Institutes*, Book II, chap. 1, pars. 8, 9.
[17] *Bondage*, p. 89. Cf. *ibid.*, pp. 82-101.

of the later history of German thought, this point would seem to merit more attention than it has received. Luther remarks that in the realm of grace "knowledge is not power, nor does it communicate power." So too, apparently in the realm of nature. His favorite simile in describing man's "free will" in nature is the relation of a man to his *possessions*. Man "may be allowed to know," he says, "that he has, as to his goods and possessions, the right of *using, acting*, and *omitting*, according to his 'Free will.'" "In those things which are beneath him . . . he has *dominion* and is *Lord*." Over them "he has a *right* and a *Free will*, that those things might do and obey as he *wills* and *thinks*."[18] The choice of words here is interesting. The modern reader cannot help noting how thinking has become part of willing, how right is related to power. The parallel to Bodin's later definition of sovereignty as the right "to give law to subjects in general without their consent" is obvious; and there is at least the suggestion of a parallel to Machiavelli's non-legal and amoral interpretation of power.

While Calvin would certainly agree with Luther that "knowledge is not power," he seems to suggest that in the realm of nature at least, knowledge does "communicate power." Calvin sees the essential meaning of the Fall as a failure of will rather than of reason, which leads him to conclude that the "principal seat" of sin is "the will."[19] His strictures on reason, while often more penetrating and devastating psychologically speaking than Luther's, are more constructive in tone. "The horrible blindness of the human mind" and the wisdom of "learned ignorance" are favorite themes with Calvin, as with Luther. "The human mind is naturally so prone to falsehood that it will sooner

---

[18] *Bondage*, pp. 79, 142, 154, 378-379 (italics not in original).
[19] See *Institutes*, Book I, chap. 15, par. 8; and Book II, chap. 2, pars. 26, 27. Cf. Niebuhr, *op.cit.*, p. 16.

inbibe error from one single expression than truth from a prolix oration."[20] But reason is not totally extinguished in man. "Being a natural talent, [it] could not be totally destroyed, but is partly debilitated, partly vitiated, so that it exhibits nothing but deformity and ruin. . . . [But] some sparks continue to shine in the nature of man, even in its corrupt and degenerate state, which prove him to be a rational creature. . . . To condemn [the power of the understanding] to perpetual blindness so as to leave it no intelligence in anything is repugnant not only to the Divine word but also to the experience of common sense."[21] Calvin's "experience of common sense" is obviously separated by a perceptible difference from Luther's.

In the subtle analysis of the powers of reason which follows, Calvin notes that although the "love of truth . . . immediately terminates in vanity . . . , yet its attempts are not always so fruitless but that it makes some *discoveries*, particularly when it applies itself to inferior things," i.e. temporal matters. The word *discoveries* is significant. Viewed in one perspective, Calvin's truth is conformity to givenness: "Man is naturally a creature inclined to society. . . . Hence it is that not a person can be found who does not understand that all associations of men ought to be governed by laws, or who does not conceive in his mind the principles of those laws. . . . The seeds of them are innate in all mankind, without any instructor or legislator." This is Calvin the medievalist. But Calvin was also a child of his times. From another perspective, truth is discovery, invention, adaptation: "Nor have [men] an energy and facility only in learning, but also in *inventing* something new in every art, or in *amplifying* and *improving* what they

[20] *Institutes*, Book I, chap. 5, par. 12; chap. 6, par. 1; Book II, chap. 2, par. 7; Book III, chap. 21, par. 2.
[21] *Institutes*, Book II, chap. 2, par. 12.

have learned from their predecessors."[22] This contrasts rather strikingly with Aquinas's well-known preference for the "liberal" over the "mechanical" arts as evidence of the dignity of human reason. In a word, Calvin not only preserves the essence of thirteenth century definitions of reason as mental conformity to objective givenness; he also infuses new meaning into the term by drawing upon contemporary conceptions of truth as a process of adaptation, invention, and discovery—in the realm of nature at least, if not in the realm of grace.

As in his anthropology, so in his theology Luther is primarily interested in the "Free will" of God, while Calvin is at least profoundly aware of the need of demonstrating the rationality of this will, so far as such a demonstration is allowable or possible. Once more the difference is difficult to illustrate by phrases torn from their context. It turns, of course, upon the problem of reconciling God's justice with God's mercy, omnipotence with beneficence. Is the reconciliation in any sense intelligible, or is the very attempt to understand it a kind of religious *lèse-majesté*?

At first glance again, it appears that both Luther and Calvin gave exactly the same answer. "God," writes Luther, "is that Being for whose will no cause or reason is to be assigned as a rule or standard by which it acts; seeing that nothing is superior or equal to it, but it is itself the rule of all things. For if it acted by any rule or standard or from any cause or reason, it would no longer be the *will of God*. Wherefore what God wills is not therefore right because He ought or ever was bound so to will; but on the contrary, what takes place is therefore right because He so wills. A cause and reason are assigned for the will of the creature, but not for the will of the Creator, unless you set up over Him another Creator."[23] What are Calvin's

---

[22] *Institutes*, Book II, chap. 2, pars. 12-14 (italics not in original).
[23] *Bondage*, p. 230 (italics in original).

words but an echo of this?—"The will of God is the highest rule of justice; so that what He wills must be considered just for this very reason, because He wills it."[24] Four centuries after these words were written, a modern observer wrote of Nazi "theology": "Since the totalitarians have no God, they must invent a Demon, a superman and magician in whom the contradictory becomes one. . . . The 'leader' is human only in the flesh. In the spirit he is beyond human fallibility, beyond human ethics, and beyond human society. He is 'always right'; he can never err. His will determines what is good or evil."[25]

Mere juxtaposition of these quotations is, of course, unfair to the Reformers. Man—even superman—is not God, and Luther might have been only slightly less horrified by the twentieth century Fuehrer than Calvin. But even the Reformers themselves were half-aware—Calvin more keenly than Luther—of the dangers of their position. "For who," Luther asks, "can direct himself according to a will inscrutable and incomprehensible?" No one. Hence God has revealed Himself in His Word. There is thus a distinction between "God preached" or "clothed" in His Word, intelligible to the man who has received faith, and "God hidden in majesty," unintelligible to man in this life even in faith. Man is to be guided therefore by God as Word, not by God as inscrutable Will.[26] Calvin, too, recognizes the difficulty, but does not take refuge in the concept of *deus absconditus.* "We espouse not the notion of the Romish theologians," he writes, "concerning the absolute and arbitrary power of God, which on account of its profaneness deserves our detestation. We represent not God as lawless who is a law to Himself; because as Plato says laws are necessary to men, who are the subjects of evil desires; but

24 *Institutes,* Book III, chap. 23, par. 2.
25 Drucker, *The End of Economic Man,* p. 229.
26 *Bondage,* pp. 172-173.

the will of God is not only pure from every fault, but the highest standard of perfection, even the law of all laws."[27]

If both Reformers were aware of the danger of preaching "the absolute and arbitrary power of God," why did they not hedge their definitions more carefully, as Aquinas did and as the "Romish" nominalists did not do? The historian's answer is perhaps too simple: the popular success of Reformation theology indicates that the age needed a God of Will, a God both transcendent and omnipotent, a God of mystery and majesty, rather than "a prime author" whose essence was "intelligence" or a Father whose essence was love. This need was reflected in the religious experience of the Reformers themselves. The "sleeping god" of Aristotle was anathema to both. A God who is not both omniscient and omnipotent is a "ridiculous God" to Luther. He never tires of castigating Erasmus for making "God and the Devil to be at a distance, spectators only, as it were, of this mutable and free will" of man. Man "cooperates with" God, but God "operates in" man. God is essentially "dynamic vitality," in Seeberg's phrase.[28] To Calvin, God's omnipotence is "not such as is imagined by sophists, vain, idle, and almost asleep, but vigilant, efficacious, operative, and engaged in continual action. . . . It is a puerile cavil to limit it to the influence and course of nature. . . . They not only defraud God of His glory but themselves of *a very useful doctrine* who confine the Divine providence within such narrow bounds."[29]

Nowhere is Calvin's awareness of the dominant need of his day more evident than in the revealing phrase, "a very useful doctrine." Undergraduates today are invariably

---

[27] *Institutes*, Book III, chap. 23, par. 2.

[28] *Bondage*, pp. 217, 242, 309, 316-317. Cf. W. Pauck, "Historiography of the German Reformation," *Church History*, IX (Dec. 1940), 332.

[29] *Institutes*, Book I, chap. 16, par. 3 (italics not in original).

struck by what they call the sophistry and inadequacy of Calvin's answer to the old objection to predestination: if God does everything, why should man exert himself? To them the question somehow seems the exact counterpart of another, more familiar in their fathers' experience: if the government does everything, what becomes of private initiative? They cannot understand that if one of the most haunting fears of our day is human unemployment, the fear of Calvin's day was divine unemployment; and that if God were actually the vigilant, operative, activistic God Calvin said he was—given the fundamental beliefs as to God and man current in the sixteenth century—the springs of human activity would inevitably be released. It is difficult to say which has been the more powerful stimulant to action in human history—a belief in man's infinite capacities as man, or a belief in the infinite capacities of forces outside man which give him the victory when they work on his side. There can be no question about where the Reformers stood on the question, however. They stood with Mohammed and Karl Marx against Benvenuto Cellini and Nietzsche. Only when man knows something of the resources of the universe—that is of predestination— can he act at all. In one of the most amusing passages in *The Bondage of the Will* Luther accuses the gentle Erasmus of fanaticism. Because he urges man to strive for salvation without first inquiring what are the rules of the game, Erasmus, he says, teaches and enjoins men "to be mad and to rush on with temerity." A poet, a farmer, or a general is stupid if he "rushes on" before he has carefully considered what *can* be accomplished in poetry, farming, or the art of war. "How can you endeavor if you know neither what you are to endeavor after, nor in what way, nor to what extent you are to endeavor?" "But now since God has put my salvation out of the way of *my* will and has taken it under *His own* . . . , I rest fully assured and persuaded that He is faithful and will not lie, and moreover great and powerful, so that no devils, no adversities can destroy Him or pluck me out of His hand." Calvin was even more plainly aware of the psychological relationship between belief in predestination and moral activity.[30]

Releasing the "free will" of God in the Reformers' day, then, was a rough equivalent of releasing the "free will" of a *Volk* embodied in a *Fuehrer* in our own day. No less than Machiavelli, but for different reasons, Luther feared the fashionable current conception of a world of autonomous wills left to fend for themselves by a blind *fortuna*. The idea that "men might be saved and damned without God's knowing anything at all about it" horrified him. Calvin added, "What can be more absurd or uninteresting than God's looking from on high to see from what quarter salvation would come to mankind?"[31] To assert the free will of God in the sixteenth century was to assert the free will of both the individual and of the godly group, against the bondage of all givenness and all mediacy which might come between free God and free man. But was this freedom a rational, or even a reasoned freedom? The Reformers insist that grace is not "compulsion" because a will cannot be compelled, but when they use a simile for the relation of God to man, it is more often the figure of the potter and his clay than that of a father and his son. Has it ever been remarked that when the Reformers *do* use the father-son metaphor, they usually have in mind the infant or child, not the grown son? "How often do parents thus play with their children," writes Luther, "when they bid them come to them or do this or that, for this purpose only that it may plainly appear to them how *unable* they

[30] See Luther, *Bondage*, pp. 32-37, 328, 384; and Calvin, *Institutes*, Book II, chap. 2, par. 1; chap. 4, par. 7; Book III, chap. 23, par. 12.

[31] Luther, *Bondage*, p. 217; Calvin, *Institutes*, Book III, chap. 22, par. 6.

are to do it, and that they may call for the aid of the parent's hand?" "God *lisps*, as it were, with us," says Calvin, "just as nurses are accustomed to speak to infants."[32] If Tertullian, Ockham, Luther, and Barth are fair tests, times of cultural crisis leave a characteristic mark upon Christian theology. It is the mark of conceiving freedom more in terms of power and dynamism than of cooperation and reason.

If the most obvious need of the Reformers' time was release of the will, the less obvious but more important was discipline of the will and (eventually) rationalization of the will. It was here that Calvinism proved its superiority to both Lutheranism and Anabaptism.

Enough has already been said of Luther to suggest reasons for this judgment. To Luther the bridge between nature and grace was too weak and too narrow to bear the weight of what we should now call a "social gospel." He was seeking "an object solemn and essential" which must be maintained and defended "although the whole world should not only be thrown into tumult and set in arms thereby, but even if it should be hurled into chaos and reduced to nothing." Temporal war and chaos were, in fact, the necessary signs of the activity of God's will in nature. To pray for peace and order, to long for a purely human and temporal justice, was to run the risk of crossing God's will. To Erasmus, the pacifist, Luther replied, "Cease from complaining, cease from doctoring; this tumult proceeds and is carried on from above." Temporal affairs were a "leprosy" to be borne rather than to be doctored.[33]

The ethical note of left-wing Protestantism was deeper. Like the Quakers today, the Anabaptists insisted upon "the relevance of an impossible ideal." Nature could and should

[32] *Bondage*, p. 145; *Institutes*, Book I, chap. 13, par. 1. (Italics not in original.)

[33] Luther, *Bondage*, pp. 54-58.

be absorbed in grace. But nature was stubborn and those in a state of grace pitifully few. In the end the Anabaptists were compelled to abandon the wide open spaces of the world to Satan in order to realize grace in a few small corners of it. In their primitivism, their heightened sense of eschatology, and particularly in their anti-intellectualism they too betrayed the influence of what we have ventured to call some of the "pathological" tendencies of their age. They bridged nature and grace, but their bridge reached only a few small islands off the continent of nature.[34]

If Calvin succeeded in his day where Luther and the Anabaptists failed, it was because of his extraordinary sensitivity to the need for disciplining and rationalizing the emancipated religious will. He saw that the bridge between nature and grace must be sturdy enough to bear the weight of a new ethic and that it must be long enough to reach into every corner of the temporal world. In extending the sovereignty of God from the realm of grace to the realm of nature, he not only opened up the whole sphere of secular life to divine activity (a process which Luther had begun but did not finish); he also provided both the possibility and the necessity for a new economic ethic (a kind of disciplined individualism), a new political theory (the famous right of constitutional resistance), and a comprehensive theory of Common Grace (which worked itself out into the characteristic conviction of the American Puritan that "among the attributes of God . . . was perfect rationality, as well as absolute will and sovereignty").[35]

[34] Cf. the brief and penetrating summary by Roland H. Bainton in *Journal of Religion*, xxi (April 1941), 124-134. "The Relevance of an Impossible Ideal" is the title of a pamphlet in "answer to the views of Reinhold Niebuhr" by G. H. C. MacGregor, reprinted by the Fellowship of Reconciliation from *The Christian Pacifist*.

[35] See the review of Perry Miller's *New England Mind* by W. W. Sweet in *Journal of Religion*, xx (July 1940), 291.

Calvin's God revealed Himself in order as well as in miracle, in form as well as in vitality, in "inferior causes" as well as in inscrutable and higher causes. The providence of God, Calvin believed, "governs all things in such a manner as to operate sometimes by the intervention of means, sometimes without means, and sometimes in opposition to all means"; but it "ought not always to be contemplated abstractedly by itself, but in connection with the means which [God] employs"; "a pious man will not overlook inferior causes." Calvinists at their best from Calvin's day to ours have never neglected "inferior causes." To Luther good works were the inevitable result of free and loving gratitude for grace; to Calvin the "diligent performance of virtuous actions" was the very "end" or purpose itself of election. God had a plan for the world, and the plan included "civil justice," "civil polity." "To entertain a thought of its extermination is inhuman barbarism; it is equally as necessary to mankind as bread and water, light and air, and far more excellent." Its object is "that there may be a public form of religion among Christians, and that humanity may be maintained among men."[36]

The "public form of religion" which Calvin maintained in Geneva is revolting to us today, and we can discern few rays of "humanity" in his treatment of Servetus. We forget that both were applauded by his contemporaries. The distinctive quality of Calvinism in its own day was that it preserved the tension between will and reason in the idea of God, between the absolute justice which is beyond human reason and the relative justice which is within human comprehension, and thus maintained the bridge over which humbler and greater Puritans than Calvin might travel to a new economic and political ethic. It is no coincidence that

[36] *Institutes*, Book I, chap. 17, pars. 1, 4, 9; Book IV, chap. 20, pars. 2-3. See also Book I, chap. 5, pars. 2-9; chap. 16, *passim*.

religio and *humanitas* are still linked today in American idealism as they once were in sixteenth century Calvinism.

IV

At this point the historian must inevitably leave the discussion to the philosopher and theologian. In the cooperative search for truth, it is the historian's first duty to offer his colleagues perspective. In this case, he has made two observations which may have something of the status of historical "laws": (1) that a voluntaristic theology in an age of voluntarism runs the risk of aggravating the very evils it professes to cure; and (2) that a theology, on the other hand, which fails to do justice to the emphasis upon will characteristic of periods of cultural crisis and change is doomed to futility. Somewhere within these two limits lay the problem of the sixteenth century. Somewhere within them lies our own problem.

It is an interesting fact that while many of Europe's non-Nazi sociologists and political scientists are bitterly bewailing contemporary man's loss of faith in reason, many of Europe's theologians (together with their followers in this country) are welcoming the Romantic-Nazi attack on reason as an unconscious ally of biblical Christianity, a kind of perverted Christian insight. Karl Mannheim, writes J. H. Randall, "is now keenly aware of the disastrous consequences of the loss of faith in the power of reason in those very groups possessed of the intelligence to bring order out of the chaos of transition."[37] "[The] disintegration of the rational character of society and of the rational relationship between individual and society is the most revolutionary trait of our times," writes Drucker. "To have given a rational explanation of the whole world . . . to have given every individual a definite place in this rational order . . . has been the great metaphysical achievement of Christian-

[37] *Journal of the History of Ideas*, ıı (June 1941), 375.

ity which sets Europe off from all others. . . ."[38] In contrast, Joseph Haroutunian glories in the fact that the "effort of the mind to understand is doomed to failure from the very start."[39] And Reinhold Niebuhr writes (more cautiously) that in the view of Christian faith, "natural vitality is not evil of itself. . . . This emphasis of Christianity is largely responsible for the superior vigor of historical action revealed by western civilization in contrast to the Orient"— a statement in interesting contrast with Drucker's interpretation of Christianity's supreme contribution to western culture. "Romanticism," Niebuhr adds, "is, in short, nearer to the Christian faith and a more perverse corruption of it than idealistic philosophies."[40]

The undercurrent of American theology, however, is still optimistic rather than pessimistic about the importance and power of reason. "If I had to choose," writes Sweet, "between the kind of Calvinism which guided the life of seventeenth century New Englanders and the kind which is coming out of Europe today, I would, without a moment's hesitation, accept the New England variety."[41] Bainton adds that unless "the ethics of love, mercy, and humanity . . . can be shown to be grounded in the very structure of life, unless there be after all a natural law which is a divine law, then morality too goes by the board." And Niebuhr agrees.[42]

In conclusion, any reconstruction of Protestant theology with a view to solving the historic Protestant dilemma must

[38] Drucker, *The End of Economic Man*, pp. 55-56.

[39] Haroutunian, *Wisdom and Folly in Religion* (New York, 1940), quoted by Virginia Corwin in *Journal of Religion*, xxi (April 1941), 207. And now see the definitive study of G. H. Williams, *The Radical Reformation* (Philadelphia, 1962).

[40] Niebuhr, *Nature and Destiny of Man*, pp. 29, 91.

[41] *Journal of Religion*, xx (July 1940), 290.

[42] *Church History*, x (June 1941), 120. Cf. Niebuhr, *Nature and Destiny of Man*, pp. 274-275.

be based upon an awareness of how thin the line is which separates the supra-rational from the infra-rational, the non-rational from the irrational. Niebuhr is certainly right in insisting that "God's will and wisdom must be able to transcend any human interpretation of its justice and meaning."[43] But God is both "will and wisdom." A strongly voluntaristic theology can do little but add fuel to the flames raging at this moment in Europe and Asia; a coldly rationalistic theology can never provide the stimulus to action which Protestantism so sadly lacks today. But it is high time that some of our adherents of "Reformation theology" realized that it is better for supra-rationality to have its roots in reason rather than in unreason, and that while their quarrel with "humanists" and rationalists may be important to themselves, it is still but a family quarrel within the Western cultural tradition. We who are the heirs of both Greece and Judea had better set our house in order before those who profess to be the heirs of neither overwhelm us.

[43] Niebuhr, *Nature and Destiny of Man*, p. 168.

10 · THE INTELLECTUAL
AS SOCIAL REFORMER: MACHIAVELLI
AND THOMAS MORE*

M Y SUBJECT here is the intellectual as social reformer, with particular reference to two sixteenth
century figures.

We may do well to start with the simple fact that the
intellectual is almost inevitably a reformer. If a man sets
himself to ponder hard and long about some big problem
—such as the nature of God or of man or of society or of
the universe—if he honestly tries to take all the relevant
facts into account and to develop an intelligible theory
about his problem, as a good intellectual does, then he is
going to become dissatisfied with what he finds. If it is
God and the universe that interest him, he may have to
limit himself to criticizing other people's *theories*. But if
it is man and society, he will be tempted to point out a few
actual things that are wrong, why they are wrong, and how
they can be remedied. Seeing things whole generally has
this effect. No sooner does Mr. Toynbee get well into his
vast *Study of History*, for instance, than we realize that he
is pointing out quite a few things that are wrong with our
Western society and calling on us to mend our ways.

At the dawn of the modern era, two supremely articulate
figures happened to exemplify most of the significant problems of the intellectual as social reformer: his strengths
and weaknesses, how he comes by his ideas, what gives him
his social passion, and what lends his work enduring qual-

* The piece that follows was originally meant to be two, to be given
at the Rice Institute in the spring of 1957 on the Anderson Visiting
Professorship. They were shortened and printed as one article by
the *Rice Institute Pamphlet* in October 1957. It is reprinted here by
permission of Rice University.

ity. They were Niccolò Machiavelli and Thomas More. Their lives and writings are perfectly familiar to educated people, and I do not expect to tell you any facts about either that you do not already know. What I propose to do is to look at them from a somewhat fresh perspective: as pioneers of the idea that society—not individuals alone—can be changed, and that for various good and sufficient reasons, it must be. The fact is that Machiavelli and More inaugurated modern political thinking by sensing and facing what proved to be some of the most crucial problems of our modern Western society. Neither had much influence on the technical political theory of his day. But between them they gave us two words which have absorbed a heavy freight of meaning in the intervening centuries: "Machiavellian" and "Utopian." And this is one measure of their stature and importance, even if Machiavelli was no "Machiavellian" and More no "Utopian"—as they were not. Together they represent the first tough-minded but imaginative thinking about modern political, social, and economic problems. Together they symbolize the perennial tension between the two polar attitudes on these problems: that of the "realist" and that of the "moralist."

It is worth recalling some of the main contrasts and coincidences between the two before we go further. Europe was culturally and spiritually more united in 1500 than it is today, but there were sharp contrasts between Machiavelli's Italy, with its welter of wealthy independent cities, and More's England, one of the better-run national monarchies of its day. Machiavelli was born in Florence in 1469; Thomas More in London nine years later. They never met nor (so far as we know) ever read each other's works. Machiavelli spent his younger years in active civil service, his later years in bitter enforced retirement. More spent his early years in private life and long resisted the call to service of his king, which he entered in his later years.

Machiavelli was driven to write by being dismissed from office, More (in part) by being invited to assume office. Machiavelli wrote his major works in Italian for the perusal of a few and never published them during his lifetime; More wrote his most famous book in Latin and published it immediately to the delight of the learned all over Europe. They wrote simultaneously. Machiavelli dedicated his final version of *The Prince* to Lorenzo de' Medici in 1516, the same year More's *Utopia* came off the presses at Louvain. Machiavelli was a thorough pagan who nevertheless never formally rejected Christianity, saw his son enter the priesthood, and died with a priest at his bedside. More was one of the great Christians of history, who nevertheless remained a layman all his life and is remembered today as much for his more worldly qualities as for his sainthood—his humor, his family life, his zest for classical learning, and his shrewd grasp of social problems. Machiavelli died a disappointed man in 1527, before word could reach him that another man had been given the public office he had long coveted. More died triumphantly on the scaffold in 1535, "the King's good servant," as he put it, "but God's first."

Polar opposites, you may conclude—and there is much truth in this. But it is important not to forget what they had in common. Each of them represented a combination, not too common even in the Renaissance, of scholarly tastes and practical experience, of humanistic accomplishment and civil service. Each was a thorough humanist in the contemporary sense of the word; that is, one who is convinced of the importance and relevance of classical study and who devotes much of his time to it. At the same time, each was saved from the dilettantism of many contemporary humanists by his strong practical interests. Both believed in the efficacy of appealing to men's intelligence, but neither believed that an intellectual could change the world merely by writing books. Both wrote with exceptional clarity, and yet both managed to set their readers to arguing violently about what they *really* meant to say. The major conclusion of these arguments, which are now over four centuries old, seems to me to be this: that Machiavelli was a curiously idealistic realist, and that More was a strikingly realistic idealist. Polar opposites with much in common, in other words.

I. MACHIAVELLI

It is hard to describe the conditions surrounding the birth of modern political thought at the close of the Middle Ages without grossly distorting the picture by oversimplification. Perhaps the most direct way is to say that the political thought of the brilliant generation that included Machiavelli and More was the result of two things: the social tensions accompanying the dissolution of medieval institutions, and the simultaneous impact of the classical revival.

At the close of the fifteenth century the medieval *respublica christiana* was disintegrating rapidly. The pattern was still there in men's minds, the pattern of a hierarchical society headed in its temporal aspects by the Emperor and in its spiritual aspects by the Pope. Most men still assumed that this pattern of feudal and ecclesiastical organization was God's design for Christendom. But the discrepancies between the form and the reality were growing at a bewildering pace. In parts of Europe—North Italy, for example—economic power lay in fact with a class which had no place in the pattern, the "middle class" of merchants, industrialists, lawyers, and scholars. Political power rested in an institution utterly unknown to the medieval pattern, the sovereign, territorial state. Within the busy, swarming cities of Italy there were careers wide open to talent—and hot competition to excel, whether as scholar or artist, professional soldier or political despot. And between the city-states there was a constant jockeying for territory and *Lebensraum,* a struggle for power untempered by any respect for higher authority of Pope or Emperor. Respect for legitimate authority, for what Burke would later call "precedent, prescription, and antiquity," was still dominant in much of Europe. But in Italy it yielded to admiration for talent and determination, inventiveness and virtuosity. In Burckhardt's famous phrase, the state was becoming "a work of art," not something given by God or rooted in immemorial custom and tradition, but something man could mould and shape and form to suit his needs. In fourteenth and fifteenth century Florence, revolutions seemed to be the chief outdoor sport, and constitution-making the chief indoor amusement. Diplomacy too became an "art," the product "of conscious reflection and calculation," as did warfare and painting and business practice. It has often been remarked that in all this Italy was a kind of microcosm of the modern world.

In other words, something like the modern sovereign territorial state and something like modern capitalistic practice in commerce, industry, and even agriculture had appeared in the Europe of 1500. But there were no categories of thought through which these developments could be understood, let alone controlled. The Middle Ages had an unshakable sense of right and justice, but never any very effective way of enforcing the right. There was always a principle to cover every incident, a law to apply to every case, but there were few effective sanctions. The typical early medieval society, someone has said, was "all law and no government." Now here were strong rulers and powerful merchants creating a kind of illegitimate order of their own. Was it enough simply to put them down as "tyrants" and "despots," "monopolists" and "usurers," using the traditional categories of thought? "The old order was not good," Machiavelli wrote "and none of us have known how to find a new."[1] He was speaking of the art of war, but the remark might serve as a symbol of the bewilderment of the thinkers of his generation as they searched for some new way of understanding what was going on around them.

Our twentieth century attitude in such a situation, I suppose, would be to say: "Get our economists and political scientists on the problem; hire a staff, apply for a foundation grant, and rent an electronic calculator; if the money holds out, we should have the answers in a few years." Fortunately or unfortunately, there were no such methods or resources available in the generation of Machiavelli and More. What *was* available was a new store of ancient political and social wisdom, and to this they turned with eagerness. Men began to reread Aristotle and Cicero, Thucydides and Polybius, Livy and Tacitus, with new purpose and understanding. Here was a literature concerned with politics and morals, with civil and foreign war, with tyranny and revolution, with justice and might—in other words, with every aspect of the struggle for power, among individuals within the state and among states themselves. To thoughtful fifteenth century readers all this was exciting— far more relevant than medieval chronicle or scholastic philosophy—and of course more practical than a "scientific method" still in its infancy. Their contemporary experience enabled them to understand the ancient writers, as schoolmen two centuries earlier could not have done; and their reading in turn deepened their understanding of contemporary politics and diplomacy. Modern political thought, in other words, resulted from the *coincidence* of rapid social change with the classical revival at the close of

[1] *The Prince* (Everyman trans.), chap. xxvi.

the Middle Ages. As new economic and political practices came into almost intolerable conflict with older habits of thought, a relatively untapped storehouse of social insight was discovered, or rediscovered. *The Prince, The Discourses on Livy*, and *Utopia* were not the only products of this fruitful coincidence, but they were perhaps the greatest.

So far we have talked in very general and abstract terms. We have left out the factor which, to men of the Renaissance at least, was always the most important: the human factor. Unless these social tensions and political problems somehow got under one man's skin, unless the man concerned was endowed with more than the usual perspicacity and sensitivity, and unless something happened to set this man writing, nothing so grandiose as "the birth of modern political thinking" would take place, of course. Therefore it is very relevant to our inquiry to ask what sort of character and experience Machiavelli brought to his writing, and how he came to write as he did.

The two most prominent traits in his character appear very early: his carefully nurtured habit of seeing things as they are rather than as they might be, and his contradictory passion to see his beloved city of Florence in the ideal state of civic peace and diplomatic security which he hoped might be, but which obviously did not exist in the 1490's. One of the earliest glimpses we get of him is in a letter he wrote to a friend in March 1497 describing Savonarola's sermons. Machiavelli saw that the prophet's public addresses were becoming more hysterical as fear for his own power grew. "He began," writes the cool young observer, "with terrifying horrors, showing with arguments that must have been very effective with people not trained to thinking, that his followers were very fine people while his opponents were the worst sort of rascals. He went on to any limit that seemed likely to weaken the hostile party

and strengthen his own." There were two armies, Savonarola argued: that of the Lord, which included him and his
own followers, and that of Satan, which was composed, of
course, of his enemies.[2] Savonarola, the "unarmed prophet"
of *The Prince*, obviously made a deep impression on
Machiavelli, but not as a model of intelligence or statesmanship.

A month after Savonarola's execution in June 1498,
Machiavelli got his first job with the republican government of Florence, and for the next fourteen years he served
as Chancellor and Secretary to the ruling council of the
city and as diplomatic envoy on numerous legations—to
Paris, to the Emperor, to the Pope, to Caesar Borgia, and
to many of the neighboring city-states. The picture we get
of him during these years is that of an exceptionally acute
observer of the political scene, unquestioningly faithful
to his government although sometimes critical of its policies, always conscious of the weakness of the city-state he
represents, always anxious to compensate by sheer intelligence for this weakness by turning up ingenious solutions
to unsolvable problems, yet usually aware of the grim limits on Florentine freedom of action. He is generally second-
in-command on any given legation, not first—which suggests that his bosses valued his brains above his judgment.
Occasionally he compares someone's policy with that of
the Roman Republic in similar circumstances, to the advantage of the ancients, which suggests that although he
is not a man of wide culture, he is reading the ancient
historians.

His two preoccupations in particular are the disunity at
home and the weakness abroad that make his government's
job the nightmare that it is. The Pazzi Conspiracy of 1478,
that lurid plot to murder Lorenzo the Magnificent in

---

[2] Machiavelli to Ricciardo Bechi, 9 March 1497, in *The Living
Thoughts of Machiavelli*, ed. Carlo Sforza (London, 1942), pp. 79-82.

church, had made a deep impression on him at the age of
nine, and all his life he was to be concerned with the problem of *parte*, or factions, and their disintegrating effect
on the State. But an even deeper impression had been left
on him by the invasion of Italy in 1494 by Charles VIII
of France, the invasion that first revealed the startling in-
feriority of a land of petty, warring city-states to a well-
organized national monarchy.[3] Five more times Italy was
to be invaded before Machiavelli's government fell—once
more by France, twice by the Emperor, and twice by Spain.
The last attack by Spain in 1512 overthrew the republican
regime in Florence and restored the Medici to power. In
her weakness Florence had made an alliance with France,
and in a stubborn display of civic honor she stuck by the
alliance long after it was clear that Spain was going to beat
France out for control of the Italian peninsula. In another
display of personal honor, Machiavelli's close friend and
superior, Piero Soderini, refused to use unconstitutional
means to save himself and his government in the crisis.
In August 1512 Soderini fled. Some two months later Machiavelli was dismissed from office. Two months after this,
a plot to destroy the new Medici rulers was discovered,
Machiavelli's name was found on a list of those to be ap-
proached, and Machiavelli himself was imprisoned and
tortured to reveal what he knew. Released in February
1513 he retired to a house of his in the country ten miles
south of the city, at Sant' Andrea, where he had a tantaliz-
ing glimpse of the Duomo from his garden. And here he
was left to put together the broken pieces of his life as well
as he could, with a wife and four children to support, no
job, and no visible prospects of getting one.

His letters during this crucial year 1513 to his friend

[3] See *The Discourses of Niccolò Machiavelli*, ed. Leslie J. Walker
(New Haven, 1950), I, 16-20ff.

Vettori (who was Florentine ambassador at Rome) and to Soderini (who had fled to Dalmatia) give fascinating glimpses of how a disappointed civil servant of a third-rate republic became the first modern analyst of political power. He was bored, frustrated, and resentful, worried about where the next meal was coming from, and acutely home-sick for the world of politics and diplomacy which was his life's blood. Occasionally he would visit the city, but since he was on the outside looking in, this was almost worse than staying in the country. There he would leave the house in the mornings and try to kill time by chatting with his wood-cutters for a while. He would have a book under his arm—Dante, Petrarch, or Ovid—and for a while he would read. Then he would walk down to the local tavern, talking eagerly to everyone he would meet on the way, "asking news of their towns, and listening to all sorts of stories as throwing light on the varying tastes and whims of men," he says. Then home for dinner at noon, then back to the tavern, where he would play cards with a butcher, a miller, and a couple of bakers the rest of the day. The stakes were small, but the emotion ran high—"just one battle after another with boundless rages and personal in-sults." "So with these lice clinging to my person," he writes, "I keep my brain dusted off somewhat and provide a vent for the cruelty of my lot," hoping the fates would soon feel ashamed of themselves for what they had done to him.[4]

He knew perfectly clearly that he was fitted for one career and one only. At forty-three he could not become a merchant or farmer overnight. If only he could talk to Vettori, he writes. "Fortune has so devised that since I cannot talk of the silk trade or the wool trade or of profit and loss, I have to talk of politics. I have only one choice:

4 Machiavelli to Francesco Vettori, 10 December 1513, in *The Living Thoughts*, pp. 101-104.

[213]

either to talk of politics or to take a vow of silence."[5] His mind runs restlessly over recent events—every state breaking treaties but Florence, every statesman forgetting the ordinary rules of morality but Soderini with his constitutional scruples. He has come to the conclusion, he writes Soderini, that the sole criterion of policies should be their *results*, not the means used to attain them. The same end can be attained by different means, just as you can get to the same place by different roads. "Just *why* different procedures should now help and now hinder, I do not know," he writes, "*but I would like to know.*" He suggests the answer is that "times and circumstances" change, and that the means suitable for one time are disastrous for another.[6] Vettori asks him what he thinks of the latest move of Ferdinand, King of Spain. Is it not foolish? Machiavelli jumps at the chance to put his rusting intellect to work and writes ten pages in reply. There is really no problem, he says, if you see that Ferdinand is not much of a statesman—just lucky. His letter will seem a jumble, he concludes apologetically, but he is in the country, never sees a human face (Machiavelli was always given to exaggeration), and knows "nothing of what is going on in the world."[7] Later he argues that Vettori overrates Venetian power; the real danger to Italy comes from the Swiss and the French. "I don't know just what Aristotle says about countries that have been destroyed. What interests me more than theory is *what is, what has been, and what may reasonably happen.*"[8]

Then in the most famous letter he ever wrote (10 December 1513)[9] Machiavelli tells Vettori how when evening comes, he is in the habit of putting off his soiled clothes,

[5] To Vettori, 9 April 1513, *ibid.*, p. 88.
[6] *Ibid.*, pp. 84-87.
[7] 25 April 1513, *ibid.*, pp. 89-96.
[8] 26 August 1513, *ibid.*, pp. 96-100.
[9] See note 4.

putting on his court dress, and spending four hours of un-
interrupted bliss in the company of his favorite classical
authors. With them he partakes of that food which alone he
can call his own and for which he was born, he says. He asks
them questions, and they answer. Since Dante says there
is no knowing apart from remembering, he has put down
on paper some of the things he has learned from these older
and wiser minds. "I have written a pamphlet which I am
calling *On Principalities*. In it I go as deeply as I can into
the subject, discussing the definition of monarchy, how
many kinds of monarchies there are, and how they are
won, held, and lost. . . . Any head of a state, and especially
a new one, should find it interesting." He explains frankly
that he is dedicating it to Giuliano de' Medici because he
desperately needs a job and hopes the Medici will give
him one. "Anybody, it seems to me, should be glad to have
the services of a man who has acquired so much experience
at the expense of other employers. Of my trustworthiness
there could be no doubt. Having so long kept faith with
people, I would not be likely to begin betraying now. A
man who has kept his word loyally for forty-three years, as
I have, could not change his nature very easily. The fact
that I am a poor man is proof of my loyalty and honor."
Four times the word *fede* (faith) occurs in these last sentences.[10] Obviously the writer is deeply concerned to im-
press even on his friend, who must know it, that patriotism
and his pledged word come before party loyalty with him.

This then was the origin of *The Prince*. Perhaps it is
evident from this account why those who have read the
book over the years have argued—and still argue violently
—over its purpose and meaning. Was it simply a cool,
disillusioned analysis of how to get and hold on to power,
with the last patriotic chapter added as a sort of after-

[10] See J. H. Whitfield, *Machiavelli* (Oxford, 1947), p. 61.

thought to give the analysis some respectable use? Or did it, on the contrary, all lead up to the last chapter? Was it an honest and passionate appeal to the Medici to become the saviors of Italy from the foreign barbarians? Did the author really mean what he said about playing the beast rather than the man, seeming to have the private virtues but not being hampered by them, breaking faith if it was to your advantage? Was this the Machiavelli who was so proud of his own word once given and of his republic's reputation for good faith? Was he perhaps being satiric in *The Prince*, showing up despotism for what it really was so that all the people could take warning? Or was he even trying to trap the young Medici into following his precepts and thus getting themselves thrown out of Florence by an outraged populace, so that Machiavelli's republican party could get back in? Was he thoroughly immoral in what he said—or simply amoral—or was he sketching a new sort of morality—or was he beneath it all as thoroughly moral as any medieval schoolman, but simply disillusioned with the way things actually were in his day?[11]

I cannot answer these questions with some nice neat formula. Nor do I know anyone who can. All of these theories about the meaning of Machiavelli's *Prince* were broached before the sixteenth century came to a close, and all of them are in one way or another still alive today. Very recent research, however, has opened up some exciting new perspectives on the development of Machiavelli's thought after 1513, and I think it is possible to report a common-

[11] See, e.g., Whitfield, *Machiavelli*, chaps. i, iv; Allan H. Gilbert, *Machiavelli's Prince and its Forerunners* (Durham, 1938); Garrett Mattingly, *Renaissance Diplomacy* (London, 1955), pp. 165-166; Felix Gilbert, "The Humanist Concept of the Prince and the *Prince* of Machiavelli," *Journal of Modern History*, xi (Dec. 1939), 449-483.

sense view of the significance of Machiavelli's thought that represents a sort of scholarly consensus.[12]

The Prince was written at white-hot speed in the fall of 1513. Into it went a good many disparate, and even contradictory, emotions and desires: resentment about his misfortune, disillusionment with legal and moral ways of doing things if this was where they landed you, desire to understand what had happened and how to avoid its happening again, desire to show off his political perspicacity to the new rulers of Florence in order to get his job back, a hope that out of writing some good would come—to him, to Florence, to Italy, perhaps even to posterity. In every chapter—some more clearly than others—he was trying to do two things at once: to understand and to reform. The two were related in a simple enough way: without understanding there could be no reform. The reason why reform schemes of intellectuals have invariably failed in the past, he is convinced, is that they have not been founded on politics as they actually are. He is acutely aware that he is breaking with tradition, with the "Mirror of Princes" literature which urged princes to act like good men and assumed everything would be all right if they did. "My intention being to write something of use to those who understand, it appears to be more proper to go to the real truth of the matter" than to imaginary states which have never existed, he says. What *is* done is so far removed from what *ought* to be done that anyone who wants to seize and hold power must "learn how not to be good." *The Prince* is a sharp but desperate appeal to certain fellow Florentines in high places—desperate because it appeals to men who have for-

[12] See particularly Felix Gilbert, "The Composition and Structure of Machiavelli's *Discorsi*," *Journal of the History of Ideas*, XIV (Jan. 1953), 136-156; and J. H. Hexter, "Seyssel, Machiavelli, and Polybius VI: the Mystery of the Missing Translation," *Studies in the Renaissance*, III (1956), 75-96.

gotten God and who have over-civilized man—to play the beast, in order to gain a certain measure of civic independence and individual dignity. It is all too easy to point out the glaring flaw in the argument. If the goal is really "to found a new realm and adorn it with good laws, good arms, good friends, and good examples," as chapter 24 seems to suggest—and this is estimating the goal at its best—will this end be achieved by the means suggested or will the means corrupt the end? Does obsession with the power factors involved in any political situation result in a regime adorned with "good laws" and "good examples," or does it result merely in irresponsible despotism and more corruption?

Machiavelli never really faced up to this question, but he was too intelligent to ignore it entirely. Whether by original design or not, *The Prince* became a sort of "Part I" to a larger work in Machiavelli's mind, a book on republics. In 1514, the year after he finished *The Prince*, Machiavelli was again bored. He wrote Vettori he was not reading the ancients or discoursing on the moderns any more because in spite of advancing middle age he had fallen in love again. But the pull of his old interests was stronger even than the delights of Venus. By 1515 he seems to have been visiting the city regularly to discuss the classical historians with congenial friends in the Rucellai gardens, and between 1515 and 1517 *The Discourses on Livy* had taken shape.

Felix Gilbert sees evidence of development from the "realism" and contemporaneity of *The Prince* to the "idealism" and classicism of *The Discourses*.[13] As Machiavelli got further away from his political career in time, he became more of an intellectual and a scholar. Influenced by his humanist friends, he saw things in larger perspective and began to elaborate his long-term ideal in a lengthy commentary on the classical historian Livy. *The Prince* was

[13] In *Journal of the History of Ideas*, XIV (Jan. 1953), 156.

for a moment of political corruption and crisis. *The Discourses* were to be for a better time, for all time. The ideal, of course, was the Roman Republic. *The Discourses* were concerned with the reasons for Rome's greatness and (by implication) the rules for success which apply to any state. Machiavelli, although probably not an atheist, had eliminated God from any effective part in history. He had eliminated eternity and infinity as the criteria by which political success is to be judged, and so was left with duration in time and extension in space. Rome was great because her regime lasted so long and because her rule extended so widely. Careful study of her history would reveal general rules for success which could be compressed into maxims and applied to the contemporary situation, since human nature never changes and history constantly repeats itself. That is, the same human beings will be continually going through the same typical political experiences in the future as in the past—and if you know the rules of the game and the record-book, you will naturally do better than if you don't.

"I have resolved to open *a new route*, which has not yet been followed by anyone," Machiavelli writes at the beginning of *The Discourses*.[14] If the results are effective, he adds, "I shall at least have shown the way to others, who will carry out my views with greater ability, eloquence, and judgment." What is this "new route"? It is the serious study of history with a view to developing a science of politics as a yardstick for social reform. Everyone reads and admires the ancients, he says, but no one *does* anything about his reading. The trouble is that men read history for fun when they ought to read it for profit. Machiavelli hopes that those who read his book will derive "those *advantages* which should be the aim of all study of history."

[14] *The Prince and the Discourses*, ed. Max Lerner (Modern Library ed., New York, 1940), p. 103. Trans. of *Discourses* by C. E. Detmold.

By "advantages" he means both knowledge and inspiration: knowledge of the rules for political success (meaning the power to endure and the power to expand), and inspiration to follow these rules through the illustrious example of the ancient Romans, both as individuals and as a people. He concludes his preface to the Second Book on a poignantly personal note, the perennial hope of the man of action turned intellectual: "It is the duty of an honest man to teach others that good which the malignity of the times and of fortune has prevented his doing himself; so that among the many capable ones whom he has instructed, some one perhaps, more favored by Heaven, may perform it."[15]

The "new route," with all its presuppositions and surprising implications, is all compressed into one arresting paragraph, which merits quoting in full: "Whoever considers the past and present will readily observe that all cities and all peoples are and ever have been animated by the same desires and passions; so that it is *easy*, by diligent study of the past, to foresee what is likely to happen in the future in any republic, and to apply those remedies that were used by the ancients, or, not finding any that were employed by them, to devise new ones from the similarity of events. But as such considerations are neglected or not understood by most of those who read, or, if understood by these, are unknown to those who govern, it follows that the same troubles generally recur in all republics."[16]

What Machiavelli seems to say here is that *because* human nature is always the same and *because* history goes round in cycles, knowledge and prediction are possible. But since the endless revolution in cycles seems to depend on men's *ignorance* of the process, knowledge of its rules and "remedies" may somehow break the cyclical process

[15] *Ibid.*, pp. 103-105.
[16] Book I, chap. xxix, *ibid.*, p. 216.

[220]

and history may straighten out into progress in a straight line. Whether he meant to say this or not, I am not sure. The important point is that Machiavelli was trying to use the best of the scientist's *and* the humanist's approach to truth, in an age which knew little real differentiation between them. The humanist finds wisdom and insight in tradition, and values continuity; the scientist finds new truth in careful observation and rational analysis, and values independence from tradition. Machiavelli went back to the ancients as authority, like a good humanist, and found in them the hope of developing a science of political behavior, like a good scientist. He had the humanist's belief in the power of direct inspiration from historical study, and the scientist's belief in the power of detached observation and rational interpretation. He was more of a scientist than any political writer of his day, more of a humanist than most political scientists today.

It is important to note, however, that it is Machiavelli the humanist rather than Machiavelli the scientist who is alive today. The carefully elaborated structure of political generalizations, theorems, and maxims which he erected with such assurance has crumbled away. It never became the foundation for our modern social sciences, which have found other more carefully tested supports. It was too early to found an experimentally grounded science of man. But to the practical politician and the statesman, to the self-seeker and the public benefactor alike, Machiavelli the humanist, the political artist, the clear-sighted but hot-blooded interpreter of power politics is still very much alive. Both dictators and democrats read him, scholars and men of affairs pay tribute to him, even theologians now appreciate him. Why? What did he really accomplish that was so important? What were his strengths and limitations as seen from four centuries away?

I suppose the answer is that he really did find a "new

route," a new intellectual and moral framework in which to set the confusing political developments of his day— a framework so satisfying to many political thinkers and actors that it is still in use today. This new perspective might be set down somewhat summarily as follows:

The world of men in which we find ourselves is a treacherous, constantly changing affair. Whether it is ultimately an ordered cosmos we do not know, but it does not look as if it were. Man is alone in this world and on his own. Most men are ignorant, ambitious, ungrateful, and not to be trusted. Among individuals and groups there is a constant struggle for power. Human desires are limitless. When ambition ceases to drive men on, fear takes over and does the job. Democracies and republics are just as insatiable for power under certain circumstances as dictatorships and despotisms. There are no "safe" courses in diplomacy and politics, only choices between evils and dangers. In this world there are a few—only a few—who have intelligence, courage, and public spirit. If these few will only exercise their brains and wills, and not be so squeamish about the means they use, perhaps some limited good may be achieved, some stability gained in the midst of flux, some virtue in the midst of corruption. The best we can do is to study the repetitive patterns of our social existence as carefully as we can, decide upon the best courses, choose our ways with intelligence and boldness, and stick by our choices with determination.

Machiavelli saw the essentially demonic nature of power. He saw that power is never tamed by moral precepts and that often the worst anarchy is the result of the best intentions. He never doubted the value of personal morality, as his own career proved, but he came to feel that there is a political morality which has its own autonomy and which must inevitably cancel out personal morality in moments of crisis. He was a ruthless critic of all who dreamed of ends without any concern for whether the means existed to attain them—and of all who saw how to attain their ends but lacked the courage to act on their insight. "It very seldom happens that a good man is willing to become prince by bad means, though his object be good," he remarked ruefully. "Men know not how to be gloriously wicked or perfectly good. . . . And when a crime has something of grandeur and nobility in it, they flinch."[17]

This last sentence suggests some of the classic caveats about Machiavelli as political analyst and reformer—because men have been "flinching" from his doctrine ever since they learned of it. The new political morality which he sketched out was purely pragmatic, to be tested not by intentions but by results. There was little if any continuity between this political morality and the traditional personal morality of the classical and Christian traditions. Machiavelli's state, it has often been remarked, was as isolated, as self-sufficient, as proud and free-standing as a Renaissance statue. He found "a new order" as he hoped, but it had too little continuity, too little organic relationship with the old for healthy, well-balanced growth. He saw two of the dimensions of power, the physical and the intellectual. And perhaps he tended to exaggerate both: not only the power of the pen (exaggeration here is par-for-the-course with intellectuals in general), but also the power of the sword (exaggeration here is what happens when intellectuals lean over backward to prove that they are tough-minded men of affairs: "Scholars and literary men often seem more given to the inverted idealism of *Realpolitik* than working diplomats," Garrett Mattingly observes[18]). But in a sense Machiavelli missed the third dimension of power, the moral dimension. It is possible to argue that Machiavelli, the consummate realist, the

[17] *Discourses,* Book I, chaps. xxvii, xxx.
[18] *Renaissance Diplomacy,* p. 40.

resolute facer of things-as-they-are, had one blind-spot which made him unable to see the reality of moral and spiritual forces in the lives of men.

This leaves us with a final paradox. The penetration and profundity of Machiavelli's thought is integrally related to his experience as a human being, as is all great thought in the humanities. What a man has learned in the venture of living, as husband, father, and citizen, has a great deal to do with how deeply he can penetrate as philosopher or poet or artist or student of literature, or even as historian and political scientist. Machiavelli's experience as a man and as a bureaucrat, taken together with his dismissal from office, were the origins of his political thought, both in its greatness and in its limitations. Two of his most famous maxims—that it is necessary on occasions for a prince to break his faith, and that deliberate frightfulness is often a good thing—are evidences of a sort of emotional high tension which can be traced to his political disappointment (there is hardly a trace of either of these doctrines in his letters before his dismissal in 1512). So it could be said— with the soundest psychiatric backing, I am sure—that if Machiavelli had only got his job back, or had learned to accept the frustration of his political ambition with more equanimity, we would have had a less cynical, less amoral, and better balanced political doctrine from him. I agree. But the paradox is that in this case he would never have written it down at all.

II. THOMAS MORE

Some five years after Machiavelli's death, a supposedly close student of his little book, *The Prince*, Thomas Cromwell, became the chief minister of King Henry VIII of England. His only rival for the King's favor, Thomas More, had resigned as Lord Chancellor the day after the clergy acknowledged Henry as Supreme Head of the Church of England in place of the Pope (May, 1532). Cromwell brought More a message from the King soon after his resignation, and they had a lengthy talk. At the end, More said: "Master Cromwell, you are now entered into the service of a most noble, wise, and liberal prince; if you will follow my poor advice, you shall, in your counsel-giving unto his Grace, ever tell him what he *ought* to do, but never what he is *able* to do. . . . For if a lion knew his own strength, hard were it for any man to rule him." More's biographer remarks that we can think of this interview "as one where the Utopian faced the Machiavellian, provided we use these words without prejudice. . . . It was not necessarily idealism facing villainy."[19]

Whatever it was, the wider issues behind this confrontation—moralism *vs.* realism, what ought to be *vs.* what is—have fascinated students of *Utopia* and *The Prince* all the way from Jean Bodin in the later sixteenth century to Gerhard Ritter in the twentieth. Ritter, a non-Nazi but nationalistic German historian writing just at the opening of the Second World War, used Machiavelli and More as pegs on which to hang reflections on the contrast between continental and English political thinking, between German realism born of continental power politics and English moralism born of insular isolation.[20] Bodin, writing four centuries earlier in the midst of a civil war, tried to find his own balance between Machiavelli's disillusionment and More's never-never land. I have found students unfailingly interested and aroused to battle by my asking them to assume that Machiavelli's Prince and More's Utopia actually exist, then to imagine what happens if the Prince lands on Utopia. Will he be helpless, or will he have the place organized in a few months? So long as men continue to be

[19] R. W. Chambers, *Thomas More* (New York, 1935), p. 291.
[20] *Machtstaat und Utopie* (1940), trans. as *The Corrupting Influence of Power* (Hadleigh, Essex, 1952).

worried about the relation between might and right, between politics and morality, these two thinkers, who were working away at their rival schemes of reform during the same years about a thousand miles away from each other, will remain alive in the memory of Western society.

The political and intellectual environment in which the young Thomas More grew up was of course different from Machiavelli's Florence. The underlying problems were the same: the decay of medieval institutions, the growth of strong centers of political power, and the spread of capitalistic practices in the economy. But there was more continuity with the immediate past in More's England, and the social tensions resulting from change took different forms. Henry VII, the first Tudor, had pretty well scotched the danger of feudal anarchy by strengthening the monarchy, building up a surplus in the treasury, holding a tight rein on the nobility, and keeping England out of war abroad. His methods were not always scrupulous, but it took hardheaded policies to deal with pretenders to his shaky throne and with overmighty subjects. Since the end result was peace and order and surcease of civil war, Machiavelli would have approved—and so have most modern historians. But a sensitive contemporary might well have been dismayed by Henry's financial exactions, his enforcement of long-forgotten laws to raise money, and his practice of getting a grant from Parliament for a war, then calling off the war and keeping the money. The same sensitive observer might well have been disturbed for different reasons by the adventurous foreign policy of his son, Henry VIII. Within five years of coming to the throne in 1509, Henry VIII had squandered his father's surplus on a futile war with France, the chief motive of which was to gain glory for the young monarch.

Machiavelli, you will remember, was impressed by two things, as he was growing to maturity; the factional fights which tore his native city to pieces, and its weakness with respect to the big powers of the day. More, on the other hand, was a subject of one of the better-run national monarchies of the sixteenth century. His country had just come through a time of troubles but was now strong, united, and in no danger of invasion or conquest. In fact, if there was any danger, it was that England would let her recovery go to her head and dissipate her new-found strength in continental adventures. There was little danger any more of organized feudal revolt or lawlessness. But there were disturbing signs that the energies of the ruling class, which had once gone into the wars with France and the Wars of the Roses, were now going into economic exploitation of the people and cut-throat competition for favor at the court. More was the son of a London lawyer, and he spent some years in his teens as a page in the household of Cardinal Morton, a churchman of integrity and devotion. It was natural for him to look at the social problems of his day through the eyes of a city-dweller or of a clergyman. The danger, as he would see it, was not so much anarchy as tyranny, not so much urban factions as feudal greed and arrogance, not so much national weakness as national aggressiveness.

The intellectual influence of overwhelming importance on More was Christian humanism.[21] It is hard today to recapture the enthusiasm of the Christian humanists—Reuchlin, Erasmus, Lefèvre d'Étaples, John Colet, and More himself—because what they believed possible seems utterly unrealistic as we look back on it. They believed they could save their society by reviving the best in both classical and Christian antiquity, going back to Plato and the Gospels, reconciling the two traditions, and stripping

[21] See J. H. Hexter, *More's Utopia: the Biography of an Idea* (Princeton, 1952), pp. 52ff.; and E. Harris Harbison, *The Christian Scholar in the Age of the Reformation* (New York, 1956), chap. iii.

off all medieval accretions and distortions. They were Christian intellectuals with an infectious belief in the power of good scholarship and proper education. They thought that if men only *knew* what Socrates said and what Jesus preached, if men could only be made to see the gulf between apostolic Christianity and sixteenth century Christianity, reform would inevitably follow. No one could stop it, once men of intelligence and good-will have been exposed to the best that had come down from ancient Greece and Palestine, Erasmus met More on his first trip to England in 1499, and for the next twenty years he and More and John Colet were in close touch with each other, plotting the strategy of a Christian humanism which would overthrow scholasticism, restore knowledge of the best in pagan and Christian antiquity, and ultimately revive a corrupt and war-torn Christendom.

Practically all of these men were pure intellectuals—writers, teachers, scholars, with no professional responsibility for carrying into practice the reforms they advocated. Thomas More was the outstanding exception: a deeply devoted Christian and a scholar in all his instincts, but one who was called early to a busy and exhausting career as a lawyer and public official. The strong streak of Christian piety in him almost led him to become a Carthusian monk, and he never entirely put aside the possibility, always admired the monastic ideal, and secretly wore a hair-shirt next to his skin all his life. But he remained a layman, married, begot a large family, and followed in his father's footsteps in the law, soon combining his private practice with the office of Under Sheriff of the City of London. The duties of this office are not clear, but More's chief job seems to have been to represent the interests of the London merchant community in legal relationships with the Crown. Henry VIII and Wolsey came to know the young lawyer and covet his services for the Crown. Just when the King began to press More to enter the royal service we do not know, but we find him a member of an embassy to the Netherlands in the summer of 1515, still merely representing the City's interests on an *ad hoc* mission and not yet a royal official.

The embassy proved to be an important event in More's life. Apparently there were lulls in the negotiations (as there always are) while both sides waited for further instructions from home. More visited an old friend, Peter Giles, in Antwerp, and there was time for talk, for thought, and for writing. Somehow, away from his family, away from his native land, temporarily unoccupied by the press of business, he began to let his imagination take flight. The world was surely in a parlous state, as perhaps it always had been. More had seen its seamy side as a lawyer. He was a good lawyer, but hated most of what he had to do. He was peculiarly sensitive to what happens to the little man in the toils of the law and the clutches of the rich. He knew that the economic revolution which had struck England—the conversion of arable land to pasture because of the profit to be made from sheep-farming—was causing misery and suffering among the poor. Unemployment led to vagabondage, vagabondage to thievery; then the thieves were punished by a savage death penalty—which did not stop the thievery or save the souls of the victims. Meanwhile the rich squandered the profits of their exploitation and monopoly on clothes, servants, and luxuries. Everywhere pride, greed, and idleness—and among princes, nothing but a ceaseless and senseless struggle for more gold and more territory. Not a pretty picture—and surely an excuse for cynicism.

How would it look, however, to a Christian humanist? There were certain unexploited resources in the classical and Christian traditions which might be utilized to help solve sixteenth century problems, if only they could be brought vividly before men's imaginations. This matter of "mine-and-thine," for instance, which was at the root of all the trouble: Plato knew that if his governors were to develop any true sense of community among themselves, private property must be denied them. The first apostles held all their goods in common, and the first rule of all truly strenuous Christian communities ever since had been renunciation of property. Granted that man will always remain a sinner, still, his nature is to a large extent the product of his environment. What if he should take seriously the ideals of Plato's Republic and the medieval monastery? Was it not theoretically possible to build a society based on communism of goods in which pride in its way of life and satisfaction with the results would curb the natural tendency to greed of its individual members? Perhaps such a society actually existed, now, somewhere in the vast expanses of the world recently opened up to wondering European eyes since Columbus's momentous voyage twenty-three years before. At any rate, the startling tales of mariners back from the New World and walking the streets of Antwerp suggested that this sort of thing was not beyond believing.

This is a not altogether fanciful account of what went through More's head in the summer of 1515 as he whiled away the time at Peter Giles's in Antwerp. It is based, of course, on what came out of his head at the end of the summer: namely, a manuscript describing the people and customs of "Utopia," and representing Book II of what we have in print today plus the first five pages of Book I as preface.[22] It was a startlingly original combination of daring imagination and hard realism, lightened by turns of sheer wit and horseplay. Almost every feature of Utopian life and thought (except the more obviously humorous bits) was designed as a remedy or palliative to some con-

[22] Hexter, *More's Utopia*, pp. 26-29, and *passim*.

crete social evil which More knew at first-hand. His realistic lawyer's grasp of his own society, its economic, social, and political problems, lay behind every flight of the imagination. He drew on his wide knowledge of classical and Christian literature for ideas, but there was no literal copying of tradition anywhere. For instance, communism in Utopia is the way of life of the whole nation, not of a few governors (as in Plato) or of an isolated group (as in the monastery); yet there is still much of Plato's and St. Benedict's spirit in it.

Not only in detail, but also in the architecture of the whole, the second book of *Utopia* is a Christian humanist's carefully developed remedy for the three key sins of English society—sloth, greed, and especially pride—as the brilliant little study of J. H. Hexter shows so convincingly.[23] Everyone is compelled to work in Utopia so that idleness may never become a badge of social privilege. Greed is nipped in the bud by providing everyone with economic security. And pride is given nothing to feed upon, at least in the individual's life. With true Christian insight, More rates pride as a deadlier sin than greed—"the princess and mother of all mischief," in fact. Without pride, without the limitless desire to outshine other persons, to show off, to out-spend and out-consume all social rivals, to play God on earth, greed would be comparatively easy to handle, More seems to suggest. At any rate, the strict and dreary egalitarianism of Utopia is designed just as clearly to exterminate pride as it is to curb avarice.

We need not enter into the tangle of later arguments about the meaning of Utopia—whether it is more "humanistic" or more "Christian," whether it looks back to the Middle Ages or forward to Karl Marx, for instance. The question whether More was fundamentally serious or just writing for fun, however, is relevant. There seems to

23 *Ibid.*, pp. 72-81.

be little doubt, since the fine biography of R. W. Chambers some years ago, that More's intent was serious: to show how an ideal society based on reason alone without the benefit of revelation, might still put to shame a Christian society which did not live up to the truth revealed to it. The literalist can of course walk heavy-footed through *Utopia* and show you that More did not mean this or that seriously, and the pedant can prove that it is all a story told by an old traveler and that *More* never said *he* believed it. But there is too much in both the design and detail of *Utopia* that has the ring of passionate sincerity about it for any thoughtful reader to doubt that the writer was trying to get something across. If we can still argue about what Erasmus was trying to do in his *Praise of Folly* and Machiavelli in *The Prince*, it is natural to wonder about what More meant to accomplish by picturing an imaginary island, remarkably like England in geography and remarkably unlike England in social customs, supposedly in actual existence here and now, removed from Europe not in time but simply by space—which was quite different from either Plato's Republic or Augustine's City of God, incidentally. I think he was trying to say: stretch your imaginations, exercise your fancy, get out of the mental ruts men have been in for centuries, stop reconciling yourselves to social evil as inevitable, and keep steadily before you the picture of *what might be* as the measure of what is. You may not, and probably will not, set up communism of goods overnight, he seems to say, but if you have seriously considered the advantages of a communist society, at least you will never again look on private property as an absolute, an untouchable right to be defended against all attempts to limit it.

One of the effects, if not one of the purposes, of *Utopia* was to answer a man whom More had never read, namely Machiavelli. Parts of Utopia, it has been remarked before this, read like a comment on *The Prince*. In judging crimes, the Utopians look not to the overt results but "count the intent and pretensed purpose as evil as the act or deed itself."[24] Agreements between princes are kept of course in Europe, says the narrator Raphael with obvious irony, but in the new world where Utopia is situated, princes find loop-holes in treaties by crafty dodges which they would loudly condemn if used in private dealings. So out there it looks as if there are two kinds of justice: ". . . the one meet for the inferior sort of people, going afoot and creeping low by the ground, and bound down on every side with many bands so that it shall not run at rovers. The other a princely virtue, which like as it is of higher majestie than the other poor justice, so also it is of much more liberty, as to the which nothing is unlawful that it lusteth after."[25] The result is that the Utopians make no formal alliances whatever in the belief that "men be better and more surely knit together by love and benevolence than by covenants of leagues."[26] Only two years before, Machiavelli had remarked, "The experience of our times shows those princes to have done great things who have had little regard for good faith . . . and who have ultimately overcome those who have made loyalty their foundation"; therefore, "a prudent ruler ought not to keep faith when by so doing it would be against his interest." "Everyone sees what you appear to be, few feel what you are," Machiavelli concluded; "the end justifies the means"; therefore let a prince aim at conquering and maintaining the state, and the means will always be judged honorable and praised by everyone, for the vulgar is always taken by appearances and the issue of the event—and the world consists only of the vulgar. . . ."[27] The issue between per-

[24] *Utopia* (Everyman ed., London, 1910), p. 87.
[25] *Ibid.*, p. 90. [26] *Ibid.*, p. 91.
[27] *The Prince*, chap. xviii.

sonal morality and "princely virtue" has never been stated better.

The chief difference between Machiavelli's thought-world and that of More, however, cannot be illustrated by direct quotation. It has to do with time and change. Utopia is a completely static society. Since its foundation by King Utopus there has been no significant change, no development, no "history" in fact, and presumably there will be no change in the future. The assumptions underlying Utopia are: first, that evil is essentially social as well as individual, and so any effective attack on it must be through the creation of a new social structure, a new environment; second, this environment, once it is created, will curb and control individual tendencies to evil, even if it will not entirely root out human sin; and third, there are timeless rules of reason which may be discovered and used in designing this new social structure. With much of this Machiavelli, especially in *The Discourses*, would agree. But Machiavelli could never escape from the time dimension as the Utopians succeed in doing. His test of a prince was ability to change with "times and circumstances," his test of a republic was ability to endure in time and expand in space. Nothing is at rest in *The Prince* and *The Discourses*; everything is at rest in *Utopia*. To Machiavelli the real world is a continuous struggle for power between competing vitalities; to More, in *Utopia*, it is a world in which power can be controlled and disciplined, nay even rendered harmless. Machiavelli is consciously an intellectual revolutionary, always striving for a "new order," a "new route." More is a conservative who pictures a society, built on reason, devoting an enormous part of its energy simply to preserving the status quo.

More's picture is worth examining more closely. Utopia is an artificial island—it was King Utopus who dug the fifteen-mile channel that separates it from the continent.

Geographical isolation both makes possible and intensifies the Utopians' psychological isolation from their neighbors. What holds the rather loose federation of Utopian cities together is national sentiment, as we would call it —pride in the Utopian way of life, which the inhabitants know is quite different from that of others and which must thus be jealously protected and preserved.[28] There are all kinds of ingenious devices to preserve the status quo, to keep the number in each family constant, to keep the population at a constant level, to balance trade, and to maintain international peace so that the Utopian welfare state may not be disturbed in its enjoyment of the good life. The Utopians are far more wealthy and powerful than any of their neighbors, and so they go to war only in "just" causes. The list of "just" causes is rather long, it must be confessed, and includes resistance to Utopian colonization of backward areas and injuries done to merchants of allied powers. The Utopians use their overwhelming power only to execute right and justice—and in Raphael's account of it, their neighbors seem to grant the Utopians' moral and cultural superiority as good grounds for their policy. In fact, there is a strong streak of moral righteousness in all that they do. They are harder on their own condemned criminals than on their foreign slaves "because they being so godly brought up to virtue in so excellent a commonwealth" still went wrong.[29] Their principal objective in going to war is "to obtain that thing, which if they had before obtained, they would not have moved battle"—an excellent principle too seldom followed by belligerents. But, the account continues, "if that be not possible, they take so cruel vengeance of them which be in the fault, that ever after they be afeared to do the like."[30] Because Utopian manhood is so precious, they prefer to fight by the crafty use of money and propaganda,

[28] *Utopia*, p. 97.   [29] *Ibid.*, p. 83.   [30] *Ibid.*, p. 93.

and by tricks which would delight a Machiavellian. They use their friends' and allies' troops before their own. But if they are finally forced to fight, they fight hard, knowing they are in the right, and they impose stiff indemnities on their defeated victims.

It took German historians like Ritter to point out that this insular self-righteousness, which is such an amusing characteristic of Utopian policy, is not unlike some later aspects of British foreign policy.[31] With no land frontier to defend, it was hard for Englishmen to understand the Machiavellism of continental powers which were caught in the continuous struggle for power, and easy for them to read the moral law to their obstreperous neighbors. The unconscious assumption of English statesmen often was that a free people's acts could not be anything but moral, whereas the acts of continental despotisms would *ipso facto* be immoral. Further, it was natural for the British to equate morality with preserving the status quo and immorality with upsetting it. It is certainly not fair to burden More with any responsibility for *forming* later British policy. But it is sound to point out, as Ritter does, that More was thoroughly medieval in his belief in timeless standards of right and justice, that he thought the use of power justified only as a means of enforcing right or justice, and that war made sense to him only as an instrument of justice meting out punishment—not as a more or less natural result of competing wills-to-live, as it looked to Machiavelli. More believed that power could be harnessed and tamed by righteousness. But his later German critics are justified in asking the embarrassing question: how would those neighboring backward peoples really feel about the high-and-mighty Utopians, with their gold which they never enjoy, their "dumping" policy in foreign trade, their big

[31] *The Corrupting Influence of Power*, pp. 74-89.

citizen army, and their high moral principles? Is the struggle for power abolished by imagining it out of existence? Or does it slip in by the back door after the moralist has bolted and barred the front? More's *Utopia* is the work of a conscientious Christian humanist, humane and civilized in spirit. But there is a streak of moralism and self-righteousness in it that is related to the later More who conscientiously supported the burning of heretics.

Now let us return to the author of this lively description of an imaginary island, back from the embassy to the Netherlands at the end of 1515, and leading his friend Peter Giles to believe that the manuscript would very soon appear in print. It did not appear for over a year, and when it did, it was expanded to include a marvelous dialogue between the narrator, Raphael Hythlodaye, Peter Giles, and Thomas More himself. This was sandwiched in between the first five pages of the original version and the actual description of Utopia. Why was this dialogue added, and what does it mean in the light of all we know about More himself?

The first to answer these questions convincingly, it seems to me, has been Professor Hexter in the study I have already mentioned.[32] In brief, there is strong indirect evidence that More was wrestling hard in the summer of 1516 with the most important problem a Christian intellectual can face: to what extent must he be responsible for carrying out his ideas *himself* if the opportunity is offered? Erasmus was with him in the summer of 1516, and the presumption is that there were long talks between them about Henry VIII's pressure on More to become a privy councilor. No one knows how Erasmus argued, but the way he lived out the answer himself is well known. The calling of a Christian scholar is a high one, he might

---

[32] *More's Utopia*, pp. 95, 102, 110. What follows is essentially Hexter's account.

have maintained. It takes all of a man's time and energy. Furthermore, it requires absolute independence and integrity. You cannot be committed to spending a certain number of hours a day at court and still study and write. More important, you cannot be the servant of a king and still think you are free to speak and write as your mind and conscience dictate. Either you commit yourself to the truly important task, the re-education of Christendom through restoration of the best in classical and Christian antiquity, or you become so entangled in worldly affairs that your tongue and pen lose their cutting edge, and you no longer are an intellectual and a reformer worthy of the name. I repeat: Erasmus may or may not have spoken thus to More, but this was really what he had bet his own life on—and More himself had strong sympathies with this point of view. Could he not argue that to have written the description of Utopia was enough? Let others read it and work out the applications. The important thing was the intellectual's task of seeing things clearly and presenting the truth persuasively.

There was another side to More, however—the lawyer, the man of affairs, the realist. In *Utopia* he remembers that his old mentor, Cardinal Morton, had served Henry VII well. "The King put much trust in his counsel, the weal public also in a manner leaned unto him," he says.[33] In sixteenth century Europe, kings had the power, and to counsel kings successfully was to put new ideas into effect and to bring about the public good. How could a Christian humanist, who honestly believed in the ideals embodied in *Utopia*, refuse the opportunity to implement them by counseling a king if offered the chance?

All this is argued out in the dialogue between Raphael Hythlodaye and More in the First Book of *Utopia*.[34] With

[33] *Utopia*, p. 20.
[34] *Ibid.*, pp. 18-20, 34-43.

his vast experience of other societies, Raphael should offer his services to a king, says More. Never, says Raphael. Imagine me in the French King's Council. The question for discussion is how the king can hold onto Milan, recover Naples, conquer Venice, gobble up the Netherlands, and still avoid a stab in the back by England. If I stand up and say: Turn over a new leaf, gentlemen; learn a new lesson; my advice is to stay out of Italy and Flanders entirely; there is enough to do in providing good government for a large country like France without wasting the nation's blood in foreign conquest—who would listen to me in such a hard-headed group? In such a situation, who listens to a man who brings up something he knows was done in times past or has seen done in some other place?

Well, says More, I did not mean that you should make yourself ridiculous by always proposing impossibly idealistic policies. This "school philosophy" naturally has no place in royal councils. But there is a more tactful and diplomatic way, a "philosophy more civil." This is to "handle the matter wittily," and to see that what you can't turn to good still does not come out too badly. "You must not leave and forsake the commonwealth; you must not forsake the ship in a tempest [simply] because you cannot rule and keep down the winds," he says to Raphael.[35]

Raphael is unconvinced. Either he must speak the truth or remain silent, he says. He is afraid that More's "crafty and subtle" approach really amounts to compromising with the truth. Furthermore, it is almost impossible to conceal your real opinions in a royal council. Unless you go along with wicked and foolish decisions of the majority, you will quickly be accounted a spy or even a traitor. And if you do go along with the decisions, the wickedness and folly will of course be attributed to you by the outside world.

[35] *Ibid.*, p. 41.

This is the last word, and Raphael, representing More's "pure intellectual" side, speaks it. But the dialogue is obviously the work of a man deeply divided in mind and heart.

This was where the argument was left when *Utopia* went to the printer in Louvain under Erasmus' supervision in December, 1516. For two more years More held out. Then what the English weathercasters call a "bright spell" seemed to pass over the political landscape. Wolsey began to defend the poor against enclosures, the King became strongly peace-minded, and the future looked bright.[36] More entered the royal service and soon he was privy councilor, Speaker of the House of Commons, and finally Lord Chancellor. His career as an independent Christian humanist, as a reforming intellectual, ceased (as he had seen it would) and his preparation for martyrdom began (as he had dimly sensed it would). Raphael's predictions came true, one by one. More made it clear to the king that he disagreed with the divorce proceedings, but that he would remain silent in public. Thomas Cromwell, however, with his clear Machiavellian vision, saw that it was More's refusal to say what he could not believe that was "making others so stiff as they be." And so, because he stood in the way of a revolution, More was condemned for treason on perjured testimony and sent to the block—twenty years after *Utopia* was conceived and three years after the appearance in print of Machiavelli's *Prince* and *The Discourses*. In a sense he had deliberately ended his career as a Christian humanist and reformer when he entered the royal service, in order to attest his belief that an intellectual must be ultimately willing to put his ideas to the test of practice, and that a Christian, like his Master, must be ready to be crucified for his beliefs.

[36] *More's Utopia*, pp. 146-155.

III. CONTEMPORARY ECHOES

I have tried to sketch the contrasting development of the two great political analysts of the early sixteenth century. Each in his own way tried to probe to the roots of the bewildering social evils of his day. Each tried like a good intellectual to see things whole, to explore every relevant resource in tradition, to use every important piece of evidence from history and contemporary experience. In trying to see things whole, they got the desire to set things straight. Or perhaps it is just as correct to say that their desire to set things straight drove them to the mental effort of seeing things whole.

They did not reach the same conclusions, of course. They differed—profoundly and fundamentally—in spite of much in common. And this points up the truth—or is it a truism?—that humanistic knowledge is not like scientific knowledge. It does not accumulate, like the sedimentary layers which eventually form a single, solid rock. Rather it grows like a group of organisms which are like each other and yet each one unique, intimately dependent on their surrounding environment of light, air, and nourishment, always subject to the possibility of annihilation. Where insight and evaluation are involved, the humanist turns to the best he knows of ancient wisdom on a subject and uses this wisdom as an essential intellectual resource in a fresh and realistic analysis of his own particular historical situation. Times change, but are never altogether different. The world of Plato, the world of Thomas More, and the world of today are very different, but they are not so different that Plato and More are irrelevant to us. A modern physicist need not know much about Aristotle or how he arrived at his ideas of motion. To be sure, he builds on Newton's laws, but he cares little about how Newton came to formulate them. The historical and biographical detail which has formed the substance of these lectures, however, is important to the humanist because the way intellectuals become social reformers, the way their human experience contributes to their social insight, is still relevant to us. And their conclusions are still alive in a way those of the medieval astrologer are not alive for the modern scientist. The antinomy of realism and moralism in the analysis of politics, for instance, must be argued through for each generation, in the light of its particular historical circumstances and needs. In their day Machiavelli and More seemed utterly irreconcilable. To Machiavelli the ceaseless struggle for power must be accepted as one of the brute facts of life. You can learn how to use it, he might say; and in certain ideal circumstances you can balance power against power and so attain a certain stability and order; but you can never tame power, never outlaw it or ignore it. To Thomas More in *Utopia*, on the other hand, the struggle for power may be so curbed and contained by the proper structure of law and right that for all practical purposes its capacity for evil can be forgotten. The causes of ambition and sedition have been so skillfully "plucked up by the roots" in Utopia that the society will "endure forever" and no foreign prince will be able to shake it, Raphael says.[37] And so the Machiavellian and the Utopian come down to us from the sixteenth century as symbols of an eternal contradiction. The Machiavellian sees nothing but material power and is blind to moral and spiritual forces; the Utopian overestimates moral forces and thinks he can exorcise the demon of power in the end.

From this distance, however, it looks as if we are dealing not with contradiction or paradox in the case of Machiavelli *versus* More, but with what our scientist friends would call complementarity. Obviously no government that ignores the pure power factors in its position will survive

[37] *Utopia*, p. 114.

long—nor will one that fails to convert naked power into some structure of right. Pascal summed it up a century later in that bitter, penetrating way he had of stabbing to the heart of the matter: "Justice without might is helpless; might without justice is tyrannical. . . . We must therefore combine justice and might, and for this end make what is just strong, or what is strong just. . . . Being unable to cause might to obey justice, men have made it just to obey might. Unable to strengthen justice, they have justified might."[38] Pascal's irony is Machiavelli's, but his underlying faith is More's.

And so the dialectic continues from generation to generation. To know the history of the argument, to know its greatest protagonists, is to add perspective and depth to our own self-understanding. Where and by whom is the dialectic being carried forward today? One would naturally look for it in the United States, the power of long isolationist tradition and strong moral beliefs, much like the Utopians in some ways, but recently shocked out of its complacency by being thrust into a deadly competition for existence with a ruthless power of equal strength. And I think you may find a hint of it at least in the writings of two distinguished statesmen who have also qualified at different times as intellectuals and reformers: George Kennan and John Foster Dulles. You notice I say their "writings." It is too early to judge the active careers of either, but each wrote books and articles around mid-century which were written rapidly and urgently for the general reader, to inform and to reform, much as Machiavelli's *Prince* and More's *Utopia* were written.[39]

In fact, there are amusing parallels here between the six-

[38] *Pensées* (Everyman ed., London, 1931), nos. 298, 300.
[39] George F. Kennan, *American Diplomacy 1900-1950* (Chicago, 1951) and *Realities of American Foreign Policy* (Princeton, 1954); John Foster Dulles, *War or Peace?* (New York, 1950).

teenth and twentieth centuries. Mr. Kennan, a distinguished career diplomat, organizer of the Policy Planning Staff of the State Department, ambassador to the Kremlin and outstanding expert on Russia, was allowed to "retire" from the foreign service in April 1953 at the age of forty-nine, because the new administration had campaigned against the "containment" policy which he had fathered and so found no use for him. He has since turned to history, like Machiavelli in his retirement, and is engaged in a full-dress study of America and the Russian Revolution, the first volume of which has won wide acclaim. Mr. Dulles, it is said, had been preparing himself for the Secretaryship of State since childhood—with somewhat more zest than Thomas More prepared himself for the royal service. As part of this preparation he wrote extensively on the general subject of foreign policy before he attained his lifelong ambition in January of 1953. And so, like Machiavelli, Mr. Kennan may be considered a statesman more or less involuntarily turned intellectual. Like More, Mr. Dulles was a lawyer and intellectual who ultimately became an active statesman. As in the case of Machiavelli and Kennan there is much in common between them, and much in sharp dispute.

Mr. Kennan urges us to see the world as it is, not as it might be if all peoples were like the American. Power is the central fact in the world of diplomacy, and it is better in the long run to devise means of balancing power by old-fashioned diplomacy, he thinks, than to ignore the power factor (which is dangerous), or to rely on legalistic restraints (which is futile). "This is a hard and cruel world we live in," he writes. Other nations do not exactly see us as we see ourselves—peace-loving, law-abiding, willing to live and let live. The rest of the world is not ready to federate in a nice reasonable way as our original thirteen states did; in fact it is not even willing to preserve the status quo which is so favorable to us. The most serious fault in twentieth century American foreign policy is what Kennan calls "the legalistic-moralistic approach to international problems": our faith in arbitration treaties, pacts solemnly outlawing war, schemes for international organization which we expect too much of and so become disillusioned with.[40] Our legalism easily becomes moral superiority; our wars too readily become wars for righteousness, which means that they are total wars and can end only in total defeats—and this will spell disaster for both sides in an atomic world. We tend to apply our individual moral standards too naively to international affairs. "We cannot, when it comes to dealings between governments, assign to moral values the same significance we give them in personal life." We can—and Mr. Kennan fervently hopes we will—follow moral *methods* in our diplomacy. But personal morality can never be a valid test of the *purposes* of a state, nor "a criterion for measuring and comparing the behavior of different states."[41] We would do better, he thinks, if as a people we were less eager to appear morally superior, and more willing to accept the fact that we are a great power which has to do some of the things great powers have always had to do to survive—and not be ashamed about it. Lest you think from this that Mr. Kennan is Machiavelli reincarnated, I hasten to add that he is a sincere Presbyterian layman and writes, "I do not wish to see the conduct of *this* nation in its foreign relations animated by anything else than decency, generosity, moderation, and consideration for others."[42] But the affinity to the best in Machiavelli's realism is evident enough, this time rooted in a kind of Christian pessimism.

Mr. Dulles is another Presbyterian layman of a some-

[40] *American Diplomacy*, pp. 95ff.
[41] *Realities of American Foreign Policy*, pp. 47-50.
[42] *Ibid.*, p. 61.

what more familiar Calvinist stamp. There is much in his book *War or Peace?* (1950) with which Mr. Kennan would agree, but the whole tone and temper is different. He believes that "in the pattern of our own national life we can find the pattern for world peace."[43] Peace can be "patterned," then, and the pattern can be found in the federation of the thirteen colonies and the drafting of the Constitution. The United States became great because of its people's moral beliefs and spiritual convictions, now unfortunately submerged by materialism. Only by recovering her faith in her spiritual destiny can America combat Communism. Where Kennan tends to emphasize the danger from Russia, the world power, Dulles tends to emphasize the threat of Communist ideology. "Power is the key of success in dealing with the Soviet leadership," he writes. But he continues: "Power, of course, includes not merely military power, but economic power and the intangibles, such as moral judgement and world opinion, which determine what men do and the intensity with which they do it."[44] As one reads on, one realizes that we are in a battle of creeds far more than a conflict of world powers. Mr. Dulles would have us fight like the Utopians, first by propaganda before we draw the sword. He has great faith in legal structures, moral arguments, and non-material forces. Like the Utopians, he has no doubt about who is right and who is wrong (he has often been ready to treat both friend and foe to little lectures on the subject as he steps aboard planes). But at his best he has the same rugged sense of right combined with realistic grasp of politics that characterized Thomas More's thinking—albeit in Presbyterian rather than papal garb.

And so there is nothing really new in the world of political thought after all. But the corollary is that the big

43 *War or Peace?* p. 19.
44 *Ibid.*, p. 16.

issues are never old and stale either. I had thought that
I was more or less "original" in my feeling that George
Kennan represents the realistic pole of contemporary
American thinking about international affairs and John
Foster Dulles the moralistic, until I picked up a little book
by a French-Swiss writer, M. Louis Brandt-Peltier, called
*Conceptions américaines de politique étrangère: Kennan,
Dulles* (Paris, 1953). The author draws the polar contrast
between the two even more sharply than I have. America
did not become great merely through her moral and spiritual convictions, he points out slyly in reply to Dulles:
geographical isolation and the protection of the British
navy had something to do with it. Europe prefers a "materialistic" to a moralistic America, he hints. Europeans can
accept American economic superiority, he says, but Lord
help them if the United States undergoes a religious reform and becomes possessed of some new sense of "Manifest
Destiny" to reform the world! He concludes dryly: "What
America needs most is to be *enlightened,* not *reformed.*"[45]

It may be that enlightenment and reform are more
closely related than M. Brandt-Peltier thinks they are. At
least Machiavelli and Thomas More thought so. To each
in different ways the impulse to reform was integrally related to the impulse to understand. The intellectual as
social reformer has his faults, as is perfectly evident in our
two subjects themselves. He is apt to see the social landscape in too sharp relief of black and white, and he is prone
to exaggerate the rationality of men. But if we are going
to have reformers—and we are, of course—there is a good
deal to be said for the proposition that it is better to have
men whose itch to change society has grown out of the
scholar's desire to grasp the complexities of the social structure than to suffer under the ignorant fanatics and "dim-

[45] *Conceptions américaines de politique étrangère: Kennan, Dulles*
(Paris, 1953), pp. 179-182.

witted saints" (the phrase is William James's) who clutter the pages of history.

Think over for yourselves whether you would vote for realism or moralism the next time you have the chance. The argument is still unsettled. Your vote can still affect the results. You may be conscious of Machiavelli and Thomas More peering over your shoulder as you debate the issue within yourself.

11 · THE IDEA OF UTILITY IN THE THOUGHT OF JOHN CALVIN*

No ONE can read very far in Calvin without being struck by his fondness for the word *utilitas*, together with its many derivatives and synonyms. The idea of utility runs "like a red thread" through almost everything Calvin wrote, says Fritz Büsser in his recent study of Calvin's judgment of himself.[1] If we had a complete concordance to Calvin's works, the references to utility and usefulness would fill columns and the titles of almost every separate work would very likely appear at least once. This broad fact has often been noted by students of Calvin. But no one, it seems to me, has sufficiently pondered both the pervasiveness and intensity of this concern with utility and tried to explain it. It is the purpose of this paper to attempt such pondering and explanation.

Calvin's concept of utility certainly owed something to Augustine's *De Doctrina Christiana*,[2] but this does not explain what was really characteristic about it. Augustine had made a sharp distinction between *use* and *enjoyment*. Temporal things are given us to use, eternal to enjoy. The

---

* This chapter grew as a more extended treatment of a point raised in my *Christian Scholar in the Age of the Reformation* (1956). I note that it is in classical scholarly form: (a) what the literature has to say on the subject, (b) why they are wrong, and (c) why I am right. The paper was presented at the Columbia Renaissance Seminar, where it had the benefit of my friend Benjamin J. Nelson's criticism among others, and at a meeting of the American Society of Church History, of which Professor John T. McNeill was chairman. The reactions of McNeill, the Dean of Calvin studies in this country, suggest that in making a point, I have exaggerated. The paper has not been published before.

[1] Fritz Büsser, *Calvins Urteil über sich selbst* (Zurich, 1950), p. 133.

[2] See e.g., T. S. K. Scott-Craig, in *A Companion to the Study of St. Augustine*, ed. R. W. Battenhouse (New York, Oxford, 1955).

first are instrumental to the second. Life is like a journey back to one's homeland: if we come to enjoy the travel itself (which is a means, to be used and not enjoyed) we will never reach home, where alone we can be really happy. "We must use the world and not enjoy it. . . . We ought to use . . . the whole temporal dispensation . . . but not with any permanent affection or pleasure."[3] There is certainly something of this *uti non frui* in Book III, chapter 10 of the *Institutes* ("The Right Use of the Present Life and Its Supports"). But Calvin's leading idea of "right use" nowhere appears in Augustine's treatment. It is characteristically Calvin's. He rejects both *dis*use and *mis*use of the blandishments of this world in favor of right use, which is defined in terms of moderation and stewardship. He insists that the use of God's gifts is never wrong when it is directed to the same end for which the Creator himself appointed them for us, namely our benefit. In other words, he does not separate use and enjoyment as Augustine does. Utility and pleasure are not divorced but united in the idea of a right use governed by moderation and directed toward the ideal of good stewardship. It is important to remember at the start, therefore, that Calvin rejects the Augustinian distinction between temporal things which are to be used and eternal things which are to be enjoyed. Right use (to Calvin) may be accompanied by legitimate enjoyment.

This helps to explain the fact that the synonyms for *utilitas* which occur most frequently to Calvin are "advantage," "advancement," "profit," and "fruit" (*prodesse, commodare, avancement, profit, fruit*). Words expressing usefulness are often coupled with words expressing "benefit" or "delight." It may have been a dour sort of delight—as when Calvin remarks that predestination, properly un-

[3] *Christian Doctrine*, Book I, chaps. 3, 4, 35.

derstood, is a "sweet and delightful doctrine"—but to Calvin a useful object gives pleasure, and the sense of being useful is accompanied by the sense of satisfaction.

The commonest appearance of the idea is when Calvin is describing his purpose in presenting some scholarly work to the public. Almost invariably, except in his more purely controversial tracts, he hopes the pamphlet or commentary or compendium will prove "useful" or "profitable" to the reader. This thought makes its modest bow in the opening paragraph of the Dedication of the first edition of the *Institutes*, dated August 1535. In the Preface which he wrote the same year to the New Testament translation of his cousin Olivétan, he urged that it was the duty of princes to see that "this holy teaching which is so useful and necessary"[4] be published and taught. In his later Preface to the Old Genevan Bibles there is much along the same line about the "profit" of Scripture and about Calvin's hope that his labors in revising Olivétan's translation will have proved "profitable."[5]

It is not till the three years at Basel and Strasbourg, however (1538-1541), that the idea of utility becomes really prominent in Calvin's writings. Now the theme of being "useful" to a wide public and to future generations begins to swell and grow. In presenting his first commentary, that on *Romans* (1539), he says that in spite of the many other fine commentaries on the same epistle, no one had yet done one with brevity and intelligibility to the ordinary reader primarily in mind. This had made him decide to try "what good he could do" (*commodare*) to the Church. He begins his Argument: "In setting forth the utility of this Epistle. . . ."[6] His first efforts to set the Psalms to music date from the same year. In introducing this work to the

[4] *Calvini Opera, Corpus Reformatorum,* ix, 791ff.

[5] *CR,* ix, 823-826.

[6] *CR,* x, part ii, 402ff.

[251]

public he argued that God means church services to re-
dound to the "profit" of his people, so what is done in
these services must be intelligible to everyone if everyone
is to receive "fruit and edification." Music "has a mysterious and almost unbelievable power to stir the hearts of
men in one way or another. So we ought to be all the more
careful to regulate it so that it is useful and not pernicious
to us."[7]

In the *Treatise on the Lord's Supper* (1541) the idea
of utility becomes more prominent than ever before. Calvin begins as usual by saying that he thought it would be
"a very useful labor" for him to write a simple, clear explanation of the sacrament because of the current confusion. The second subdivision of the argument is an answer to the question, "What fruit and utility we receive
from the sacrament." The author shows "how profitable
the Lord's Supper is to us, on condition that we turn it
well to our profit: for we shall know its utility in realizing
our own indigence, which it remedies." The "communication" with Christ himself is the first and principal "fruit"
of Holy Communion. The second "fruit" or "singular
utility" of the sacrament is that it stimulates us to constant
thankfulness to God for all his mercies; and the third that
it affords "a vehement exhortation to holy living." The
Devil knows that Our Lord left "nothing more useful to
his Church than this holy sacrament," and so he has done
his best "to corrupt and destroy its fruit" by spreading
errors and superstitions about it. Utility, fruit, profit, efficacy: the words recur like a refrain throughout the little
treatise.[8]

Examples could be multiplied. The famous Preface to
the *Commentary on the Psalms* (1557) begins: "If the
reading of these commentaries brings as much advantage

[7] In *Oeuvres choisies* (Geneva, 1909), pp. 169, 174.
[8] *CR*, v, 429-460, *passim*.

[*utilitas, avancement*] to the Church of God as I have gained profit [*fructus, proufit*] in writing them, I will have no reason to regret having undertaken this work."[9]

Finally, the 1559 edition of the *Institutes* contains many familiar examples of Calvin's interest in usefulness. In the Preface of that year he writes that God has devoted him to two aims: the enlargement of the Kingdom and "the promotion of social utility"[10]—in other words, "to profit the Church by maintaining the pure doctrine of godliness." After the famous chapter on "God's preservation and support of the world by his power and his governance of every part of it by his providence" there follows a chapter on "The proper application of this doctrine to render it useful to us."[11] Utility provides the transition from Book II on Christ to Book III on the Spirit: "We are now to examine [Book III begins] how we obtain the enjoyment of those blessings which the Father has conferred on his only begotten Son, not for his own private use, but to enrich the poor and needy. And first it must be remarked that as long as there is a separation between Christ and us, all that he suffered and performed for the salvation of mankind is useless and unavailing to us." And so "Christ is rendered profitable to us by the secret operation of the Spirit," as the chapter title declares.[12] Later on in the same book, the Spirit renders profitable to us the doctrine of predestination. Some would like to hush-hush this doctrine, Calvin recognizes, but "the Scripture is the school of the Holy Spirit, in which, as nothing necessary and useful to be known is omitted, so nothing is taught which

[9] *CR*, XXXI, 14.

[10] "Nam quamvis Deus et propagandi regni sui et adiuvandae publicae utilitatis studio animum meum penitus addixerit. . . ." Cf. Jean Belin, *La logique d'une idée force: L'Idée d'utilité sociale et la révolution française, 1789-92* (Paris, 1939).

[11] I, 16 & 17.

[12] III, 1, 1.

it is not beneficial to know."[13] The very obscurity of the doctrine, which excites dread in some people, "not only displays the utility of this doctrine, but shows it to be productive of the most delightful benefit."[14]

So much for our sampling of the evidence. I believe enough has been offered to suggest that Calvin was much concerned—perhaps the proper word is obsessed—with the concept of utility. Precisely what did he mean by it? Obviously not what Bentham or William James or John Dewey meant by it. So far as I can discover, Calvin used the idea at different times on three different levels: the religious, the ethical, and the intellectual.

By "useful" Calvin meant first of all: instrumental in fostering awe, reverence, and true piety. Or to put it in his more objective terms, it meant favoring the actual transferral to the believer of the graces gained by Christ's obedience and passion. The religious meaning of the term is always the fundamental one.

The second or ethical meaning, however, was more frequently emphasized by Calvin. "Useful" in this sense meant issuing in Christian living, resulting in ethical action. This is such an all-pervasive and familiar strain in Calvin's thinking that it needs no emphasis here. Karlfried Fröhlich has underscored the predominantly social and ethical character of Calvin's thought. Doctrine and ethics, belief and action, are inseparable in everything he wrote: "the right ethic is implicit in the right belief."[15] God does not mean men merely to contemplate truth or just to win salvation for their own souls. He has a Kingdom to build, and men are his instruments. "It is certainly the part of a

---

[13] III, 21, 3.

[14] III, 21, 1.

[15] K. Fröhlich, *Die Reichgottesidee Calvins* (Munich, 1922), pp. 37-39; *idem, Gottesreich, Welt, und Kirche bei Calvin* (Munich, 1930), pp. 28-30.

Christian man," Calvin wrote in his *Reply to Sadoleto* (1539), "to ascend higher than merely to seek and secure the salvation of his own soul." "The end proposed in our election," say the *Institutes*, "is our diligent performance of virtuous actions."[16] The most prevasive and obvious meaning of "useful" to Calvin is having ethical implications, resulting in action, advancing the Kingdom.

There is a third meaning of "useful" which can easily be missed in Calvin's thought. While not so prominent in the texts as the first two, it is certainly there. This is the connotation of helping to clear up intellectual difficulties, to straighten out knotty doctrinal points, to replace confusion with clarity. In the broadest sense, this is the utility of sound scholarship. Calvin could never abide confusion. His sense of order and his passion for orderliness were not only the mark of his writing but often the main stimulus to take pen in hand. In the important years immediately after his expulsion from Geneva in 1538 when he was finding himself as a young scholar and writer, the problem of why God allows controversy and confusion to exist seems to have troubled him a good deal. At least three times in three years—in the *Reply to Sadoleto*, the *Commentary on Romans*, and the *Treatise on the Lord's Supper*—he raised the question of why men of both learning and devotion could come to quite contradictory conclusions, why "those who have treated the mysteries of God with zeal for learning, devotion, and sobriety, have not always agreed with each other."[17] For instance, he points out, Luther and Zwingli had differed violently about the sacrament. Calvin's answer is that God permits his servants to disagree in order to humble them. He observes further that if there were a larger measure of agreement in the world, men might either reach the *wrong* conclusion, or depend too

[16] *Institutes*, III, 23, 12.
[17] *CR*, X, part II, 405.

little upon God's grace in reaching the truth. One very important purpose of Calvin's writings becomes evident in such passages as these: to throw light in dark places, to offer intellectual clarification, to allay controversy by searching out God's answer to disputed questions in his Word. "I do not demand at all," he once wrote, "that people agree with me or my opinion or my say-so, except upon condition that they first recognize that what I teach is useful."[18] Calvin's works are to be useful to the reader for piety, for holy living, and for understanding. Any writings that do not contribute to these ends are by implication useless, and may be pernicious.

It seems to me there are three possible ways of approaching this evidence of Calvin's concern with utility. The first is, of course, to deny that any problem exists. The argument would run thus: Christianity is perhaps the most this-worldly of all the great world religions. Any Christian writer must be concerned sooner or later with the practical implications of belief. The doctrine of the Incarnation has prevented all but the most extreme mystics in the Christian tradition from transforming the Christian religion into pure contemplation. Any Christian who puts pen to paper, it can be argued, is concerned to foster piety and moral conduct. And as a matter of fact, as Benjamin Nelson says, the concept of utility in a general sense is something of a commonplace with the Schoolmen.

This will hardly do as an explanation, however. There is an unmistakable difference of tone between Calvin and Aquinas, or even between Calvin and Luther. A great deal that Aquinas wrote is "useful" in Calvin's sense, but St. Thomas does not feel compelled to keep *telling* the reader that it is in quite the same way. Nor does Luther (in spite of his use of *nützen* in the sense of being useful to one's

---

[18] "Contre la secte des libertins," *CR*, VII, 248; Büsser, p. 106.

neighbor, as W. Pauck puts it). I submit that in spite of the religious utilitarianism perhaps inherent in all Christian thinking, there *is* something here to be accounted for, *an almost obsessive concern to be thought useful and practical.*

The second possible approach is to say that Calvin's preoccupation with utility is simply participation in the *Zeitgeist* by a thinker who was peculiarly sensitive to nearly all the major thought-currents of his day. This is to say that there is a strong utilitarian undercurrent in humanism which comes to the surface in Calvin as it does in others who were influenced by humanist thought.

There is obviously much in this line of thinking. The Italian humanists absorbed the strong ethical interests of the Greek and Roman writers whom they read with such avidity. Their main quarrel with scholasticism was that it was useless—useless for better living here in this world. Imperceptibly the test of truth with many of them became its utility, here, now, in this life. As the prestige of dialectic declined, that of grammar and rhetoric rose. In Quattrocento Italy dialectic tended to be "useless," rhetoric "useful."[19] Quirinus Breen suggests that in the long conflict in European thought between the philosophers like Aristotle whose aim it was to contemplate truth and the rhetoricians like Isocrates and Cicero whose business it was to present truth in persuasive and usable form, it looked as if the rhetoricians were finally winning out. Erasmus echoed the objections of earlier humanists to scholasticism: it was useless for Christian living. The "Philosophy of Christ" was properly not a "philosophy" at all in any systematic sense, but an attitude, a way of life, something practical. The general utilitarian temper affected even those relatively untouched by humanism, like Ignatius of Loyola.

[19] Quirinus Breen, in *Church History*, XVI (Dec. 1947), 197-209, and in *Archiv für Reformationsgeschichte*, XLIII (1952), 13-27.

It is not hard to see how these various influences reached Calvin, during his student days, through his friends and his reading, both before and after his conversion. His mastery of the Latin and French languages is evidence of his interest in rhetoric. Even before his conversion Calvin had no great interest in abstract ideas which had no practical implications. In his *Commentary on Seneca* he wrote, "Human nature is such that we are more affected by considerations of utility or pleasure than by these Stoic paradoxes which are so far removed from ordinary sentiment."[20] In the *Reply to Sadoleto*, Calvin echoed the usual humanist criticism of scholasticism, but with characteristic intensity. The real trouble with the older education, he maintained, was that there was no "profit" or "fruit" in it.

The direct influence of Melanchthon, whom Calvin knew and admired, should not be ignored. Professor Breen has emphasized the "fundamentally rhetorical or homiletical" character of Melanchthon's writings. "They are handbooks for preachers," he says, "shot through with warning, comfort, and practical admonition," like Calvin's *Institutes* in many respects.[21] In 1558, the year before Calvin published the definitive edition of his *Institutes*, Melanchthon wrote a refutation of Pico della Mirandola's argument of 1485 to Ernolao Barbaro that philosophy was superior to rhetoric, contemplation to persuasion.[22] Me-

---

[20] *CR*, v, 39.   [21] *Church History*, xvi, 207.

[22] However, Pico's nephew reported (in Thomas More's translation) that Pico valued his learning only so far as it was "profytable to ye chyrche and to ye extermynation of errours," cared not whether his works came out under his own name or not so long as they were of "profite" to readers, and would have liked to devote himself solely to biblical studies except that many people were anxious to see the great works he had spent so much time on—and "ye commune profyte pricked him." (*Giovanni Pico della Mirandola: His Life by his Nephew Giovanni Francesco Pico*, trans. Sir Thomas More, ed. J. M. Rigg [London, 1890], pp. 19-20.) Even to a defender of "pure scholarship," the argument of scholarly utility was a commonplace.

lanchthon subordinated philosophy to rhetoric and argued that wisdom is useless if it is merely enjoyed in contemplation; it must be declared and explained to ordinary people in clear and intelligible terms.[23] Certainly Calvin was not the only theologian of his generation to insist upon the dignity of the popularizer's calling, the importance of rendering Christian doctrine "useful."

If a man is simply and purely a product of his age, if his mind is an accurate reflection of its currents of thought, then this is explanation enough. But the uneasy suspicion remains that there was something more to it than this, something more personal and peculiar to Calvin. Luther was relatively uninfluenced by the utilitarian current, and one could cite many a monk or mystic who was utterly untouched by it. Why was *Calvin* such a religious utilitarian? Why did he feel compelled to point out over and over again that what he was writing was designed to be "useful"?

I think one answer lies in a third approach, through Calvin's conception of his own calling and the way he attained it. I have sketched this out elsewhere,[24] and there is not space here to go into detail. But the outline of an answer may be suggested. The clue is hidden, I think, in Calvin's well-known account of himself and his career in the Preface to his *Commentary on the Psalms* (1557).[25] Looking back on his life at the age of forty-eight, he saw it as a long conflict between his natural temperament and God's will, in which the latter eventually won out through unexpected and sometimes traumatic events. By nature a shy, timid, and retiring person, with a strong bent toward study, he was constantly being seized by God and thrust out into the hurly-burly of life. His father had destined him for theology, then had changed his mind and sent him

[23] *Archiv*, XLIII, 17.
[24] In *The Christian Scholar in the Age of the Reformation* (New York, 1956), chap. v.
[25] *CR*, XXXI, 14-36.

into the more lucrative study of law. God had other plans for him, however. By a "sudden conversion" God "reduced his heart to docility." His first taste of true piety had the effect of making him lose his taste for the humanistic studies in which he was engaged, although he dutifully stuck at them. His friends flocked to him to learn of the Gospel, even though he was but a beginner himself, and he began to look for seclusion. "Being by nature a bit anti-social and shy, I always loved retirement and peace, and I began to look for some hide-out where I could be away from people; but far from gaining my desire, every retreat and hide-away became like a public-school to me. In short, although my aim was always to live a private life without being known, God has so taken me about and whirled me around by various vicissitudes that he has never let me rest anywhere, but in spite of my natural inclination, has thrust me into the limelight and made me 'get into the game,' as they say."[26]

The rest of his life Calvin saw as a kind of commentary on this passage. First he sought seclusion in Basel. Here he was shocked by the persecutions in France into reworking his *Institutes* into an apology. A year later he was stopped by Farel while passing through Geneva. "Master William Farel kept me in Geneva not so much by counseling and persuasion as by a terrifying imprecation, as if God had stretched out his hand over me from on high to arrest my steps." When Calvin protested that he had some special studies in hand for which he wished to keep himself free, Farel went to the length of calling on God to curse "the studious quiet and tranquillity" which Calvin was looking for if he refused to stay and help out in Geneva. This so frightened and disturbed him, Calvin says, that he stayed. Exile from Geneva three years later came as a relief, and once more he sought seclusion for scholarly

[26] *CR*, XXXI, 22-24.

work at Basel. This time it was Martin Bucer who routed him out of his retirement by using somewhat the same technique Farel had used. Bucer told him that he was like the prophet Jonah, who thought that by boarding ship he could run away from the Eternal's command to go warn Nineveh of the wrath to come. Once more Calvin was frightened and gave in, this time to become a minister and lecturer in Strasbourg. Not long afterward, reverent regard for his duty to his first flock and further personal pressure led to his return to Geneva. There he had been engaged in a bitter struggle ever since, he wrote, a struggle that reminded him of David's with the Philistines outside the city walls and with the traitors within.

This self-portrait surely demonstrates that Calvin thought of himself as a man cut out by nature for one thing, a life of scholarship, but called by God to something rather different. Naturally "shy," he was called to deal with people rather than with books alone; naturally "timid," he was called to be general of a crusading army of God; naturally "peaceful" in his instincts, he was constantly aroused to do battle for truth and righteousness. In other words, Calvin thought of himself as a God-frustrated scholar.

And yet think of those 59 volumes in the Strasbourg edition! Quite an output for a frustrated scholar! The truth is of course that Calvin constantly withdrew all his life to read and write and re-write, but the significant thing is that *he seems to have felt guilty about it.* At least this is the implication of his own account. On the one hand, he thought of himself as cut out for scholarship and seclusion. On the other, as his conversion shows, he knew that faith must result in action, such as resigning one's benefices in a corrupt church (as he did) or accepting the clear call of God to preach or teach. And so Calvin felt guilty about his love for learning, as many a Christian had before him all the way back to Jerome—and as many a seminary student has since. This is why he was so disturbed by Farel and Bucer when they called down the divine curse on him if he retreated again to his books. Something in him agreed with them, and he obeyed their exhortations as the call of God. But he was still a scholar at heart, and throughout a busy and hectic career he kept returning to the occupation he loved.

Only one thing could justify this continual yielding to his early zest for scholarship. This was the idea that the products of his pen could be "useful," could bear "fruit" in thousands of readers miles away in space and perhaps years away in time, readers who would never be reached by his living voice. Scholarship for its own sake, reading and writing for the sheer fun of it—this could never be justified. But if Calvin could keep persuading his readers, and himself, that this was a particular sort of scholarship—productive of Christian piety, sensitive to human needs and relevant to social ills, conducive to better understanding of fundamental Christian beliefs, concrete and vital where the older tradition of Christian learning had been abstract and dead—then he could keep on writing in the confidence that his efforts had high importance in the eyes of God. And this I think is the ultimate reason why he made so much of "utility."

JOHN T. MC NEILL COMMENTS ON
"THE IDEA OF UTILITY
IN THE THOUGHT OF JOHN CALVIN"

I have had both pleasure and profit in reading and hearing this paper, which, all will agree, offers a competent treatment of an aspect of Calvin's thought by one who reads Calvin for what Calvin has to say and not with some extraneous test to be applied or some preshaped mold into which Calvin's ideas have to be crushed. It is true that when, as in this instance, a single concept or favorite word of an author is selected and pursued through many contexts, we sense the possibility of some perverse emphasis creeping in. But we find that Dr. Harbison does not ask us to think of *utilitas* as the exclusive gateway to the stronghold of Calvin's system. He has, however, fully alerted us to the importance of this concept in Calvin, and he has good reason to hope, with Calvin, that his discussion will prove useful, or profitable, or serviceable, to his hearers and readers. I for one will not cease to watch for instances of the idea in reading Calvin—like a child who with help has found a four-leafed clover and soon by attentive search finds many more. Nevertheless, I have some reservations to offer, and, before stating these, some supplementary comments.

The examination of the idea of the useful has rightly led Dr. Harbison beyond the occurrence of the words *utilis* and *utilitas*. Perhaps more than most writers, Calvin has a habit of employing interchangeable terms, synonyms or near synonyms, to lend variety to his discourse. Some of our scholars, who, like our President, Dr. Breen, are interested in the rhetoric of Calvin's age, could present another helpful (i.e., useful) study of this element in his style. Thus what is useful may be called fruitful, profitable, needful, efficacious, beneficial, or edifying. We today, in arguing for any cause, use much the same reassuring words, though we habitually translate the old word "edifying" by "constructive"—one of our most over-used words of commendation. Almost anything that Calvin commends is likely to be accorded one of these adjectives; or the idea may be conveyed by nouns and verbs with the same effect.

Now, when a thing is useful, or when a course of action is constructive, it is implied that it is useful or constructive toward some end. Useful, we ask, for what? I have therefore been greatly interested to observe the interpretation placed upon Calvin's terms by Dr. Harbison. What I have to say of this will amplify a little, and attempt to give further point to his argument.

About the time I received a copy of this paper I was working over a passage on Ceremonies in which the Reformer gives a scathing judgment of those unscriptural ceremonies which "hypocrites and light-headed little women" just adore. These are, he says "trifles because they have no usefulness (*nugae quod nihil utilitatis habeant*)" when they are judged "according to the rule of piety (*secundum pietatis regulam*."[27] A few pages further on he charges that the ceremonies that are of human tradition and invention "are in no respect edifying (*nihil aedificent*)," but are "useless and amusing employments (*inutiles ac lusoriae occupationes*)," rather than true exercises of piety.[28] These are instances of a common association of "piety" and "utility" in Calvin: others are mentioned by Dr. Harbison. Now "piety" is one of Calvin's most favored words, and it represents something substantial in his thinking.

In the beginning of the *Institutes*[29] he affirms that "there is no knowledge of God where there is no religion or piety" and he there describes piety in a sentence: "Piety I define as reverence combined with love of God (*Pietatem voco conjunctam cum amore Dei reverentiam*) which a knowledge of his blessings induces (*quam beneficiorum eius notitia conciliat*)." This definition is expanded when he speaks of men becoming "aware that they owe everything to God, that they are supported by His paternal care, that

[27] *Inst.*, IV, x, 12.
[28] *Inst.*, IV, x, 16.
[29] *Inst.*, I, ii, 1.

He is the author of all the blessings they enjoy." It is not surprising then that in the first edition of the *Institutio* (1536) the substantive title is followed by the words: "in which is comprehended a summary of piety, and what is needful to know of the doctrine of salvation." Nor is it remarkable that in the Author's Preface to the 1559 Latin edition he should make bold to say: "God has wholly disposed (*addixerit*) my mind to zeal (*studio*) for the expansion of His kingdom and the promotion of public usefulness," and should very solemnly affirm that he has had no other object than "to profit the church by maintaining the true doctrine of piety."

It has been said that for Calvin piety and sound doctrine are interchangeable terms. At least they are so closely related that they are habitually mentioned in association. His *Institutio* is in his view a book of piety, and if it is useful, it is useful for its service to piety.

It is a curious fact that neither the old indexes of Calvin's *Institutes,* such as that of Augustin Marlorat, nor the new English one by Leroy Nixon, so much as mention the word "piety," though it is scattered abundantly, and heavily stressed, in the work. Nor do they contain the word "utility," which Dr. Harbison shows to be also a favorite. But I believe that a full study of the piety concept in Calvin would have no surprises for Dr. Harbison. In his analysis of the meaning of utility he points out that the useful is "instrumental in fostering awe, reverence and true piety." He says further that this meant "favoring the actual transferral to the believer of the graces gained by Christ's obedience and passion," and he regards this religious meaning of utility as fundamental. With this I fully agree.

To this religious sense of the word he adds the ethical and the intellectual; but I have a feeling that these do not stand out with great distinctness. Dr. Harbison's use of the term "ethical" seems to gather in something of the religious. That is useful, he says, which promotes the Kingdom of God. I am reminded of the letter Calvin wrote from his death-bed to his old companion, Farel. In this brief word of farewell, his last letter, Calvin's message is: "Live mindful of our fellowship (*vive memor nostrae conjunctionis*): which, as it was useful to the Church of God, so the fruits of it are laid up for us in heaven." With Calvin's conception of the Kingdom and of the Church of God in mind, it is only with reservation that I can think of such references as "ethical."

I appreciate the difficulty that confronts Dr. Harbison in this three-fold classification of the meaning of the useful for Calvin. It is perhaps impossible to devise any scheme of classification that would be without some objection. In the intellectual bearing of the useful again we cannot disentangle ourselves from the religious. Intellectual activity has for him a religious purpose. That is a striking quotation, presented in the paper, from the Treatise against the Libertines.[30] Calvin wants people to agree with him only so far as they recognize that what he teaches is useful. The passage is from the conclusion of the book. In it he has assailed at length the "false and damnable impiety" found in the teachings of the sect.[31] This impiety is confuted by a very considerable intellectual effort, a clarification of certain doctrines that have been thrown into confusion by his opponents. Again, the end is "piety," with its doctrinal implications.

Calvin never doubted that the intellect can do an indispensable service in behalf of religion. In reading him we see that nothing is more striking than the frequency of his words of contempt for stupidity. Words like *stultus, insulsus, imperitus, indoctus, inscitus, rudis,* and the related nouns and adverbs are like arrows from his bow shot

[30] *Opera Calvini, Corpus Reformatorum* VII, 248.
[31] *CR*, VII, 225.

in all directions against his doctrinal and ecclesiastical foes. To be useful, a discourse must escape these banalities, and must clarify true doctrine. The province of the intellectual within the useful is still the service of religion.

Now I must advert to the principal point at which Dr. Harbison leaves me unconvinced. He finds the clue to Calvin's emphasis on, or obsession with, the useful in the conflict of his natural temperament with what he was convinced was God's will for him, as shown in the Preface to the Commentary on the Psalms. Now I would not minimize this experience, and I have always made a good deal of it. Intensely bookish as a boy, Calvin had little social courage. Largely for this reason his participation in the affairs of the disturbed Church cost him distress and even anguish. He longed to live off Main Street in an ample library surrounded by wide lawns, in complete quietness and intense study. I do not deny that there may have been some sense of guilt engendered in him over this craving, especially by Farel's helpful suggestion that God would curse that studious quiet. But it is possible to carry the ascription of motive beyond safe evidence. Are we to suppose that when after Farel's conditional malediction he signed up for Geneva, and came there as lecturer in the Scriptures, he felt that he was abandoning, or was obligated to abandon, entirely the intellectual life? Or that he always had a sense of guilt when he undertook to study and write? Might it not be argued in reverse of this that simply because Calvin wanted to do nothing useless and was anxious to be as useful as possible, he felt called upon to drive that brain of his while other men slept, and to live a life of dedicated intellectual effort in the midst of his practical activities? The passage cited itself has far other suggestions of the motivation of his writing than those stressed in the paper. Calvin hastened to finish his book on hearing of the persecutions, the sufferings, of his "brethren" in France "whose death was precious in the sight of the Lord."

I am asking why it was needful for him to keep arguing with himself, as Dr. Harbison seems to think he did, that this lovely scholarly endeavor was after all justifiable as a useful thing. That it was useful and justifiable was, I think, axiomatic with him. It is not necessary to think that it required much self-persuasion, or persuasion on the part of his readers, to reach a judgment that this kind of work had validity, and insofar as it was well and truly done did not need apology before the bar of conscience. Indeed it is of his intellectual labor in revising the *Institutio* that he expresses himself with most self-approval. "I was not sorry for (did not repent of) (*me non poenitebat*) the labor . . . my diligent application to the accomplishment of this service to God and to the Church." We should not forget Dr. Harbison's remark that his was "a particular sort of study." It may be argued that his conscience would have suffered if he had gone on commenting on Seneca, or like Melanchthon had edited Cicero—though the prominence of the classics in the Geneva Academy makes even this doubtful. But all his work was directed to the same end, the Reformation of the Church, so that from his point of view it was "useful to the Church of God" whether it was performed in the consistory or in the study. He felt the command of God to write, as well as to take the lead in Church affairs, and one half of him did not need to apologize to the other half.

There would of course be conflict in the timetable. His favorite Church fathers, especially Augustine, who wrote so voluminously, had been through the same trial, and Calvin knew that this was not exceptional in the experience of a Christian leader. There may have been a running struggle, but, if so, I suspect that it was not connected with any problem of the justification of intellectual endeavor, but rather with the doing of two or more full-time jobs. It would be easy to illustrate this point of view from his let-ters and from the life of Calvin written by Beza. I should be inclined to think that he freely rejoiced in putting forth his mental energy, and to hazard the guess that it was more, and not less, satisfying to his soul than his always partly frustrated efforts at reform within the routines of the ex-ternal Church. He felt himself a God-directed, not in Dr. Harbison's phrase, a God-frustrated scholar.

And I remind myself of the fact that for Calvin there is an excellence that is linked with piety but expressly ex-empted from the test of utility. It is the excellence of beauty. "Shall the Lord have adorned the flowers with such beauty and sweetness of smell and shall it be unlawful for our eyes to be affected by their beauty (*pulchritudine*) our olfactory nerves by their odors. . . . Has He not made many things, commendable to us, regardless of any neces-sary use (*citra necessarium usum*)."[32]

This is not to account for the prevalence of the concept of the useful in Calvin. But it seems to me that if we are to attempt this we should not fail to examine the same con-cept in Calvin's chief source of all, the Bible. Although the word "useful" is very rare in Scripture, the idea is deeply embedded in it, and is often represented by such words as "profitable," "expedient," "needful," and in the RSV "helpful," and by the negatives matching these. Paul finds a happy pun in the name of the runaway slave, One-simus, whom he has been instrumental in converting to Christianity and has thus brought to a condition to cor-respond to his name: he "was useless and has become use-ful to you and to me" (Philemon 11). And he writes to the Corinthians: "All things are lawful but not all things are helpful; all things are lawful but not all things build up" (I Cor. 10:23). And here perhaps lies another suggestion for research.

[32] *Inst.*, III, X, 2.

12 · CALVIN'S SENSE OF HISTORY*

THIS IS a big subject, and in spite of the increasing flood of literature in recent years on the meaning of history, not much of scholarly substance has been written on it. We have a large book by a Belgian Franciscan, Pontien Polman, on the use of historical arguments in the long debate between Protestants and Catholics during the sixteenth century (1932). We have several monographs on Luther, the best by Hans Lilje (1932). We have two brief but suggestive treatments of Calvin by Karlfried Fröhlich (1930) and Josef Bohatec. (The recent doctoral study by the Swiss, Heinrich Berger, assembles much data from Calvin's works, but does little to illuminate it.) Karl Dannenfeldt has done a paper on "Concepts of History in Reformation Thought," and two graduate students of Roland Bainton have entered the field (Frank Wray on Anabaptists and John Headley on Luther). But there is nothing definitive yet. With all our interest these days in the Christian understanding of history, there has been remarkably little concern about tracing the historical development of this understanding, especially during the Reformation.

Now, I am no expert on this subject, but I am interested in it as a historian, and Professor Herberg thought it might interest you—even though it is not directly and explicitly concerned with "social science." What I am going to sketch this evening is a sort of hypothesis—still unproved, still to be fully tested, but supported by what evidence I know.

* 1559 was a momentous year in the history of Calvinism—the final, definitive edition of the *Institutes*, founding of what came to be the University of Geneva, first national Synod in France, beginnings of a Calvinist revolution in Scotland, and so on—but it took a Baptist seminary, the Colgate-Rochester Divinity School, descended from some of Calvin's bitterest enemies, to celebrate the year with a conference. I had long been interested in the place of the Reformation in the history of historiography, and this seemed a good excuse to adumbrate my ideas.

And I feel a good deal of hesitation in venturing even this far in such a company of theologians. In fact, as a layman and a historian, I feel a bit like a lion in a den of Daniels this evening.

My hypothesis might be stated briefly and baldly thus: the Protestant Reformation restored a sense of the dynamism and divine purpose in history at a moment in European development when this sense was in peril of being lost. The immediate result was to imbue several generations of Protestants with a fresh interpretation of the past and a vivid sense of historical destiny. The key figure here, I believe, was Calvin. The end result—unanticipated and perhaps undesired, as so often in history—was the modern idea of progress, the secular shell of the Augustinian-Protestant conception of history with the religious kernel removed.

In all this I will be making two pretty obvious assumptions: (1) that there is always a close relation between the sense of history and the sense of destiny—the sense of the past and the future—in any age; and (2) that a man's sense of history is usually deep-rooted in a man's personal experience, particularly his religious experience.

Let us begin by asking where speculation about the meaning and importance of history had arrived by the time Luther posted his 95 Theses in 1517. The two great rival disciplines in the universities of the time were what we call "scholasticism" and "humanism," and each had its characteristic attitude toward history.

The scholastic method as it developed in the High Middle Ages was an utterly unhistorical, if not anti-historical, method. A question is propounded; opinions and proof-texts are marshalled on both sides from all sources regarded as authorities, regardless of context, author's general intent, or historical background; then a resolution of the problem is proposed by rational argument, and truth emerges in the form of a proposition valid in all times and places. This was the process which fascinated the best minds of the thirteenth century. "History" had little if any real interest for the profoundest thinkers of this age. They were primarily interested in Being, not in Becoming. They were philosophers, not historians. "Events" were unimportant except as symbols or allegories of eternal truths. Time brought no essential change. God had incarnated himself in Christ, and Christ had founded the Church. This Church was visible, tangible, present. In its form, being divine, it was also perfect and therefore unchanging. The passage of time would make no difference either to ideal truths or to institutions, which were patterns from the mind of God. Time had passed, of course, but since the Resurrection, history was realized in the Church. Men wrote chronicles, but no one traced "development" because development could not occur in any significant sense. Men recorded events, but only as "wonders" or as examples of timeless truths. I am exaggerating, of course, in order to make the point, but I think it true to say that a theologian like Thomas Aquinas was not really interested in history at all. In his and his contemporaries' *Summae*, the dynamism of the Augustinian conception of history was almost totally lost. *Scientia*, not *Historia*—timeless truth, not the truth that time brings—was what the Schoolmen wanted. The sense of *Kairos*, the feeling for the significant event which happens in the fullness of time, and the passion to read the signs of the time—these were utterly lacking in the great medieval theologians.

Scholasticism represented faithfully the dominant interests of the educated classes in late medieval Europe, but there was a counter-current at a deeper social level, the vague and inchoate hopes of a new age that sprang from the writings of Joachim of Flora. In the idea of the Three Ages—the Age of the Father (or Old Testament), the Age of the Son (or New Testament), and the Age of the Spirit (to be ushered in in the near future by a purified order of monks)—Christian Europe rediscovered something of the sense of *Kairos* that breathes through the New Testament, something of the dynamism and feeling for spiritual progress that suffuses parts of Augustine's *City of God*. But to speak of a new age in which the Church would be superseded was, of course, to talk heretically, because it was to say that history was *not* realized in the visible Roman Church. And so the sects that sprang from the Joachite writings were generally suppressed. Joachite ideas are undoubtedly the remote progenitors of the modern idea of progress, but apart from their influence on Dante and fourteenth century mystics, they had little immediate impact on the thought of the educated.

Much more immediate was the impact of the revived study of the classics which we call humanism. From one point of view, humanism was an assertion of historical and literary interests over and against the logical and philosophical interests of the Schoolmen, within the medieval university curriculum. The modern disciplines of history, archaeology, and philology were born in the humanistic revival. Something of a scholarly revolution was involved here. When Lorenzo Valla in the fifteenth century proved the Donation of Constantine a forgery by analyzing its anachronisms and incongruities, that is, by placing an ecclesiastical document in its purely historical context, he was following a method that would have seemed either unintelligible or unfruitful to a thirteenth century Schoolman. Valla assumed that times had changed, and that the change was significant. One result was the idea of anachronism, the idea that each age has a self-consistent pattern of its own which is unlike that of any other age. It dawned on Petrarch and his successors that a society quite unlike their own had lived and died in Greece and

Rome, that this "Antiquity," as they called it, had been succeeded by a "Dark Age," and that the Dark Age was beginning to give way in their own day to a "Revival" or "Rebirth" of culture and civic vigor. This vision of history as consisting of three stages—a Golden Age, a Dark Age, and a Rebirth—was a genuinely new perspective, roughly parallel to the Joachite picture of three ages, but now thoroughly secular in its substance. In a secularized form, it had something of the dynamic feeling and the sense for *Kairos* which characterized the Augustinian conception of history. As in Augustine's view, history was periodized into meaningful stages. But there was a new element here, the ambiguous idea of revival or rebirth. In the humanist view, mankind was trembling on the verge of a *re*birth that was also a *new* birth, a revival of a Golden Age that was also in some sense a New Age. Was this essentially a *re*turn or a *new* turn in the road of history? Was history cyclical or linear?

In spite of the Augustinian and Joachite background of the humanists' historical perspective, there was a strong tendency among them to follow their Greek and Roman models and to say that history was essentially *cyclical* in character. Machiavelli, the keenest of them all, was fascinated by the possibility of developing a science of politics from the study of history. This was possible only if human nature is always the same and if history constantly tends to repeat itself. If this is so, as Thucydides dimly sensed, then the laws of human behavior which are always true everywhere and at all times can be worked out, and man can in some sense control his destiny through knowledge of the laws that govern society.

Machiavelli was a passionate reformer, however, as well as a scientific analyst. He was fascinated by the problem of *Kairos* in its secular form, the problem of diagnosing the spirit of the times and recognizing the crucial moment.

In the last chapter of the *Prince* he wonders whether the present moment was not the proper one for the appearance in Italy of a new prince who would throw out the barbarians and unite the Italians under his leadership—and he concludes, "I do not know of any time more fitting for such an enterprise." His thought moves between two poles, *virtù* and *fortuna*—the man of virtuosity pitting his will and intelligence over against Fortune. The providential framework of history is not attacked; it is simply ignored. The idea of a history realized in the visible Church is for Machiavelli, of course, simply an unmentionable absurdity.

Erasmus (as Myron Gilmore has recently shown[1]) combined the cyclical view stemming from Greco-Roman thought and the linear view stemming from Christianity in a unique and interesting way. He saw a kind of recurring pattern or analogy between the age of the birth of Christianity and his own times. "As in time past there had been a development from learning to piety [from the Greeks to Christ], from classicism to Christianity, so in time present learning could restore piety"—and he devoted his life to proving that it could. The present moment was both a unique development in the historical process—and something which had happened before. But Erasmus was not much concerned about the problem of history. He never developed these insights into the historical process, nor did he get his contemporaries excited about them.

Here then were the broad alternatives in attitudes toward the past at the opening of the sixteenth century: a scholastic theology which assumed that history was realized in the Church and looked for timeless divine truth; and a humanistic philosophy which tended to search for a more secular, but equally timeless, truth in the ethical and political laws to be discerned operating in a history

[1] *Teachers of History: L. B. Packard* (Cornell, 1954).

essentially cyclical in character. From the history of revelation, scholasticism pretended to develop a theological "science." From the history of secular states, humanism hoped to establish a political "science." These pretensions to timeless, supra-historical knowledge were not unchallenged, as I have suggested. Joachite ideas of a New Age and Petrarchan conceptions of "Rebirth" introduced a more dynamic and progressive conception of history, from both the religious and secular points of view. But these more dynamic and progressive views were, from the point of view of a thoughtful Christian, either heretical or predominantly secular—except perhaps in Erasmus. Neither the Joachite nor the humanist was very closely related to the original Christian understanding of history which came mainly from St. Paul and St. Augustine.

It was Luther's work to reject both scholastic and humanistic notions of history in favor of a more biblical and Augustinian understanding. Luther's study of Paul, together with his own personal experience of God's grace and power, persuaded him that no bounds whatever can be set to the will of God, no channel dug by man which God's will may not overflow, no law envisaged by man which exhausts the possibilities of divine action. "God is that being for whose will no cause or reason is to be assigned as a rule or standard by which it acts; seeing that nothing is superior or equal to it, but it is itself the rule of all things."[2] How absurd to think to channel such a will within institutional walls, even those of God's own Church! How blind to think to define such a will by the rational propositions of scholasticism! God's will is too majestic and mysterious for that. It works in history, but history is no simple revelation of its character. To Luther God reveals himself in historical events, but he also *conceals* himself. God is *Deus absconditus, Der fremde Gott,* as

[2] *The Bondage of the Will,* p. 230.

well as the God who rewards the just and punishes the unjust. If his will were plainly and completely revealed in history, then history might be a "science," as both schoolmen and humanists had maintained in different ways. But it is not. God shows only his backside in history —the phrase is "posteriona Dei." History is God's "theatre," says Luther, his "jousting place." But the meaning of the play, the significance of the tourney, are not evident to everyone in the audience. There is mystery as well as meaning in the stream of historical events, which destroys any assurance of the easy attainment of a "science," whether theological or social.

Events do have a meaning which is evident to the eye of faith, however. In a few striking passages, Luther recaptures the New Testament feeling for *Kairos*, the significant unique event in linear history. "For since God's work goes on without interruption," he writes, "as Christ says, 'My Father worketh hitherto, and I also,' so *something noteworthy* must without fail happen in each period of time, which men should justly mark."[3] And in an oft-quoted letter to the city councillors of Germany in 1524, he urges them to seize the present moment to do something for education, since God by his grace has supplied so many teachers and such a rich opportunity.

Such a view of history obviously rejected the cyclical view revived by humanism, and at the same time shattered the static, church-centered view of scholasticism. The divine will was too "free," too "hidden," to work only within the channels of an ecclesiastical institution. God was still doing decisive things in history—converting Luther himself, for instance, to a true understanding of the Gospel, calling him to lead a revolution in spite of his gnawing doubts ["Are all the authorities of past and present wrong, and I alone right?" he used to ask himself], raising up

[3] Luther's *Werke*, Weimar Aufgabe v. 50, p. 384.

Anti-Christ and stirring the Devil to final furious resistance, bringing events to a crisis of mysterious but decisive importance in these latter days. This is the way Luther saw it. Luther's view of Church history was a very complex mixture of old and new ideas, as a recent study has shown. There are hints and suggestions in his writings of a relatively new periodization of history, a view closely parallel to both the Joachite and the humanist conceptions. There had been a kind of "Golden Age" in Christian history, Luther thought, the age of the Early Church. Luther was never very clear about how long this age lasted—perhaps through Gregory the Great, perhaps to Hildebrand in the eleventh century. But it was succeeded by a Dark Age, the age of the papacy, that is, of Anti-Christ, when the simplicity and purity of the Early Church was corrupted by human inventions and superstitions. Now a New Age was dawning which was at the same time a "Last Age" as well. The Gospel was preached in its original form once more, while Satan raged even more furiously than ever. This vision of the three ages of church history since the Resurrection independently developed by the Anabaptists was to become the standard with Protestants for many years to come.[4]

It is difficult to generalize about the historical views of those left-wingers of the Reformation whom we lump together under the name of Anabaptists. Their ideas were hazy at best and there was no very large area of agreement among their authors. They went further than Luther. All historical continuity with the early church had been utterly broken, they believed. God's work of restitution had just begun, in them, as the true divine community. They were the bearers of divine destiny, the historical instruments of God's will. They were divided about just *how* the restoration would take place. The vast majority be-

[4] Luther's *Werke*, Weimar Aufgabe v. 11, p. 36.

lieved it would be by and through their *suffering*, but a few thought it would be by *violence* and threw themselves into the lurid attempt to establish the Kingdom by bloodshed at Münster in 1534. The communism and polygamy of Münster discredited the violent apocalyptic tradition for years to come. Together with the earlier Peasants' War of 1525, the affair of Münster tended to push Luther, Calvin, and the other Protestant reformers in a conservative direction. Each of them was careful to say in his own way that the Kingdom of God is not to be realized *in history*, but only beyond it.

This brings us to Calvin, the great systematizer and organizer of Protestantism. Calvin's mind was formed by his scholastic, legal, and humanistic studies, and his superb intellect reflected the influence of *more* of the main currents of thought in his day than did any other Reformer. His understanding of history, like his understanding of other great Christian doctrines, was an attempt to expound the biblical answer according to the best scholars' consensus, in terms so clear and convincing that Christians would be moved to action by it.

Calvin had little sympathy with scholasticism. Naturally, like Luther, he rejected its static view of history as realized in the Roman Church and its attempt to develop a theological science based largely on reason. But his training in scholastic method left its mark on him, I think, in his passion for ordering, arranging, and systematizing. Certainly he took kindly to scholasticism's tendency to tidy things up, to tie up all the loose ends of an argument. In a more general sense he conceived of God as the supreme ordering power, waging constant warfare against the disintegrative activities of Satan. "Regno Dei oppositus omnis ἀταξία et confusio," he wrote,[5] "The Kingdom of God is opposed to all anarchy and confusion." Calvin's main

---

[5] Bohatec, 279; 45, 197.

objection to the Anabaptist sects of his day was that they were disruptive, subversive of social order, contemptuous of God's plan. The Gospel is a re-ordering power, Christ's lordship consists in restoring the order of creation [Bohatec].

The influence of humanism on Calvin was more subtle, and we have only begun to unravel it in recent years. His early humanistic training had one positive effect on him. As a working scholar and biblical commentator he subscribed wholeheartedly to the humanist program: get back to the sources, make sure you know what a document says in its original language, place a document in its whole historical context before you draw lessons from it, and get its whole intent before you wrench proof-texts from it. These were as yet only the most elementary tools of the historian's profession, but Calvin mastered them probably better than any of the Reformers.

Humanism had some more important negative effects on Calvin's intellectual development, however. He did not look at history through a humanist's eyes. He did not look back nostalgically to a golden age of pagan antiquity like Petrarch, nor did he think to draw simple political lessons from recurrences in history like Machiavelli. Humanist history, in fact, provided him with the two false theories of history in answer to which he developed his own theory of predestination. We sometimes forget that his doctrine of predestination was not simply an answer to free will, but a middle road, as it were, leading up and out of the dilemma posed by *two* wrong theories: the theory that history is the product of sheer chance (Fortune) and the theory that history is the result of inexorable determinism (Fate). To Calvin, Greek and Roman thought knew no way out of this dilemma of limitless free will and equally limitless necessity. The picture of the man of *virtù* battling alone against *fortuna* was anathema to him, as also the picture of a blind Fate governing history. The truth to Calvin was that every event that happens in time is "predestined" by an inscrutable but purposeful will. Thus to talk about either chance or determinism is equally blasphemous. (I will never forget the horror I caused my strict Calvinist grandmother when as a boy I innocently said, "Well good-by, grandmother—good luck.") History assuredly has meaning, but it is neither the strivings of man nor the laws of nature that give it this meaning. It is God.

Calvin's debt to Luther was, of course, very large. He adopted Luther's division of Christian history into three ages: an age of primitive purity, a "Dark Age," and a new age or Age of Reform (which Calvin tended even more clearly than Luther to see as a last or decisive age). Like Luther also, Calvin developed the idea of a God who "hides himself" in events. As Bohatec points out[6] he distinguished between the "revealed" and the "hidden" justice of God in history, God's "ordinary" and his "extraordinary" justice—"justice manifeste, notoire, ordinaire," by which the evil get what is coming to them—and "justice cachée, secrète, incompréhensible," by which the godly are persecuted and the evil rewarded. The hiddenness of God in history does not deny or contradict the manifest revelation: both are part of the same single purpose. Behind the apparent chaos and senselessness of history lie purpose and meaning. The times of concealment are balanced by what Calvin calls "opportune times" when God reveals himself with particular clarity to his elect, as well as to the reprobate.

Every leading idea of Luther about the meaning of history, in other words, is picked up by Calvin and woven into the structure of his thought. *But somehow the result is different.* Somehow the tone and temper have changed. There seems to be something new. What is it?

[6] Bohatec, 292-295.

We can get at the heart of it, I think, if we say that *Calvin took Luther's sense of history and transformed it into a sense of destiny.* He took the idea of revival or rebirth, which was not much more than a scholarly theory of cultural revival in humanism, with pietistic overtones in Erasmus, and not much more than a mystical expectation in Joachitism, and transformed it into a powerful ideology which could move multitudes. To Calvin, even more self-consciously than to Luther, the present moment was a decisive moment of time in the realization of God's Kingdom, a *Kairos,* a crisis reached in the fullness of time, like the age of the Prophets or the age of the Apostles. (Calvin often felt a close kinship with the Prophets and with David.) So his conception of history became a strong stimulus to action, here, now, in this world.

Here we must be careful. It is too easy to give the impression that Calvin was a sort of "social gospel-ler" before his time, or an early advocate of the "evangelization of the world in this generation." Needless to say, he had never heard of Walter Rauschenbusch—or even of Reinhold Niebuhr. The "realization of the Kingdom" was to him a spiritual concept from beginning to end. Such realization as there was in history was invisible, and the process would not be complete until the end of time. In fact, the word "history," with its eighteenth and nineteenth century connotations to us of secular evolution and development, would have been unintelligible to him. But what a man says to his generation is sometimes more than he intends to say. What the tone of his voice or the style of his written word suggests often has more influence than what he actually says. And so it was, I think, with Calvin. His end in view was other-worldly through and through, but his immediate objectives always had to do with this world. "No other of the Reformers [Karlfried Fröhlich argues] saw the tasks of Christianity in this world and for this world so clearly and on such a grand scale, no other sought to realize the idea of the sovereignty of God on this earth in so comprehensive a way. . . ."[7] "The dynamic of the Calvinist Kingdom [he continues] is a systematically forward-moving and forward-pressing power, ordered by the mysterious will of God. . . ."[8] Whatever the continuity with medieval and Lutheran doctrine, Calvin emphasized strongly the *secular* tasks facing the Elect, the *social* and *structural* character of evil, the *dynamic* aspects of the battle with Satan, the peculiar and decisive aspects of the *present* moment of time, and the *responsibility* of the Elect. All of which was a powerful stimulant to secular activism.

To document this, let us look briefly at some familiar attitudes and styles of thinking in Calvin which have always seemed important to historians because of their results, but which have sometimes been lost sight of in the current emphasis on his Christology. First, Calvin's conception of *God* is shot through with dynamism. He is not interested in the divine Essence, because we can never know it, but he is enormously interested in the divine action, which we experience in history. He is shocked by the "philosophers'" notion of God as either mere essence or mere law, a do-nothing God. God, he says, is "not such as is imagined by sophists, vain, idle, and almost asleep, but vigilant, efficacious, operative, and engaged in continual action . . . a power constantly exerted on every distinct and particular movement."[9]

Second, his conception of *Christ*. It is dangerous for a layman to generalize about Calvin's conception of Christ. But certainly it is not the helpless infant that captures his imagination, nor the suffering figure on the cross, but

[7] Karlfried Fröhlich, *Die Reichgottesidee Calvins* (Munich 1922), Vol. I, p. 7.

[8] Fröhlich, *Gottesreich, Welt, und Kirche bei Calvin* (Munich 1930), p. 92.

[9] Calvin, *The Institutes*, Vol. I, p. 16.

Christ as man, living, working, and teaching among men, and above all Christ as risen Lord, seated at the right hand of the Father and endowed with power.

Third, his concept of the *Kingdom*. However traditional and other-worldly this concept may be at heart, he presents the Kingdom over and over as a living, growing, dynamic thing. God does not simply call individuals to salvation. He calls them to work collectively for the coming of the Kingdom. A Christian man, Calvin says in his Reply to Sadoleto, must certainly "ascend higher than merely to seek and secure the salvation of his own soul."[10] "It is not very sound theology to confine a man's thoughts so much to himself and not to set before him, as the prime motive of his existence, zeal to illustrate the glory of God. For we are born first of all for God, not for ourselves."[11] Here is the heart of Calvinism: the emphasis on the *objectivity* of the task and of the Great Taskmaster. "We are not our own." God means men to *work* for his Kingdom, not to sit about saving their souls.

The Kingdom in some mysterious sense *grows* in time. "It grows from day to day and progresses toward the better," Calvin says, although he hastens to point out that it has not yet reached perfection, nor will it until the Last Day.[12] In another place: "The Kingdom grows by continuous stages up to the end of the world."[13] This sense of "growth," "advance," "improvement" in the Kingdom has recently been traced in Luther's thought also, but I do not think it had the organic connection with the whole drift of Luther's thinking which it had with Calvin's. The "progress" Calvin suggested is still entirely spiritual, but it takes place in this world, and could easily be translated

[10] Fröhlich, *RGI*, 34.
[11] Fröhlich, *RGI*, 33.
[12] In *Opera Calvini, Corpus Reformatorum*, Vol. 80, p. 29.
[13] *CR*, 73, 197; *RGI*, 105.

into secular progress by later interpreters or followers. If we ask *how* this growth or progress of the Kingdom takes place, the answer of course is by God's will alone. Just because we see hints of growth taking place today is no reason to count upon its inevitably continuing (Bohatec). God can speed it up or slow it down. But he works always through human agencies—sometimes through special individuals, *"viri singulares"*—sometimes through ordinary men (Berger). The Elect, who are his instruments, have therefore a peculiarly significant task. A real fight is going on, not a mock combat. The efforts of the Elect are God's efforts, and so they count. Although God is omnipotent and the ultimate issue is certain, it is true in a way to say that without his Elect, God would fail.

With such a God, such a Christ, and such a Kingdom to be increased in history, the Elect have every reason to feel a peculiar sense of historical mission and destiny. If he had only his own interests to take into account, Calvin wrote to Bullinger in May 1549, he would immediately move somewhere out of Geneva. "But" [he added] "when I consider how important this corner of the world is for the spread of Christ's Kingdom, I have reason to be concerned about protecting it."[14] Geneva, in more modern words, was a small but crucial beachhead from which the task forces were already fanning out which would infiltrate and overthrow the enemy throughout Europe.

Both Luther and Calvin used the analogy of the theatre in describing God's activity in time and space, but in significantly different ways. To Luther the world of history is the scene of God's wonder-working, his jousting-place with Satan. Man is an awe-struck spectator. I do not suppose that Luther, a peasant by origin and a monk by training, ever in his wildest moments imagined himself a knight on horseback taking part in a tourney—and it was generally as an

[14] *Opera*, XIII, 268.

awe-struck spectator that he looked at the worlds of business and politics all his life. Calvin, on the other hand, says that because the span of each of our lives is short, God has set us in a theatre with all history spread before us so that we may learn and profit by what we see, that is, by the evidence of God's actions in history. We are not merely spectators, but participants. The ancient idea of the utility of history, so dear to Machiavelli, is thus adapted to Christian purposes.[15] To Luther the world is the *scene* of God's saving activity, to Calvin it is rather an *object* to be transformed by his sovereignty.[16]

Calvin's understanding of history and destiny, as revealed by his conceptions of God, Christ, and the Kingdom, was not learned from books. It was deep-rooted in his own intimate experience of God—as is evident to anyone who takes the trouble to read the fascinating autobiographical preface to his *Commentary on the Psalms* of 1557. There he pictured himself as a somewhat shy, timid, and antisocial person with a strong, life-long urge to get away from society and devote himself to scholarship. Over and over this urge had been frustrated by God, as he saw it. First he underwent a "sudden conversion" through which God brought his mind into "submission" to the Gospel, he says. Then Farel called down God's curses on him if he should return to his scholarly work rather than help Farel evangelize Geneva, and Calvin obeyed, "terrified." Then Martin Bucer dragged him out of retirement to an active pastorate in Strasbourg, "terrifying" him again, this time with the example of Jonah. And finally the people of Geneva called him back against his will to what turned out to be a life's work of teaching, preaching, city-government, and direction of ecumenical Protestant strategy. God, he says, constantly "turned him about" and "thrust him out onto

---

[15] Bohatec, 283-284.
[16] Fröhlich, *RGI*, 37.

the stage," frustrating his scholarly urge and terrifying him into the work of ecclesiastical statesmanship. [To be sure, the frustrated scholar managed somehow to turn out 59 thick volumes of writing in his life-time].

God's dealings with Calvin are the model of God's activities in history. God works in history to build his Kingdom, calling his Elect through his Elect, relentlessly recruiting the *militia Christi* from the most unlikely groups, even from scholars. "We are not our own," wrote Calvin in a famous passage in the *Institutes*,[17] "We are God's; to him, therefore, let us live and die."

What can we conclude from this hasty survey? A conception of history's meaning shaped to a vivid sense of destiny is the most powerful social force known to man. "Calvin," says Tawney, "did for the bourgeoisie of the sixteenth century what Marx did for the proletariat of the nineteenth. . . . The doctrine of predestination satisfied the same hunger for an assurance that the forces of the universe are on the side of the elect as was to be assuaged in a different age by the theory of historical materialism."[18] The analogy is faulty in some respects (Calvin had no such relation to an economic class as Marx had), but it is disturbingly suggestive. The Calvinist international underground organized from Geneva was strangely like the twentieth century Communist apparatus, for instance. Oliver Cromwell was in the authentic Protestant tradition when he insisted over and over upon seeing the hand of God in historical events—in "dispensations." Cromwell was "one of the very last," Norman Cantor once wrote, "of that race of giants who bestrode Europe for more than thirteen centuries—those men who dared and achieved great things because they took God seriously." It is no longer Christians who see "dispensations" in the turn of events as Cromwell,

[17] III, 7.
[18] *Religion and the Rise of Capitalism*, R. H. Tawney (New York, 1926), p. 112.

[287]

who eagerly read the "signs of the times" and search out the *Kairoi* of our day. It is the Communists who treasure every revolt of a colonial people, every native massacre, every lynching, and every wave of unemployment, as secular "dispensations" in the relentless progress of capitalism's decay. While half the world—our half—seems to have lost all sense of *Kairos* and destiny, believing again that history is meaningless chance, the other half—the Communist half—seems to see in it relentless secular determinism.

So these are the problems I leave with you—the problems which seem to me to be raised by this quick look at the Protestant Reformers' sense of history: How can the Christian reject the view of history as governed by Fate or Fortune in favor of a view of history as governed by a predestining Providence, without falling into the sin of playing God and saying "Lo, here—Lo, there," or "here is a dispensation"? How can he refute the humanist or Marxist who sees a too-evident meaning in history, and at the same time confound the cynic or mystic who sees no meaning whatever in the process? What is the balance of mystery and meaning in history? Is it meet and right for a Christian to deduce a sense of destiny from his conception of history? And how are we to face the paradox that history sometimes shows unmistakable signs of cyclical recurrence, and at other times looks like a straight-line succession of unique events? The Protestant Reformers rescued the sense of history from both chance and determinism, and left it in the predestining power of the living God.

INDEX

Rauschenbusch, Walter, 282
Reply to Sadoleto, see Calvin, John
Republic, see Plato
Reuchlin, Johann, 227f
Revue Thomiste, 40n
Ritter, Gerhard, 225, 236
Robinson, James Harvey, 47
Roman Catholic Church, 141ff
Roman Catholicism, 104
Rostovtseff, 62
Rousseau, Jean Jacques, 166-68
Roosevelt, Franklin D., 168
Rust, E. C., 37n

Savonarola, 210-11
Schweitzer, Albert, 115, 173f
Schwiebert, E. G., 46n
Second Isaiah, *see* Isaiah
Seeberg, Reinhold, 195
Servetus, Michael, 104, 200
Society of Jesus, 84-85, 89-91
Socinians, 146
Socrates, 87, 228
Soderini, Piero, 212-14
Sorokin, Pitirim, 11, 50, 115
Spengler, Herbert, 11, 47
Stoics, 166
Study of History, see Toynbee, Arnold
Sturm, Johann, 84
Supreme Court, 168
Sweet, W. W., 199n, 202

Tacitus, 56, 123, 209
Tawney, R. H., 287
Taylor, H. O., 37n
Tertullian, 81, 183, 198
Thils, G., 37n, 40n
Thucydides, 54, 56, 123, 128, 209, 274

Tillich, Paul, 35-36, 36n, 63f, 82, 151f, 177n
Toynbee, Arnold J., 9, 43, 47f, 63f, 115-37, 204; *Study of History,* 120ff
Treatise against the Libertines, see Calvin, John
Treatise on the Lord's Supper, see Calvin, John
Trent, Council of, 145
Troeltsch, Ernst, 143f

Unitarians, 146
University of Paris, 82-83
Utopia, see More, Sir Thomas

Valla, Lorenzo, 5, 186, 273
Van Doren, Mark, 95
Vergerius, Peter Paul, 80
Vettori, Francesca, 213f, 218
Voltaire, 5, 16, 36, 57-58, 171, 174

War or Peace? see Dulles, John Foster
Weed, Paul C. Jr., 98ff
Weil, Simone, 106
Wesley, John, 115, 171
White, Lynn Jr., 12n, 46n
Whitehead, Alfred North, 51, 64, 96
Wilder, Thornton, 97
Williams, G. H., 202n
Wimpfeling, Jacob, 83
Wolsey, Thomas, Cardinal, 228, 240
Wood, H. G., 36, 36n
Woodward, E. L., 42
Woolman, John, 115
Wray, Frank, 270

Zilsel, Edgar, 74
Zwingli, 255